'This is a groundbreaking book in the series "Wellbeing and Self-care in Higher Education: Embracing Positive Solutions" that delves into the crucial yet often overlooked topic the contextually sensitive and culturally responsive approaches to wellbeing and self-care in higher education, with a specific focus on the unique challenges and opportunities present in the Global South. This book is a timely and much-needed contribution to the field, as it sheds light on the diverse experiences and perspectives of students, faculty, and staff in non-Western contexts, challenging the assumptions and norms that have long dominated the discourse on wellbeing in higher education.'

Professor Narelle Lemon, *series editor, Edith Cowan University, Perth, Australia*

Understanding Wellbeing in Higher Education of the Global South

This edited book gives voice to previously unheard narratives on wellbeing in higher education and provides novel implications for higher education policy and practice.

Offering contextually sensitive and culturally responsive perspectives, the book problematizes wellbeing in higher education as it is currently theorized in the Global North, bringing to the fore perspectives and multi-disciplinary insights from the Global South region. Chapters present an alternative conceptualization of wellbeing in higher education based on stories, perceptions, and experiences of university students, faculty, and leaders from the Global South region, challenging a reductionist view of wellbeing and embracing its complexity, multi-dimensionality, and context-sensitivity. The authors present an alternative non-Western approach to thinking, researching, and doing wellbeing in higher education, offering clear guidelines to support teachers, educational researchers, and leaders in fostering a more holistic teaching and learning experience.

This volume will stimulate policy development and enactment, as well as university-wide interventions and practices that can make a difference in the lives of students in higher education.

Youmen Chaaban is a Research Associate Professor at the Educational Research Centre, College of Education, Qatar University, Qatar.

Abdellatif Sellami is a Director of the Educational Research Centre, College of Education, Qatar University, Qatar.

Igor Michaleczek is a Research Assistant in the Educational Research Centre, College of Education, Qatar University, and a PhD student at the University of Dundee, UK.

Wellbeing and Self-care in Higher Education: Embracing Positive Solutions

Prioritising Wellbeing and Self-Care in Higher Education
How We Can Do Things Differently to Disrupt Silence
Edited by Narelle Lemon

Sustaining Your Wellbeing in Higher Education
Values-based Self-Care for Work and Life
Jorden A. Cummings

Exploring Time as a Resource for Wellness in Higher Education
Identity, Self-care and Wellbeing at Work
Edited by Sharon McDonough and Narelle Lemon

Navigating Tensions and Transitions in Higher Education
Effective Skills for Maintaining Wellbeing and Self-care
Edited by Kay Hammond and Narelle Lemon

Passion and Purpose in the Humanities
Exploring the Worlds of Early Career Researchers
Edited by Marcus Bussey, Camila Mozzini-Alister, Bingxin Wang and Samantha Willcocks

Supporting and Promoting Wellbeing in the Higher Education Sector
Practices in Action
Edited by Angela Dobele and Lisa Farrell

Understanding Wellbeing in Higher Education of the Global South
Contextually Sensitive and Culturally Responsive Perspectives
Edited by Youmen Chaaban, Abdellatif Sellami and Igor Michaleczek

For more information about this series, please visit: www.routledge.com/Wellbeing-and-Self-care-in-Higher-Education/book-series/WSCHE

Understanding Wellbeing in Higher Education of the Global South

Contextually Sensitive and Culturally Responsive Perspectives

Edited by Youmen Chaaban, Abdellatif Sellami and Igor Michaleczek

LONDON AND NEW YORK

Designed cover image: © Getty Images

First published 2025
by Routledge
4 Park Square, Milton Park, Abingdon, Oxon OX14 4RN

and by Routledge
605 Third Avenue, New York, NY 10158

Routledge is an imprint of the Taylor & Francis Group, an informa business

© 2025 selection and editorial matter, Youmen Chaaban, Abdellatif Sellami and Igor Michaleczek; individual chapters, the contributors

The right of Youmen Chaaban, Abdellatif Sellami and Igor Michaleczek to be identified as the authors of the editorial material, and of the authors for their individual chapters, has been asserted in accordance with sections 77 and 78 of the Copyright, Designs and Patents Act 1988.

All rights reserved. No part of this book may be reprinted or reproduced or utilised in any form or by any electronic, mechanical, or other means, now known or hereafter invented, including photocopying and recording, or in any information storage or retrieval system, without permission in writing from the publishers.

Trademark notice: Product or corporate names may be trademarks or registered trademarks, and are used only for identification and explanation without intent to infringe.

British Library Cataloguing-in-Publication Data
A catalogue record for this book is available from the British Library

ISBN: 978-1-032-78807-4 (hbk)
ISBN: 978-1-032-79365-8 (pbk)
ISBN: 978-1-003-49161-3 (ebk)

DOI: 10.4324/9781003491613

Typeset in Times New Roman
by KnowledgeWorks Global Ltd.

Contents

List of contributors ix
Series preface xii
Opening editorial notes xv

1 **Introduction** 1
   YOUMEN CHAABAN

2 **Wellbeing odyssey: Integrating Afrofuturist theory with academic literacy** 10
   OSCAR EYBERS

3 **Exploring wellbeing in the Arab higher education context: A scoping review** 27
   IGOR MICHALECZEK, WEAM IBRAHIM, AND YOUMEN CHAABAN

4 **Student wellbeing in the Pacific Islands: Challenges and opportunities for enhancing academic success** 52
   ANNIE CROOKES

5 **The science of wellbeing and success in higher education: Applying positive psychology and PERMA+4 across cultures** 74
   STEWART I. DONALDSON AND JANA KOCI

6 **University students' wellbeing: Diversity across contexts** 87
   NOOR AL-WATTARY, HESSA AL-THANI, AND AISHA AL-AHMADI

7 **Students' wellbeing in online and blended Arabic as second and heritage language courses: Challenges and suggested solutions** 104
   MOHAMED MAHGOUB, HANY FAZZA, AND MARTINE ELIE

8 **Beyond borders: Understanding wellbeing in higher education through culturally appropriate measures**   125
HERDIYAN MAULANA AND GUMGUM GUMELAR

9 **Challenges to wellbeing of faculty and leaders in higher education in the Gulf Cooperation Council**   142
RITA W. EL-HADDAD AND STAVROS P. HADJISOLOMOU

10 **Conclusion**   164
ABDELLATIF SELLAMI AND IGOR MICHALECZEK

Index   *170*

Contributors

Aisha Al-Ahmadi is an Experienced Assistant Professor with a demonstrated history of working in higher education. She is skilled in Counseling Psychology, Mindfulness, Crisis Intervention, and Case Management. Her research focuses on Clinical Mental Health, Positive Psychology, character strengths, and wellbeing.

Hessa Al-Thani is passionate about promoting holistic teaching, experiential learning, and incorporating methods related to institutional wellbeing. Her work focuses on students' interests, motivations, and diverse backgrounds. Al-Thani is dedicated to exploring and adopting diversified approaches in curriculum transformation and renovating those to become experiential, entrepreneurial, and collaborative. Al-Thani strongly advocates programs that focuses on building generations of responsible and engaged citizens.

Noor Al-Wattary is a faculty member at the College of Education, Qatar University, Qatar. Her main research interest is about Islamic Well-being, Social Emotional Learning, and Character Education.

Youmen Chaaban is a Research Associate Professor at the Education Research Center, at the College of Education, Qatar University. She has over 18 years of teaching experience expanding the levels of students' primary, secondary, and tertiary education. Her research interests include professional learning, teacher education, and higher education.

Annie Crookes joined USP in 2019 after 15 years of building psychology programs for British universities in UAE. She has extensive experience in program management, curriculum development, and various roles to support the development of psychology and mental health services. Research interests: mental health and wellbeing in students and the role of positive psychology in mental health support.

Stewart Donaldson is a Distinguished University Professor and Executive Director of the Claremont Evaluation Center (CEC) and the Evaluators' Institute (TEI) at Claremont Graduate University. He is deeply committed to improving lives through positive psychology research, evaluation, and education. He has published hundreds of peer-reviewed articles, chapters, evaluation reports, and more than 20 books on positive psychology topics and evaluation science.

Rita El-Haddad is an Assistant Professor of Psychology at the American University of Kuwait. She received her Ph.D. in Psychology from the Graduate Center of the City University of New York. She conducts research on neurodevelopmental disorders and cross-cultural studies on wellbeing.

Martine Elie is the Manager of Research and Evaluation at Pre-University Education Research Office, Qatar Foundation. She is a Speech-Language Pathologist whose research has focused on teaching and learning, dual language, multicultural issues, global health, interprofessional practice and education, clinical precepting, and the assessment and treatment of culturally and linguistically diverse populations.

Oscar Eybers is a Lecturer at the University of Pretoria, who specializes in academic literacies. He focuses on developing novice scholars' confidence and sees academic literacies as essential to disciplinary identities and cultures. He has published extensively, including works on artificial intelligence in higher education, promoting ethical and culturally relevant practices.

Hany Fazza is an Arabic Language Lecturer at Georgetown University in Qatar. His research focuses on teaching Arabic and technology-enhanced learning. He holds an M.A. in Teaching Arabic as a Foreign Language and is currently a Ph.D. candidate at Lancaster University. He is also a principal investigator for the Qatar Linguistic Digital Map Project.

Gumgum Gumelar is a Senior Lecturer in Psychology, University of Jakarta, where he has been a faculty member since 2006. He holds a doctoral degree in psychology from Universitas Indonesia. His research focuses on Organizational and Communication Psychology. He has published numerous articles in peer-reviewed journals in psychology and relevant fields.

Stavros Hadjisolomou is an Associate Professor of Psychology and Associate Dean at the American University of Kuwait. He holds a Ph.D. in Psychology from the City University of New York. His research spans behavioral neuroscience, cross-cultural psychology, and wellness, focusing on learning processes and technology's impact on cognition.

Weam Ibrahim is a Research Assistant at the College of Education at Qatar University. She holds a Master's in Education in Curriculum Studies (teaching English as a Second Language). Her research interests include adult second language learning, language assessment and professional development in the educational context and literacy.

Jana Koci is an Assistant Professor of Well-being and Health Education at Charles University and a Visiting Professor at Ganesha University of Education in Bali,

Indonesia. She is the author of the book *Well-being and Success for University Students: Applying PERMA+4* and she is currently conducting study on student wellbeing among universities in Europe, North America, South America, Asia, and Australia.

Mohamed Mahgoub earned his Ed.D. in critical sociology of assessment from the IOE, UCL's Faculty of Education and Society. He teaches education policy – on an adjunct basis – at the Doha Institute for Graduate Studies. His research focuses on teaching and learning from learners' perspectives, Arabic heritage learners and dual language development.

Herdiyan Maulana is a Senior Lecturer at the Faculty of Psychology, State University of Jakarta, with a special interest in wellbeing and quality of life studies. He graduated from the Queensland University of Technology, Australia. He is interested in cross-cultural approaches to understanding wellbeing to assist policymakers in improving the quality of life.

Igor Michaleczek is working at the Educational Research Center within the College of Education, Qatar University. Prior to that, he taught Modern Foreign Language in the UK and North Africa after having worked with International NGOs in Africa and Southeast Asia. He is focusing on education in intercultural context and decoloniality.

Abdellatif Sellami is the Director of the Education Research Center, College of Education at Qatar University in Qatar. Previously, he served as an Educational Programs Manager at Qatar Foundation in Qatar and a senior researcher and a faculty member at Qatar University. Prior to that, he had served as a faculty member in the UAE, the UK, and North Africa.

Series preface

As academics, scholars, staff, and colleagues working in the context of universities in the contemporary climate, we are often challenged with where we place our own wellbeing. It is not uncommon to hear about burnout, stress, anxiety, pressures with workload, having too many balls in the air, toxic cultures, increasing demands, isolation, and feeling distressed (Berg & Seeber, 2016; Lemon & McDonough, 2018; Mountz et al., 2015). The reality is that universities are stressful places (Beer et al., 2015; Cranton & Taylor, 2012; Kasworm & Bowles, 2012; Mountz et al., 2015; Ryan, 2013; Sullivan & Weissner, 2010; Wang & Cranton, 2012). McNaughton and Billot (2016) argue that the "deeply personal effects of changing roles, expectations and demands" (p. 646) have been downplayed and that academics and staff engage in constant reconstruction of their identities and work practices. It is important to acknowledge this, as much as it is to acknowledge the need to place wellbeing and self-care at the forefront of these lived experiences and situations.

Wellbeing can be approached at multiple levels, including micro and macro. In placing wellbeing at the heart of the higher education workplace, self-care becomes an imperative both individually and systemically (Berg & Seeber, 2016; Lemon & McDonough, 2018). Self-care is most commonly oriented toward individual action to monitor and ensure personal wellbeing; however, it is also a collective act. There is a plethora of different terms that are in action to describe how one approaches their wellbeing holistically (Godfrey et al., 2011). With different terminology comes different ways self-care is understood. For this collection self-care is understood as "the actions that individuals take for themselves, on behalf of and with others in order to develop, protect, maintain and improve their health, wellbeing or wellness" (Self Care Forum, 2019, para. 1). It covers a spectrum of health-related (emotional, physical, and/or spiritual) actions, including prevention, promotion, and treatment, while aiming to encourage individuals to take personal responsibility for their health and to advocate for themselves and others in accessing resources and care (Knapik & Laverty, 2018). Self-love, -compassion, -awareness, and -regulation are significant elements of self-care. But what does this look like for those working in higher education? In this book series authors respond to the questions: *What do you do for self-care? How do you position wellbeing as part of your role in academia?*

In thinking about these questions, authors are invited to critically discuss and respond to inspiration sparked by one or more of the questions of

- How do we bring self-regulation to how we approach our work?
- How do we create a compassionate workplace in academia?
- What does it mean for our work when we are aware and enact self-compassion?
- What awareness has occurred that has disrupted the way we approach work?
- Where do mindful intentions sit?
- How do we shift the rhetoric of "this is how it has always been" in relation to over working, and indiscretions between workload and approaches to workload?
- How do we counteract the traditional narrative of over work?
- How do we create and sustain a healthier approach?
- How can we empower the "I" and "we" as we navigate self-care as a part of who we are as academics?
- How can we promote a curiosity about how we approach self-care?
- What changes do we need to make?
- How can we approach self-care with energy and promote shifts in how we work individually, collectively, and systemically?

The purpose of this book series is to

- Place academic wellbeing and self-care at the heart of discussions around working in higher education;
- Provide a diverse range of strategies for how to put in place wellbeing and self-care approaches as an academic;
- Provide a narrative connection point for readers from a variety of backgrounds in academia;
- Highlight lived experiences and honor the voice of those working in higher education;
- Provide a visual narrative that supports connection to authors' lived experience(s);
- Contribute to the conversation on ways that wellbeing and self-care can be positioned in the work that those working in higher education do;
- Highlight new ways of working in higher education that disrupt current tensions that neglect wellbeing.

References

Beer, L. E., Rodriguez, K., Taylor, C., Martinez-Jones, N., Griffin, J., Smith, T. R., Lamar, M., & Anaya, R. (2015). Awareness, integration and interconnectedness. *Journal of Transformative Education*, *13*(2), 161–185.

Berg, M., & Seeber, B. K. (2016). *The slow professor: Challenging the culture of speed in the academy*. University of Toronto Press.

Cranton, P., & Taylor, E. W. (2012). Transformative learning theory: Seeking a more unified theory. In E. W. Taylor & P. Cranton (Eds.), *The handbook of transformative learning* (pp. 3–20). Jossey-Bass.

Godfrey, C. M., Harrison, M. B., Lysaght, R., Lamb, M., Graham, I. D., & Oakley, P. (2011). The experience of self-care: A systematic review. *JBI Library of Systematic Reviews, 8*(34), 1351–1460. Retrieved from http://www.ncbi.nlm.nih.gov/pubmed/27819888

Kasworm, C., & Bowles, T. (2012). Fostering transformative learning in higher education settings. In E. Taylor & P. Cranton (Eds.), *The handbook of transformative learning* (pp. 388–407). Sage.

Knapik, K., & Laverty, A. (2018). Self-care individual, relational, and political sensibilities. In M. A. Henning, C. U. Krägeloh, R. Dryer, F. Moir, D. R. Billington, & A. G. Hill (Eds.), *Wellbeing in higher education: Cultivating a healthy lifestyle among faculty and students*. Routledge.

Lemon, N., & McDonough, S. (Eds.). (2018). *Mindfulness in the academy: Practices and perspectives from scholars*. Springer.

McNaughton, S. M., & Billot, J. (2016). Negotiating academic teacher identity shifts during higher education contextual change. *Teaching in Higher Education, 21*(6), 644–658.

Mountz, A., Bonds, A., Mansfield, B., Loyd, J., Hyndman, J., & Watton-Roberts, M. (2015). For slow scholarship: A feminist politics of resistance through collective action in the neoliberal university. *ACME: An International E-Journal of Critical Geographies, 14*(4), 1235–1259.

Ryan, M. (2013). The pedagogical balancing act: Teaching reflection in higher education. *Teaching in Higher Education, 18*, 144–155.

Self Care Forum. (2019). Self Care Forum: Home. Retrieved July 27, 2019, from http://www.selfcareforum.org/

Sullivan L. G., Weissner C. A. (2010). Learning to be reflective leaders: A case study from the NCCHC Hispanic leadership fellows program. In Wallin D. L. (Ed.), *Special issue: Leadership in an era of change. New directions for community colleges, No. 149* (pp. 41–50). San Francisco: Jossey-Bass. https://doi.org/10.1002/cc.394

Wang, V. C., & Cranton, P. (2012). Promoting and implementing self-directed learning (SDL): An effective adult education model. *International Journal of Adult Vocational Education and Technology, 3*, 16–25.

Opening editorial notes

The importance of contextually sensitive and culturally responsive approaches to wellbeing and self-care

"Wellbeing in Higher Education: Contextually Sensitive and Culturally Responsive Perspectives from the Global South" is a groundbreaking book that delves into the crucial yet often overlooked topic of wellbeing and self-care in higher education, with a specific focus on the unique challenges and opportunities present in the Global South. This book is a timely and much-needed contribution to the field, as it sheds light on the diverse experiences and perspectives of students, faculty, and staff in non-Western contexts, challenging the assumptions and norms that have long dominated the discourse on wellbeing in higher education.

The book comprises a collection of chapters, each offering a distinct perspective on the topic and contributing to a rich, nuanced understanding of wellbeing and self-care in higher education. The chapters cover a wide range of themes, from the conceptualization and assessment of wellbeing in different cultural contexts to the implementation of culturally responsive interventions and support systems. Together, they paint a compelling picture of the challenges faced by higher education institutions in the Global South and the innovative strategies being developed to address them.

One of the key strengths of this book is its emphasis on the importance of contextually sensitive and culturally responsive approaches to wellbeing and self-care. The authors consistently highlight the need to move beyond Western-centric models and frameworks, and to develop approaches that are grounded in the specific cultural, social, and economic realities of the Global South. This is evident in chapters that explore the unique challenges faced by students and faculty in the Gulf Cooperation Council (GCC) region, the importance of incorporating indigenous knowledge systems and epistemologies into academic literacy programs, and the development of culturally appropriate measures of wellbeing in Asian contexts.

Another major contribution of this book is its focus on the wellbeing and self-care of often-marginalized groups within higher education, such as female leaders, expatriate academics, and students from diverse cultural backgrounds. The chapters that address these issues provide valuable insights into the specific challenges faced revealing lived experiences that support proactive actions in wellbeing and success. This includes the development of leadership training programs for women, the creation of supportive networks for expatriate academics, and the implementation of culturally responsive interventions to address the mental health needs of international students.

The book also highlights the transformative potential of positive psychology and the PERMA+4 framework in promoting wellbeing and academic success across cultures. The chapter on this topic provides a comprehensive overview of the science and practice of positive psychology and demonstrates how the PERMA+4 framework can be adapted and applied in diverse cultural contexts to enhance student wellbeing and positive functioning. This chapter offers practical strategies and tools that can be implemented by higher education institutions to create more supportive and inclusive learning environments.

Throughout the book, the authors emphasize the need for a holistic, multidimensional approach to wellbeing and self-care in higher education. This involves addressing not only the academic and professional needs of students and faculty but also their social, emotional, spiritual, and physical wellbeing. The chapters that focus on the development of academic literacy programs and the implementation of social-emotional learning interventions provide concrete examples of how this holistic approach can be put into practice.

The book also underscores the importance of collaboration and partnership in promoting wellbeing and self-care in higher education. This includes collaboration between different stakeholders within higher education institutions, such as students, faculty, staff, and administrators, as well as collaboration with external partners, such as community organizations and mental health professionals. The chapters that discuss the implementation of wellbeing interventions and support systems highlight the critical role of collaboration in ensuring their effectiveness and sustainability.

Looking forward, this book lays the foundation for a new era of research and practice in the field of wellbeing and self-care in higher education. It challenges us to move beyond one-size-fits-all approaches and to develop contextually sensitive and culturally responsive strategies that are grounded in the specific needs and experiences of diverse student and faculty populations. It also illuminates the need for more research on the wellbeing and self-care of marginalized groups within higher education, and the importance of developing culturally appropriate measures and interventions.

The insights and recommendations presented in this book have the potential to transform the way we think about and approach wellbeing and self-care in higher education, not only in the Global South but also in other non-Western contexts. By prioritizing the specific needs and experiences of diverse student and faculty populations, and by developing culturally responsive and contextually sensitive approaches, we can create more supportive and inclusive learning environments that promote the success and flourishing of all members of the higher education community. As the field of wellbeing and self-care in higher education continues to evolve, this book will undoubtedly serve as a valuable resource and guide for researchers, practitioners, and policymakers. It lays the foundation for a new era of research and practice that is grounded in contextually sensitive and culturally responsive approaches, and that prioritizes the specific needs and experiences of diverse student and faculty populations.

Professor Narelle Lemon

Series Editor, Wellbeing and Self-care in Higher Education: Embracing Positive Solutions
Vice-Chancellor Professoriate Research Fellow & Professor in Education
Lead, Wellbeing and Education Research Community (WE)
Edith Cowan University, Perth Australia

Chapter 1

Introduction

Youmen Chaaban

The past decade has witnessed a proliferation of policy and popular discourses on student wellbeing, mainly triggered by challenges external to academic institutions, including social problems, economic crises, environmental disasters and human-made conflicts. Several government reports documenting the status of mental health and wellbeing among university students have found staggering high levels of mental illness and distress and low wellbeing (Byrne & Surdey, 2021; Houghton & Anderson, 2017; Thorley, 2017). These reports allude to the importance of promoting wellbeing in higher education and identify several pedagogical benefits. The recent COVID-19 pandemic may have pushed these discussions and debates even further, prompting academic institutions to take reactive measures to mitigate the challenges facing students during educational disruptions. Interest in student wellbeing in higher education has been steadily growing over the past decade (Hernández-Torrano et al., 2020) and has seen a spike in volume during this time (e.g., Van de Velde et al., 2021).

This growing interest is important as it accentuates the need for proactive measures that take into consideration the inherent challenges of experiencing higher education, despite external demands. For instance, students must still navigate the challenges inherent in higher education, such as making important decisions, managing academic demands, adapting to a less-structured learning environment and interacting with a diverse group of people, mostly on a short-term basis. In comparison to the school environment, universities and colleges are larger, sometimes spread over a wide geographic area and incorporate a large student body with far more variation in demographics and experiences. Additionally, it is a time when many students leave home for the first time and are required to manage finances, housing and livelihoods. These challenges combined add to the pressure on higher education institutions to balance their obligations toward student academics and develop workplace-ready graduates, but also their responsibilities toward vesting interest in promoting student wellbeing.

Few would dispute, though, that universities have come to pay greater attention to supporting students, evidenced by the increasing number of support and guidance centers spread across campuses. Higher education institutions are considered unique contexts for promoting wellbeing among students as they encompass a range of academic, professional and social activities, as well as health and counseling services (Hernández-Torrano et al., 2020). However, the number of students benefitting from such services may not be up to par, as services struggle to keep up with the rapid expansion of higher education and the mounting challenges facing students in recent years (Van de Velde et al., 2021). The obligation of higher education institutions to prepare workplace-ready graduates has prompted most universities to offer programs to teach students remedial skills and ways to cope with academic stress, anxiety and depression, while overlooking opportunities for students to learn about themselves and their strengths (Lambert et al., 2019).

Defining wellbeing

While discussions about wellbeing abound, there is much less consensus on how the concept is defined and understood. There are large variations within and among different disciplines, which consider wellbeing a core concept and conceptualize it in ways compatible with their disciplinary perspectives. While these different perspectives enrich our understandings, we contend that any definition that does not allude to the complexity of the construct is necessarily limited. Clearly, a definition of wellbeing is important as it sets the stage for the way the concept may be explored in particular settings. In this volume, wellbeing is conceptualized in relation to learning in higher education, where the welfare of all students is concerned and not only of specific vulnerable students who traditionally occupy educators' concerns.

Though not initially directed toward student wellbeing, psychologists have offered multiple conceptualizations on wellbeing, which may arguably be considered the backdrop and reference for other disciplines. One of the most recognized contributions distinguishes two broad approaches to wellbeing, namely a hedonic view of wellbeing versus a eudaimonic perspective (Hernández-Torrano et al., 2020; Huppert et al., 2009; Ryan & Deci, 2001). Generally speaking, the adoption of the former would necessitate a focus on what makes life pleasurable and what makes individuals feel good (Kahneman et al., 1999), while taking the latter perspective would require a focus on aspects of self-actualization, purpose and meaning (Ryan & Deci, 2001). Researchers continue to point out the limitations of adopting one view over the other, and recent attempts at exploring wellbeing in diverse contexts have considered the need to draw on both approaches (McLellan & Steward, 2015). However, these dimensions are far from their seemingly clear-cut and definitive appearance. For example, Martela and Sheldon's (2019) literature review revealed 45 different ways of operationalizing eudaimonic wellbeing, using measures of at least 63 different constructs. If anything, these findings reveal the variations in the way researchers approach the concept and its constructs, leading to obvious variations in recommendations to policy and practice.

On a similar note, we have observed a widespread propensity to use mental health interchangeably or in conjunction with wellbeing (Hernández-Torrano et al., 2020). Accordingly, mental health is sometimes considered synonymous to wellbeing, while in other instances the two terms are used in a way that *you can't have one without the other*. According to the World Health Organization (WHO), mental health is a term that stems from the medical field and has been posited as "a state of well-being in which every individual realizes his or her own potential, can cope with the normal stresses of life, can work productively and fruitfully, and is able to make a contribution to her or his community" (2014, para 1). However, researchers caution that the absence of mental health issues, or mental illness, does not necessarily imply wellbeing, neither are low levels of wellbeing an indication of mental illness (Hernández-Torrano et al., 2020; Ryan & Deci, 2001). Given the diverse demographic composition of higher education institutions, it may be important not to conflate mental health with wellbeing in a higher education context in order to take a wellbeing-for-all stance, rather than illuminate on instances where only specific groups of students receive support, and the majority of students are left to their own resources. This necessitates navigating away from a deficit perspective to wellbeing in higher education, which equates mental illness to the absence of wellbeing, and consequently as a problem to be fixed. This deficit approach has been the driver behind student support centers which implement interventions in a reactive manner, offered to certain groups of students and in a disconnected and unsystematic approach to wellbeing. Though important, these reactive measures cannot account for the vast majority of students who do not seek help if they are or are not mentally ill, but nonetheless would benefit from proactive and preventative structures for promoting wellbeing in the university context.

Clearly, wellbeing as a construct has been considered and developed in various disciplines, yet positive psychology has taken the lead in this endeavor. In comparison to scholars and researchers in other disciplines, positive psychologists have perhaps been the most influential in moving public policy on wellbeing toward action. It seems logical if not imperative then to consult the literature on wellbeing from a positive psychological perspective, though we caution that our conceptualization of wellbeing is centered on students in higher education, not so much on measuring their wellbeing per se, but on investigating the conditions and sources likely to influence their wellbeing. Therefore, while we have and continue to consult on the positive psychology literature on wellbeing, we contend that other disciplines, including medicine, public health, sociology and education can add to our understanding of wellbeing and its conceptualization.

In this regard, Lomas et al. (2021) provide a glimpse on how the field of positive psychology has undergone several developments since its first inception over 20 years ago (presidential address to APA). Metaphorically speaking, Lomas et al. (2021) categorized these developments into three waves, which are complementary, rather than mutually exclusive. Thus, following the initial instantiation of the field with its emphasis on *positive* phenomena during the first wave, Lomas et al. (2021) argued that the second wave constituted a shift toward acknowledging the subtle interplay between the positive and negative, including the dialectical nature of wellbeing. As opposed to the narratives of dysfunction, or the deficit approach, positive psychologists were behind the promotion of wellbeing-for-all approach. The third wave beginning to form, they argue, involves going beyond the individual and embracing greater complexity. Accordingly, this involves (1) broadening the focus of inquiry to incorporate super-individual processes, (2) becoming more multi-disciplinary, (3) incorporating a multi-cultural and global perspective and (3) embracing other ways of knowing and researching wellbeing.

Therefore, it is our intention to draw on a holistic conception of wellbeing that goes well beyond psychopathological and biomedical perspectives and encompasses social, emotional, physical, intellectual and spiritual dimensions. This is in line with positive psychologists who also make clear the need to be concerned with every individual's wellbeing, and not only the most vulnerable. But again, we are particularly focused on an educationalist perspective, which investigates wellbeing in relation to human and non-human components of university contexts that make teaching and learning processes more meaningful and accessible. Some useful concepts that we draw on from the positive psychology literature include, for example, Seligman's (2011) PERMA model that posits positive emotions, engagement, relationships, meaning and accomplishments as important wellbeing constructs. Another influential model includes Ryff and Singer's (1998) model, which comprises six components, namely autonomy, environmental mastery, personal growth, positive relationships, purpose in life and self-acceptance. A third popular model is attributed to Ryan and Deci's (2001) self-determination theory, which regards autonomy, competence or mastery and positive relationships as the basic psychological needs for individuals to experience wellbeing. These models have been used extensively in educational research (e.g., Butler & Kern, 2016) and provide a springboard for much of our thinking on wellbeing in a higher education context.

Despite the R for relationships in these models, the conceptualization of wellbeing in the field of positive psychology has been criticized to under-theorize the social context (Lomas et al., 2021; McLellan & Steward, 2015). Relationships constitute an important element of educational research due to their essentiality in any teaching and learning process. A reverse influence may happen here, where positive psychology can benefit from educationalists' theorizing on socio-cultural dimensions. It may be useful at this point to distinguish between categorical and relational conceptions of wellbeing (Wyn, 2009). A categorical conceptualization defines wellbeing as a product or outcome that can be operationalized, measured and delineated in a universal way, much like that which has been documented during the first wave of positive psychology literature. Accordingly, wellbeing becomes a personal property, skill or capacity that individuals can possess. In opposition, a relational conceptualization considers wellbeing as a social process or social construct that is a function of the relationships that individuals share with others; invented and reinvented in different times and places and for different purposes (Wright & McLeod, 2015). As such, individuals' perceptions of not only receiving social support, but also contributing social support to others play an important role in their wellbeing from this educational perspective (Huppert et al., 2009).

Clearly, there is little consensus on how best to approach the definition of wellbeing, which has been deemed a "wicked problem" in the research arena

(Svane et al., 2019). This is problematic because a lack of clear definition ultimately influences how wellbeing is operationalized and measured, how interventions are designed and implemented and what kinds of results and outcomes are expected. With some exceptions (Boulton et al., 2019; Byrne & Surdey, 2021), we suggest that there should be a consideration of the higher education context, not only as a place for examining and promoting student wellbeing, but as contributing to wellbeing through its values, purposes and support systems.

Why wellbeing?

Despite its fluid and elusive nature, there is good reason to promote student wellbeing. Generally speaking, wellbeing is considered an essential component of education in light of several studies linking wellbeing and education. For instance, student wellbeing has been positively associated with academic performance, as well as students' holistic engagement with learning (Boulton et al., 2019). In a longitudinal study of student wellbeing, Boulton et al. (2019) suggested a possible feedback loop where increasing student engagement increases academic performance, which in turn increases student wellbeing, which then increases engagement. As an alternative, they also suggested that students with greater background levels of wellbeing are more likely to engage with learning.

Further, Koydemir and Sun-Selışık (2016) emphasize students' wellbeing to be connected with higher positive affect, stronger relationships and satisfaction and effective coping, while Maddah et al. (2021) provided empirical evidence for effectiveness of university interventions in enhancing students' life skills, including self-care, work and study, career and education planning and goal setting. These findings are further validated by Lambert et al. (2019) who argue for connections between student wellbeing, character strengths, career readiness and employability. Further, wellbeing support in the form of interventions and programs offered to students particularly during the demanding transition from high school to university has been shown to buffer against emotional exhaustion and reduce dropout rates among students (Byrne & Surdey, 2021; Thorley, 2017).

What these studies have in common is the notion that wellbeing is strengthened by conditions such as having economic security and safety, sense of purpose and meaning, control over decisions and positive relationships with others. In this respect, we see relevance in Hale et al.'s (2019) modified version of Maslow's (1943) Hierarchy of Needs, whereby the conditions of higher needs, including belonging, self-esteem and self-actualization, are no longer seen as being contingent on the fulfillment of basic physiological and safety needs. Rather, each need supports all others in an integrated framework of wellbeing. Also valued are the contributions made by large-scale studies on wellbeing in educational contexts (Butler & Kern, 2016), which further support developing understandings of wellbeing among education stakeholders from a multi-dimensional perspective.

While there is increasing interest in wellbeing among researchers and practitioners (e.g., Hale et al., 2019), there is nonetheless little understanding and guidance for infusing wellbeing into the higher education context, including its policies, culture and practices. Our own experiences in higher education indicate little and opaque understanding by faculty, staff and senior leaders about where wellbeing fits into higher education and about the most effective approaches to *doing* wellbeing on a university-wide scale. Without clear guidelines for a wellbeing-for-all approach, students will continue to receive isolated and sporadic interventions that will do little to build a culture that sustains their wellbeing.

Context, culture and wellbeing

While there is growing recognition in the literature that both context and culture are important in more than just providing a backdrop to wellbeing studies, most of these reports or studies have emerged from the Global North (Lomas et al., 2021; McLellan et al., 2022), with far fewer research conducted in the Global South (Lambert & Pasha-Zaidi, 2019). According to the bibliometric analysis of student mental health and wellbeing in higher education (Hernández-Torrano et al., 2020), over 50% of publications were from researchers based in the United States. Despite methodological limitations of the study and the fact that only English databases were consulted, its findings provide evidence for the domination of Westernized conceptualizations of wellbeing, which do not necessarily provide the contextually sensitive and culturally responsive view needed (McLellan et al., 2022). While an evident lack of diversity in research is a viable concern, the issue concerning cultural relativism versus universals in human nature adds another layer for researchers to grapple with (Ryan & Deci, 2001). In this regard, Lomas (2015) offered a synthesis of the two perspectives in what he labels "universal relativism," and recognizes the possibility of connecting universal similarities and cultural diversity. We take a similar stance to Western models and theories as Lambert and Pasha-Zaidi (2019), in that we cannot claim that *one size fits all* and that they can be applied indiscriminately in a non-Western context nor do they accurately reflect local cultural landscape, yet may provide an important departure point for many of the discussion in this volume.

Another strong argument has been made when Western views not only dominate the literature and research but also are exported to non-Western settings, thus diluting local understandings (McLellan et al., 2022). This is especially relevant in the Global South which has witnessed a form of neo-colonialism with the introduction of Western understandings and conceptualizations of *just about everything* into the educational contexts, including notions of wellbeing. With the domination of such views, it may be time to recognize indigenous understandings as potentially different from the normalized Western notions and respond to calls for the development of a body of knowledge grounded in multi-cultural contexts (Lambert & Pasha-Zaidi, 2019; Lomas et al., 2021). Therefore, problematizing wellbeing as embedded within socio-cultural, political and economic contexts allows local voices to emerge, and local policies, research and practices to follow suit.

From an ecological and systems-thinking perspective (Kern et al., 2020; Lomas et al., 2021), students cannot be isolated from the systems of influence on their wellbeing, nor can they consequently have more or less wellbeing if the conditions that enhance or hinder such wellbeing are not accounted for within the contexts where they learn, develop and grow. This is particularly important given the focus of this volume on student wellbeing in higher education institutions. A focus on the decontextualized and deculturated individual student would at best provide a narrow illustration of wellbeing, yet at worst would fail to account for the multitude of factors and conditions that influence and shape the wellbeing of students from diverse socio-cultural, political and economic settings. Inspired by this systems-thinking approach (Kern et al., 2020), multi-cultural perspectives carry implications at the epistemological level with non-Western cultures perhaps challenging the very nature of what constitutes wellbeing (Lomas et al., 2021). As predicted by Lomas et al. (2021), the third wave will likely involve greater contributions from non-Western contexts using constructs and methodologies developed locally.

Considering the approaches and concerns thus far noted, we propose the following principles for a structured framework for defining student wellbeing in higher education: (1) previous theorizing of wellbeing is necessary yet insufficient for the purpose of grounding student wellbeing within the socio-cultural context of higher education and the cultural context of the Global South, (2) the concept itself needs to be extracted from its customary affiliations with mental health to incorporate familial and social elements, but also socio-cultural, political and economic forces too, (3) individual perspectives are important, but they should not dominate the discourse on wellbeing, as subjective and objective dimensions are equally important, (4) wellbeing must be seen as a multi-dimensional construct that is influenced by multiple factors that cross individual, relational and contextual boundaries and (5) a reductionist view of wellbeing is rejected, as any conceptualization that does not take into consideration the complexity of wellbeing will not do justice to those involved.

This volume therefore presents an alternative conceptualization of wellbeing in higher education in the Global South region. It offers contributing authors the opportunity to re-conceptualize taken-for-granted definitions and, understandings of wellbeing based on Western values and social norms, and delineates a contextually sensitive and culturally responsive perspective. We encourage the exploration of wellbeing in higher education from a range of approaches and intellectual scholarship and support the investigation of its different dimensions and complexity as called for by Lambert and Pasha-Zaidi (2019) and Lomas et al. (2021). By challenging a reductionist view of wellbeing and embracing its complexity, multi-dimensionality and context-sensitivity, we hope that this volume will stimulate policy development and enactment, as well as university-wide interventions and practices that can make a difference in the lives of students in higher education.

References

Boulton, C. A., Hughes, E., Kent, C., Smith, J. R., & Williams, H. T. P. (2019). Student engagement and well-being over time at a higher education institution. *PLoS ONE, 14*(11), e0225770. https://doi.org/10.1371/journal.pone.0225770

Butler, J., & Kern, M. L. (2016). The PERMA-Profiler: A brief multidimensional measure of flourishing. *International Journal of Wellbeing, 6*(3), 1–48. https://doi.org/10.5502/ijw.v6i3.526

Byrne, D., & Surdey, J. (2021). *Embedding well-being across the curriculum in higher education*. Union of Students in Ireland and the National Forum for the Enhancement of Teaching and Learning in Higher Education. Available: https://usi.ie/wp-content/uploads/2021/10/Supporting-Wellbeing-in-Practice-October-2021.pdf

Hale, A. J., Ricotta, D. N., Freed, J., Smith, C. C., & Huang, G. C. (2019). Adapting Maslow's hierarchy of needs as a framework for resident wellness. *Teaching and Learning in Medicine, 31*(1), 109–118. https://doi.org/10.1080/10401334.2018.1456928

Hernández-Torrano, D., Ibrayeva, L., Sparks, J., Lim, N., Clementi, A., Almukhambetova, A., Nurtayev, Y., & Muratkyzy, A. (2020). Mental health and well-being of university students: A bibliometric mapping of the literature. *Frontiers in Psychology, 11*(1226). https://doi.org/10.3389/fpsyg.2020.01226

Houghton, A., & Anderson, M. J. (2017). *Embedding mental well-being in the curriculum: Maximising success in higher education*. Higher Education Academy. Retrieved from: https://s3.eu-west-2.amazonaws.com/assets.creode.advancehe-document-manager/documents/hea/private/hub/download/embedding_wellbeing_in_he_1568037359.pdf

Huppert, F., Marks, N., Clark, A., Siegrist, J., Stutzer, A., Vittersø, J., & Wahrendorf, M. (2009). Measuring well-being across Europe: Description of the ESS well-being module and preliminary findings. *Social Indicators Research, 91*, 301–315. https://doi.org/10.1007/s11205-008-9346-0

Kahneman, D., Diener, E., & Schwarz, N. (Eds.). (1999). *Well-being: The foundations of hedonic psychology*. Russell Sage Foundation.

Kern, M. L., Williams, P., Spong, C., Colla, R., Sharma, K., Downie, A., Taylor, J. A., Sharp, S., Siokou, C., & Oades, L. G. (2020). Systems informed positive psychology. *Journal of Positive Psychology, 15*(4), 705–715. https://doi.org/10.1080/17439760.2019.1639799

Koydemir, S., & Sun-Selışık, Z. E. (2016). Well-being on campus: Testing the effectiveness of an online strengths-based intervention for first year college students. *British Journal of Guidance and Counselling, 44*, 434–446. https://doi.org/10.1080/03069885.2015.1110562

Lambert, L., Abdulrehman, R., & Mirza, C. (2019). *Coming full circle: Taking positive psychology to GCC universities*. In: Lambert, L. & Pasha-Zaidi, N. (Eds.). *Positive psychology in the Middle East/North Africa*. Springer. https://doi.org/10.1007/978-3-030-13921-6_5

Lambert, L., & Pasha-Zaidi, N. (Eds.). (2019). *Positive psychology in the Middle East/North Africa: Research, policy, and practise*. Springer.

Lomas, T. (2015). Positive cross-cultural psychology: Exploring similarity and difference in constructions and experiences of well-being. *International Journal of Wellbeing, 5*(4), 60–77. https://doi.org/10.5502/ijw.v5i4.437

Lomas, T., Waters, L., Williams, P., Oades, L. G., & Kern, M. L. (2021). Third wave positive psychology: Broadening towards complexity. *Journal of Positive Psychology*, 1–15. https://doi.org/10.1080/17439760.2020.1805501

Maddah, D., Saab, Y., Safadi, H., Abi Farraj, N., Hassan, Z., Turner, S., Echeverri, L., Alami, N. H., Kababian-Khasholian, T., & Salameh, P. (2021). The first life skills intervention to enhance well-being amongst university students in the Arab world: 'Khotwa' pilot study. *Health Psychology Open, 8*(1). https://doi.org/10.1177/20551029211016955

Martela, F., & Sheldon, K. M. (2019). Clarifying the concept of well-being: Psychological need satisfaction as the common core connecting eudaimonic and subjective well-being. *Review of General Psychology, 23*(4), 458–474. https://doi.org/10.1177/1089268019880886

Maslow, A. H. (1943). Preface to motivation theory. *Psychosomatic medicine*, 5(1), 85–92.

McLellan, R., Faucher, C., & Simovska, V. (2022). *Well-being and schooling: Cross cultural and cross disciplinary perspectives*. Springer.

McLellan, R., & Steward, S. (2015). Measuring children and young people's well-being in the school context. *Cambridge Journal of Education*, 45(3), 307–332. https://doi.org/10.1080/0305764X.2014.889659

Ryan, R. M., & Deci, E. L. (2001). On happiness and human potentials: A review of research on hedonic and eudaimonic well-being. *Annual Review of Psychology*, 52, 141–166.

Ryff, C. D., & Singer, B. (1998). The contours of positive human health. *Psychological Inquiry*, 9(1), 1–28. https://doi.org/10.1207/s15327965pli0901_1

Seligman, M. (2011). *Flourish*. Simon & Schuster.

Svane, D., Evans, N., & Carter, M. A. (2019). Wicked well-being: Examining the disconnect between the rhetoric and reality of well-being interventions in schools. *Australian Journal of Education*, 63(2), 209–231. https://doi.org/10.1177/0004944119843144

Thorley, C. (2017). *Not by degrees: Improving student mental health in the UK's universities*. IPPR.

Van de Velde, S., Buffel, V., Bracke, P., Van Hal, G., Somogyi, N., Willems, B., Wouters, E., & C19 ISWS consortium. (2021). The COVID-19 international student well-being study. *Scandinavian Journal of Public Health*, 49(1), 114–122. https://doi.org/10.1177/1403494820981186

Wright, K., & McLeod, J. (Eds.). (2015). *Rethinking youth well-being*. Springer.

Wyn, J. (2009). *Youth health and welfare: The cultural politics of education and well-being*. Oxford University Press.

Chapter 2

Wellbeing odyssey

Integrating Afrofuturist theory with academic literacy

Oscar Eybers

Introduction

The main purpose of this chapter is to emphasize the critical need for sound policies and pedagogical systems in Higher Education, particularly focusing on academic literacy development, to safeguard the wellbeing of novice African scholars. This protection is identified as urgent due to the challenges faced within contemporary Higher Education systems in Africa. The chapter explores the concept of an African Renaissance, defined as a collective effort to overcome neo-apartheid and neo-colonial challenges while envisioning a prosperous future prioritizing the wellbeing of all Africans. Additionally, the analysis highlights the role of academic literacies rooted in African epistemologies and Afrofuturistic perspectives in shaping this Renaissance and safeguarding African cultural identities within disciplines.

This chapter also contrasts the experience of epistemic captivity under colonialism and apartheid with Afrofuturist visions, illustrating how colonialism aimed to dominate African ontologies and erase Africans' cultural memory, indigenous modes of social organization, and knowledge systems. A key claim is that coloniality extends beyond physical and mental domination, targeting every aspect of indigenous peoples' existence, including pedagogies and knowledge facilitation, thereby harming the wellbeing of novice scholars in Higher Education. Central to the chapter's argument is the crucial role of academic literacies in Higher Education, particularly in safeguarding the wellbeing of novice African students from colonial and apartheid violence (Luiz, 1998). The reasoning stresses the need for robust policies and pedagogical methods aimed at developing academic literacies among students. Emphasis on academic literacy is vital for nurturing the intellectual growth and overall wellbeing of students amid the challenges faced within contemporary Higher Education systems in Africa.

This chapter advocates for an African Renaissance integrally rooted in the revitalization of indigenous African languages, epistemologies, and institutions. The logic strives to highlight the transformative potential of academic literacies grounded in African epistemologies and Afrofuturistic perspectives as generators of the African Renaissance. By equipping students with essential literacies to survive in their disciplines and degrees, educators play an important role in fostering cultural identity, belonging, and intellectual agency within academic disciplines. Consequently, African cultural identities, belonging to disciplines and intellectual agency, are essential aspects of holistic wellbeing. This initiative-taking method aims to not only empower students but also to contribute to envisioning a future that prioritizes the academic, individual, communal, disciplinary, and professional wellbeing of all African scholars enrolled in institutions of higher learning.

This chapter's discussion concludes by critically examining colonial legacies in South Africa that sought to erase African peoples' indigenous knowledge systems and perpetuate epistemic captivity through university disciplines. By acknowledging and countering this historical erasure, educators, academic literacy facilitators and scholars can reclaim and celebrate Africa's diverse ontologies (Na'Puti, 2019). Moreover, through the lens of Afrofuturistic and Afrocentric theoretical paradigms, the chapter advocates for a decolonial approach to education that recognizes and validates indigenous ways of knowing. By doing so, this investigation aims to dismantle the intellectual and existential darkness imposed by coloniality, thereby promoting disciplinary illumination and holistic wellbeing in pan-African universities that are responsible for developing future leaders.

Coloniality and the attempted erasure of African knowledge systems

When European states from the Global North committed themselves to colonizing Africa and enslaving Africans as chattel labor for newly acquired territories, monarchs, missionaries, and businesspeople recognized that physical violence alone was insufficient to consolidate the emerging globalized capitalist economy. Therefore, alongside physical aggression to acquire African labor and land, epistemic brutality and violence were deemed essential for capturing African minds. The key point here, particularly concerning Southern Africa, is that under colonialism, the Global North aimed not just to physically dominate Africans but also sought to eradicate indigenous knowledge systems and ways of life, perpetuating epistemic violence that impacted all aspects of indigenous social ontologies. Consequently, capitalism was founded on deliberate efforts to erase and manipulate various aspects of African socioeconomic organization through pedagogies, literacies, and knowledge facilitation within newly established colonial institutions.

The South African state emerged from colonial and apartheid rule less than 35 years ago. As a result, there are still knowledge structures, curricula, and ideologies within the country's universities that inadvertently perpetuate epistemic violence against indigenous, Black, African students. This chapter argues that persistent presences of coloniality and apartheid ideology in African university disciplines and degree programs fosters epistemic trauma among African students. Zunguze (2019) posits that due to centuries of coloniality and apartheid, global Africans endure significant social breakdown. This induced social pathology, stemming from colonialism and apartheid, currently results in unprecedented levels of epistemic marginalization based on race, gender, and economic identities, directly permeating university disciplines. Hence, Africans continue to face unavoidable social trauma within university disciplines, entrenched in Eurocentric, colonial, and apartheid frameworks. Zunguze (2019), drawing on Frantz Fanon's concept of trauma, highlights educators' responsibility to alleviate human suffering within this enduring legacy of colonialism and apartheid.

Multi-academic literacies, operating at the intersection of disciplinary epistemologies and students' abilities to master specific knowledge fields, disciplinary vocabularies, and modes of argumentation have been exploited by colonial and apartheid educators, institutional administrators, and academic literacy developers in various ways. These exploitations aimed to either exclude indigenous African students from Higher Education disciplines or subject them to epistemic trauma. Examples of how academic literacies continue to be facilitated in manners that cause epistemic harm to African university students, and at times exclusion from disciplines, include monolingual instruction in languages inherited from colonialism and apartheid, assessment strategies that disregard indigenous epistemic approaches, and the discouragement of knowledge generation and individualist pedagogies (Seroto, 2011). By perpetuating these methodologies within university disciplines and academic literacy development, this chapter holds that African and global institutions of higher learning inadvertently jeopardize new university entrants' epistemic, cognitive, and cultural wellbeing while navigating disciplinary domains where Eurocentrism is normalized under the guise of academic freedom for some scholars, testers, and instructors. For these reasons, the current chapter advocates for Afrocentric and Afrofuturist pedagogic frameworks to safeguard the wellbeing of African scholars in disciplinary environments that are often hostile to their indigenous orientations to life.

Afrofuturist literacies as generators of wellbeing

The current chapter argues that Afrofuturism, as a dynamic educational framework, offers a transformative conceptual lens for addressing the historical and enduring impact of colonial and apartheid legacies on African wellbeing in Higher Education. The Afrofuturist theoretical paradigm aims to integrate Africa's ancient histories and cultures with futuristic visions that encompass imagination, creativity, and innovation. Samatar's (2017) analysis, "A Planetary History of Afrofuturism," explores the interplay between Black peoples' cultural past and alternative liberatory visions of the future. Examining the intersections of African knowledge systems and futuristic technology applications, Hamilton's (2017) study, "Afrofuturism and the Technologies of Survival," explores the relationship between Black visions of emancipation and technological advancements. Similarly, this chapter posits that a fusion of global African aspirations for liberation from colonialism can be achieved by bridging indigenous epistemologies, creativity, and technology.

Afrofuturism emerges as a transformative curriculum framework for redefining and reconstructing academic literacies for new university entrants by integrating African histories, knowledge systems and contemporary disciplines. This change in thinking empowers educators and facilitators of academic literacy to weave critical teaching, learning, and assessment strategies that transcend traditional curricula boundaries, reflecting colonial, and apartheid epistemic boundaries, by actively safeguarding students from residual Eurocentrism in the lecture hall. Adopting Afrofuturist principles initiates a healing process and fosters a deliberate revisualizing of the future of African academia. Afrofuturism enables the integration of global African knowledge systems and literacies with the ways local communities produce knowledge. Moreover, Afrofuturism aligns with disciplinary advancements, technological innovations, and addresses the social and economic needs of these communities. In this light, through Afrofuturism, there is a synergistic marriage of indigenous knowledge systems that not only heal trauma but also innovate and adapt to enhance wellbeing.

In the quest for avant-garde pedagogical frameworks within Higher Education, Afrofuturism acts as a pivotal mechanism for nurturing academic literacy and new students' wellbeing. Afrofuturist paradigms allow educators to identify a spectrum of literacies – ranging from reading and writing to critical thinking, analysis, problem-solving, and context-specific learning – rooted in the academic and personal development of African students. By integrating Afrofuturist principles into educational methods using innovative technologies like GenAI and other online platforms, academic literacy can disrupt the long-standing effects of systemic trauma which harm African scholars' wellbeing through innovative methods. By tapping into diverse individual and community knowledge through these new digital tools, we can guide academic discussions toward inclusivity and empowerment, thereby reducing the weight of colonial and apartheid knowledge structures in disciplinary discourses.

Emphasizing digital tools as enablers of decolonized pedagogies that draw on ancient African knowledge systems within innovative GenAI technologies is central to re-envisioning academic literacy through an Afrofuturist lens (Rabaka, 2022). In the contemporary era, educators and emerging disciplinary members have access to digital tools that have transformed the development of teaching, learning, and core communicative strategies. These current digital technologies, including Generative Artificial tools, empower multilingual, multicultural African disciplinary members to overcome colonial and apartheid pedagogic structures, such as monolingual and ethnocentric practices, thereby excelling in their respective knowledge domains. ChatPDF and Quillbot, respectively, are illustrative examples of the advantages of digital tools in enhancing students' engagement and learning outcomes.

ChatPDF offers an integrated platform for navigating disciplinary texts. Here, students are empowered to actively engage in the co-creation of knowledge through questioning and discussions with the ChatPDF chatbot. ChatPDF enables students to analyze complex texts, ask questions, and seek clarification as they navigate challenging disciplinary concepts. This personalized approach to developing disciplinary reading fosters students' understanding and critical thinking literacy as they interact with peers and educators, sharing insights and perspectives while receiving valuable feedback. In essence, ChatPDF serves as more than just a tool for collaborative analysis; it becomes a dynamic space for inquiry and exploration, enriching the learning experience and empowering students to grasp disciplinary content with confidence and clarity.

Afrofuturism, as a pedagogic framework, allows academic literacy facilitators' integration of ChatPDF in ways that guard students' wellbeing. Recognizing the symbiotic relationship between reading and writing, comprehension and knowledge representation in academic success, ChatPDF and Quillbot synergize to advance literacies. ChatPDF's interactive functionalities enhance comprehension through questioning and annotation, while Quillbot aids in refining students' writing, promoting clear and coherent expressions of disciplinary knowledge. Together, these applications nurture diverse academic literacies, including critical thinking – empowering multilingual African learners to interpret and contribute to disciplinary knowledge, thereby safeguarding their holistic wellbeing. This digital synergy stresses the iterative progression inherent in reading and writing development, in environments where students feel supported and enabled to thrive academically and personally.

Interplays of Afrofuturism, Afrocentricity, and wellbeing

Like Afrofuturism, Afrocentric theory is capable of protecting students' wellbeing. Afrocentricity, as conceptualized by Asante (1991), functions to center African perspectives, experiences, and values in the interpretation of disciplinary knowledge. The Afrocentric paradigm is particularly relevant in analyzing wellbeing through academic literacies, by empowering African scholars to interpret their experiences of wellbeing through indigenous frameworks, thus challenging the historical dominance of Eurocentric viewpoints in disciplinary and cultural realms (Mazama, 2001). Philosophized by Asante (1991), Afrocentricity emphasizes the imperative for Africans to reclaim agency in shaping their academic experiences, fostering an indigenous methodology for safeguarding the academic wellbeing of novice African scholars. Incorporating Afrocentric principles not only promotes self- and cultural pride, identity, and wellbeing among scholars of pan-African heritages but also contributes to a more inclusive and diverse academic literacy field.

Afrofuturism combines African cultures with science fiction, creativity, and cutting-edge technologies. The pedagogic framework can provide valuable perspectives on students' wellbeing in disciplines, similar to Afrocentrism. Holbert and colleagues (2020) suggest that the Afrofuturist framework provides a means for scholars, curriculum planners, and academic literacy facilitators to contemplate the future of the oppressed through alternative disciplinary lenses. In Higher Education, and as pertaining to protecting new students' wellbeing, this methodology includes African students critically examining social, economic, and environmental aspects of their disciplines. Such criticality is achieved by educator's utilization of Afrofuturist principles to connect students' personal, family, and community cultures to disciplines modes of producing knowledge (Holbert et al., 2020). One might suggest that the Afrofuturist framework supports interpreting students' wellbeing through developmental lenses rather than through Eurocentric frameworks that perpetuate deficit constructs. Similar to Afrocentricity, Afrofuturism challenges Eurocentric analyzes of African scholars' academic literacy development in disciplines, advocating for an indigenous, holistic methodology.

This chapter suggests that clues to protecting the wellbeing of students in disciplinary communities within African universities may be found in art, fiction, writing, and creativity. While not conducting a literary analysis of Afrofuturist fiction, it would be incomplete to overlook the influential works and ideas of Octavia Butler, a foundational Afrofuturism theorist in the pan-African community. Butler's narratives, such as "Kindred" Duffy et al. (2017) and "Parable of the Sower" (1993), embody values, themes, and concerns relevant to the wellbeing of African scholars, resonating with the experiences of the pan-African community. These narratives prompt educators to reconsider traditional pedagogical approaches and explore innovative strategies aligned with Afrofuturistic principles.

Some key Afrofuturist themes and concepts, evident in Butler's theory and art, which are relevant to academic literacy developers and educators aiming to protect African university students' wellbeing include Butler's emphasis on community and addressing historical challenges faced by the pan-African community. This focus encourages a holistic methodology, inspiring educators to design learning environments that draw on communal and Black history while integrating Afrofuturistic elements, such as new technologies, into teaching practices. In doing so, educators decolonize their pedagogies, acknowledging and fostering the resilience of new disciplinary members. Likewise, bell hooks (1989) stresses the significance of marginalized spaces within pan-African ontologies, frequently influenced by coloniality and apartheid within academic disciplines. hooks indicates that within disciplinary realms marked by colonialism and Eurocentrism, African intellects can exhibit resistance, aiming toward alternative futures. This Afrofuturist perspective, coupled with resilience and historical consciousness, enables contemporary educational analysis in African universities that may safeguard novice African scholars through academic literacies.

Challenges to Afrofuturist literacy models

The convergence of academic literacy and Afrofuturist principles occurs at multiple junctures. However, challenges emerge in safeguarding the wellbeing of novice African scholars when grappling with interplays of colonial and apartheid-influenced autonomous frameworks of literacy in academic disciplines. Colonial, apartheid, and autonomous literacy models tend to be restricted to sentence-level and textual aspects of discourses within faculties, making it challenging to discern the connections between academic literacies and Afrofuturist principles. Therefore, it is crucial to distinguish between autonomous and ideological models of literacy (Street, 2006).

The differentiation between autonomous and ideological academic literacy models is crucial for overcoming conceptual obstacles that impede pan-African academic literacy facilitators from theoretically integrating Afrofuturistic principles, including ancestral knowledge, into their curriculum design, teaching methods, learning approaches, and assessments. Street's (2006) autonomous model of literacy, extensively standardized in numerous South African academic literacy units, takes center stage in this examination. This model not only undergoes scrutiny but also raises concerns specifically related to its impact on the wellbeing of novice African scholars. Positioned as a universally advantageous skill detached from contextual nuances, the autonomous model conceals ideological biases within academic literacy constructs, curricula, and assessments. Furthermore, its inadequacies become particularly harmful to multilingual, indigenous disciplinary scholars, exacerbating the challenges they face within the academic landscape.

By presuming literacy as a mechanistic skill, the autonomous literacy model (Street, 2006) imposes Eurocentric standards onto pan-African academic disciplines, disregarding diverse pre-colonial literacy practices. This imposition carries implications for the wellbeing of novice African scholars. The autonomous literacy model fails to recognize the impact of literacies in various disciplinary cultures, as it also disregards pre-colonial knowledge systems and alternative approaches to shaping disciplines. Consequently, autonomous literacy models fail to address specific threats posed to the academic wellbeing of novice African scholars in disciplines.

Drawing on the philosophies of hooks and Butler, Afrofuturism not only confronts challenges posed by autonomous literacy constructs that can harm students' wellbeing but also presents opportunities for academic literacy facilitators to be innovative and impactful in their craft. The Afrofuturist principle of creativity emerges in two pivotal ways, offering a pathway to transcend the boundaries of generic, basic skills and courses influenced by transfer-oriented, monolingual structures. First, educators possess the agency to infuse creativity into curriculum planning, thereby safeguarding the status of novice scholars as vulnerable members of disciplines. This stance aligns with hooks' (1989) acknowledgment of marginalized spaces as domains of vulnerability and possibilities.

Highlighting Afrofuturist principles sheds light on the crucial roles of students' creative, futuristic, ancestral academic literacies within various disciplines, such as psychology, criminology, sociology, political science, philosophy, and economics. This illumination serves a dual purpose: safeguarding their wellbeing and empowering literacy facilitators to overcome the constraints imposed by generic, autonomous course models. The ideological literacy framework (Street, 2006), in contrast, resonates with Octavia Butler's emphasis on drawing on the pan-African community's ancestral epistemologies to design new, alternative futures. Therefore, informed by Butler and hooks' insights, Afrofuturist principles will now guide how the current analysis blends Afrofuturism and Afrocentrism with academic literacies, to visualize pedagogies that confront risks to the wellbeing of African scholars in Higher Education.

Risks in safeguarding novice African scholars' wellbeing

If pan-African academic literacy facilitators fail to integrate Afrofuturist precepts and indigenous knowledge into academic disciplines, they risk diminishing the importance of indigenous future realities and further marginalizing them. The neglect to incorporate indigenous values and knowledge systems into pedagogical frameworks may exacerbate concerns raised by Street (2006) regarding the autonomous model of literacy. This neglect has the potential to negatively impact the wellbeing of scholars and disciplinary communities. Street (2006) contends that educators employing autonomous literacy models approach critical thinking, reading, and writing as culturally sterile and mechanistic practices, devoid of acknowledgment of the cultural and epistemic peculiarities of discipline-specific literacies. Such a construal of literacy proves detrimental to university students on the African continent.

During South Africa's apartheid era, linguists collaborated with government officials in using literacy to sustain social inequality and a colonial order, thereby harming indigenous African scholars. The autonomous model of literacy was utilized to manipulate, control, and restrict the academic literacy development of indigenous African scholars, impeding their access to influential disciplinary knowledge and discourses (Reagan, 1987). The autonomous model of literacy, as applied within the framework of academic literacy in education, furthered Verwoerd's aims by perpetuating the concept of "whiteness" and reinforcing social divisions in Higher Education spaces.

Hendrik Frensch Verwoerd, a key architect of the apartheid-era Bantu Education Act, designed this system with the explicit goal of segregating and controlling the education of African scholars. The deliberate exclusion of indigenous African people from scientific and expert disciplines and discourses in Higher Education, as seen in the Bantu Education Act, was a prime example of this strategy. Consequently, African individuals were systematically deprived of access to essential literacies required for meaningful engagement in mainstream academic fields. This deprivation had far-reaching implications, hindering Africans' opportunities for entry into various industries, professional roles, and expert positions after completing their university education. As a result, the wellbeing of novice African scholars was significantly compromised.

The awareness among academic literacy and disciplinary facilitators regarding the use of academic literacies as tools for apartheid social engineering, perpetuating "racial" segregation and economic inequality through higher learning disciplines reflects the value of historical contexts in Afrofuturist paradigms. Threats posed by autonomous literacy models, as maintained by apartheid-era applied linguists in cahoots with the government of that day, are evident in their potential to reinforce discriminatory practices, further entrenching apartheid ideologies and exacerbating socioeconomic disparities. For example, in Southern Africa, most students entering university do not have the option of highlighting their intellectual and disciplinary capabilities in assessments based on their primary languages. Hence, within

Afrofuturist and Afrocentric paradigms, it is vital to acknowledge the historical contexts of African universities' academic literacy history under colonialism and apartheid. This recognition is essential for appreciating the complexities and risks associated with autonomous academic literacy models that marginalize university students' realities, cultural orientations, languages, worldviews, and multiple ways of being.

Autonomous, ideological models relations to wellbeing

The presence of autonomous academic literacy models (Larson, 1996), of which the harmfulness toward student wellbeing is often underestimated within universities, poses substantial risks to the wellbeing of first-year and multilingual African scholars. Without mastering academic literacies tertiary-level students cannot progress. Autonomous academic literacy models are founded on a narrow perspective of academic literacy, overlooking cultural, disciplinary, and contextual differences in the ways communication displays in distinct knowledge fields. This oversight of the autonomous literacy model has detrimental effects on students' wellbeing if they are not introduced to and cannot apply discipline-specific genres.

In contrast to the autonomous literacy model, Street's (2006) ideological construct of literacy surpasses its limitations by recognizing diverse and context-specific disciplinary literacies, acknowledging the influences of cultural, social, and economic factors on academic discourses. Alternatively, the ideological model of literacy acknowledges the social features of knowledge production, whereas the autonomous construct reduces knowledge generation to culturally sterile mechanisms. Aligned with the ideological literacy model, Hubbard (2021) and Howell et al. (2021) define discipline-specific discourses as specialized communication forms and unique literacies within academic domains, encompassing their terminologies, conventions, and communication styles. Therefore, according to this chapter – prioritizing disciplinary literacies is a means of safeguarding new university students' wellbeing. In correlation, the ideological model of literacy shields students from the detrimental effects of the autonomous construct of literacy, which neglects African knowledge systems, languages, and students' disciplinary distinctions, thereby jeopardizing their wellbeing.

By examining current academic literacy practices through the Afrofuturist synthesis of Afrocentrism and Street's (2006) ideological model, this chapter exposes the continuum of academic literacy models in universities from the colonial and apartheid eras to the present day. This historical analysis enables us to uphold Afrofuturists' appreciation for past and future African educational practices and literacies, in conjunction with Afrocentrism's emphasis on centering African scholars' aspirations, hopes, and indigenous analytical modes in the study of literacy acquisition. Proceeding, the three primary features and pieces of evidence of autonomous models of literacy development in Southern Africa that this chapter presents as harmful and inducing epistemic trauma among new scholars include generic academic literacy courses, ICELDA TALL literacy tests, and the separation of scholars' indigenous identities from disciplinarity. These obstacles to transforming academic literacy development in Southern African Higher Education contexts will now be examined.

Generic ICELDA TALL tests

The Inter-institutional Centre for Language Development and Assessment (ICELDA) in South Africa has obtained permission to administer autonomous Tests of Academic Literacy (TALL), predominantly in former-Afrikaans universities. While the current thesis argues that academic literacy tests can evaluate novice scholars' application of literacies rather than quantitatively measure them since literacies are qualitative, social, and cultural phenomena, they are crucial mechanisms for certain instructors. However, this chapter highlights a concern that TALL tests, being based on autonomous models of literacy, overlook indigenous African knowledge systems, languages, and the disciplinary goals of students and their communities. Consequently, in some South African universities where ICELDA TALL tests are normalized, there is a perpetuation of discrimination reminiscent of the apartheid era. This displays, in some cases, in the actual physical segregation of indigenous African new disciplinary members into generic, discipline-specific literacy modules. The isolation of African scholars into academic literacy modules due to the quantitative measurements from TALL tests creates perceptions of their stigmatization, leading to harm to their holistic wellbeing.

The autonomous model of literacy, as demonstrated by TALL tests, contributes to harm experienced by new university students. By divorcing the evaluation of literacies from disciplinary histories and African knowledge systems, TALL tests create a barrier to understanding the full intellectual capabilities of indigenous, multilingual African disciplinary members. For example, TALL tests are exclusively available in Afrikaans or English, limiting the opportunities for African students to display their multilingual, intellectual prowess effectively. The multiple-choice format of TALL tests suppresses multimodality and multiliteracies while marginalizing indigenous literacies, further disadvantaging African students. In certain Southern African universities, novice university entrants are segregated into generic, disciplinarily sterile literacy modules due to deficit characterizations of multilingual students resulting from TALL test scores. Consequently, the wellbeing of novice, multilingual African scholars in South Africa is jeopardized as they are forced into academic literacy modules that under-emphasize meaningful connections to mainstream disciplines.

Afrofuturist literacies as guardians of wellbeing

It is evident that academic literacy, as a set of practices and a field of study, is far from being ideologically neutral. As a result of historical trauma under colonialism and apartheid, and conflicting approaches to developing literacies in African Higher Education systems, the present chapter proposes that effective learning requires novice scholars to master the specific literacies of their disciplines (Shanahan & Shanahan, 2012). Students in universities cannot avoid developing disciplinary literacies to understand the specialized knowledge in degree streams. Hence, it is vital for educators and academic literacy facilitators to be aware of the differences between disciplinary and content area literacy, analysis from expert-novice comparisons, and consider implications for literacy programs (Shanahan & Shanahan, 2012). Whereas disciplinary literacies emphasize epistemologies of academic fields, content methods incorporate data from fields without exposing students to the methodologies that generated them. To safeguard the wellbeing of university students, Afrofuturism and Afrocentric paradigms support disciplinary academic literacy pedagogies by offering a culturally relevant framework that resonates with African students' experiences and indigenous epistemologies. This proposed framework enhances engagement, motivation, and mastery of discipline-specific genres.

Recognizing the active presence of African students' cultural orientations, community aspirations, and family values in engaging with knowledge is crucial for protecting their wellbeing. This recognition is a departure from Street's (2006) autonomous model and highlights the necessity of embracing a more disciplinarily, epistemically, and culturally sensitive method of analyzing academic literacy. Overcoming the legacy of apartheid applied linguistics, which marginalized indigenous knowledge systems and languages in disciplinary literacies, demands intentional efforts. By emphasizing multimodality and collaboration, history and culture – educators can infuse Afrofuturist and Afrocentric principles not only into the curriculum but also into student-student and student-lecturer interactions. This pedagogical approach promotes a pre-colonial method that revitalizes indigenous modes of communication, in harmony with Afrocentric principles that value students' indigeneity. Therefore, by critiquing the restrictions of autonomous, generic academic literacy models, this chapter underscores the necessity to shift toward a more culturally and contextually inclusive paradigm for academic literacy development in Higher Education. In the sections that follow, case studies will be shared to illustrate how Afrofuturist theory may be put into practice to develop students' knowledge and communication abilities.

Case Study 1: Wakanda: Opening the High School Classroom to Afrofuturism

Case study 1 is based on a project by Mattern (2023) called "Wakanda: Opening the High School Classroom to Afrofuturism." Despite this study being located in secondary schools, there are lessons for Higher Education practitioners too. Situated in the English subject, Mattern (2023) adopts Afrofuturist principles by acknowledging her identity of being "a white educator of Black, Indigenous, and students of Colour [aiming] to disrupt their whitewashed curriculum [...] and to also decenter [her] whiteness as [she] work[s] to disrupt the canon." The researcher's statement is significant as she indicates that embedding Afrofuturist principles into curricula transcends educators' complexion. Instead, and in Afrocentric fashion,

Mattern (2023) equally recognizes that somehow, Black and indigenous students' cultures and knowledge systems need to be centered in the curriculum.

According to Mattern (2023), the incorporation of Afrofuturism into the English classroom serves a twofold purpose. It encourages students to explore works by Afrofuturist authors often excluded from Eurocentric high school canons and acts as a continual and objective reminder that the framework itself is as significant as the literary works it encompasses. In achieving pedagogical objectives, Mattern (2023) integrates Afrofuturist fiction into the curriculum to expose novice scholars to indigenous African worldviews. This method not only introduces students to futuristic perspectives but also illuminates African worldviews in the evolution of the discipline of literary studies.

Specific Afrofuturist creations, such as a music video by Missy Elliott, Womack's (2013) theoretical Afrocentric reasoning, the Afrofuturist movie "Wakanda," and even The Bible, are introduced to students. Through these pedagogical methods, Mattern (2023) applies Afrofuturist principles by exposing students to and integrating African heritages in linguistic development across various genres and literacies. This approach aims to broaden students' individual epistemologies and wellbeing, contributing to a more inclusive understanding of the discipline of English studies.

Case Study 2: Exploring the phenomenon of Afrofuturism in film in decolonizing the university curriculum: A case study of a South African university

The second case study, conducted by Waghid and Ontong (2022), also integrates Afrofuturist and Afrocentric principles. It was selected for its similarity in incorporating the film medium within the secondary school domain. Additionally, its abundant empirical data, specifically focusing on fourth-year Further Education and Training students' perspectives of this Afrofuturistic method, contributes to its selection. Similar to case study 1, the participants in Waghid and Ontong's (2022) project interacted with the *Black Panther* film. They have posed the question: "Do you feel that the film empowered you as an African student? Explain" (Waghid & Ontong, 2022; 32). Proceeding, students' responses will be reinterpreted within the context of academic wellbeing and literacy.

Student A, when asked to respond to the researchers' questions answered partially as follows: "I would somewhat say the film instilled some sort of empowerment as it directs attention to the African continent's minerals [and] emphasizes on the intellectual ability of African minds as well as ways and means of using these in a manner that is beneficial for the country, Wakanda." Through an Afrofuturist lens, Student A's narrative, when framed by the philosophies of Butler (1993) and hooks (1989), reflects a sense of community empowerment derived from the film's focus on the potential of African resources and the intellectual prowess of its people. This sense of empowerment, according to the thesis at hand, strengthens the educational students' sense of wellbeing.

Envisioning a future where Africa's natural resources are harnessed for the benefit of the people, the student echoes themes of progress and innovation that resonate with Afrofuturist principles (Butler, 1993; hooks, 1989). Further, from an Afrocentric perspective, the student's response reveals the vitality of recognizing and celebrating African intellectual capabilities and the strategic use of the continent's resources, connecting to cultural heritage and an appreciation for the value that these elements bring to the advancement of Africans, Wakanda.

Case Study 3: Tripping Black Fantastic at a PWI

In Reed and Lohnes' (2019) study titled "Tripping Black Fantastic at a PWI: Or How Afrofuturist Exhibitions in an Academic Library Changed Everything," insights are provided into the manner in which spaces of an academic library present diverse and inclusive exhibitions. Consequently, PWI stands for predominantly White institution. Focus is on showcasing Afrofuturistic art that represents Black culture among diverse populations, thereby creating a theoretical and practical framework for other libraries to exhibit rich resources. Reed and Lohnes' (2019) work holds critical implications for facilitators of academic literacies and disciplinary knowledge who aim to safeguard the wellbeing of novice scholars. The powers and capabilities of visual literacies to enhance the acquisition of knowledge by library science members emerge from Reed and Lohnes' (2019) analysis, particularly in the context of Black art.

The project methodology of Reed and Lohnes (2019) comprised two essential components: the exhibit "Black Space: Reading (and Writing) Ourselves into the Future" and an art installation titled "Branding the Afrofuture Black Space," which showcased the library's futuristic book, film, and music collections, providing a multiliteracies and genre exploration of Afrofuturist themes. Simultaneously, Branding the Afrofuture Black Space featured digital print collages with graffiti wall drawings, delivering a visually striking portrayal of Black cultural production through the Afrofuturist lens. In this manner, Union College's library activated Afrofuturist and Afrocentric principles by integrating indigenous modes of expression and disciplinary analysis into an academic ecology. As such, the academic community's wellbeing was safeguarded through the experience of art and futuristic African ideas.

Reed and Lohnes (2019) report that prospective library science students and families felt a sense of welcome and actively engaged with the Afrofuturist exhibition, capturing the vibrant atmosphere in the university's library Learning Commons. The positive reception created a welcoming environment and contributed to the academic wellbeing of those involved. Additionally, Reed and Lohnes stressed the noticeable implications of the Afrofuturistic display for developing academic literacies and disciplinary knowledge, highlighting how exposure to visually engaging content positively impacted the academic wellbeing of new members of Higher Education, and in particular the discipline of library science. It is necessary not to note, however, that concerns about racially sensitive imagery prompted careful consideration and exclusion of specific pieces, underlining the need for thoughtful curation and communication with Afrofuturist artists to maintain a supportive academic environment for participants' wellbeing.

Discussion and conclusion

This chapter presents key findings, insights, and implications of integrating Afrofuturist principles into methods aimed at safeguarding the holistic wellbeing of new university entrants and disciplinary members in Higher Education. The goal is to strengthen the capabilities of academic literacy and disciplinary knowledge practitioners in integrating the chapter's key theories, concepts, and practices into their work. This integration is specifically focused on sustaining and safeguarding the wellbeing of new African university students. It is crucial for African Higher Education practitioners, including academic literacy developers, to acknowledge their responsibility in actively guiding the continent toward a tangible departure from colonialism and apartheid economies, particularly as manifested in Higher Education.

In the context of Afrofuturist reasoning, this thesis argues that the conventional notion of pursuing knowledge solely for its own sake within African disciplines is flawed and potentially harmful to the holistic wellbeing of new entrants to academia. Instead, by embracing Afrofuturist methodological frameworks, particularly when combined with Afrocentric theory, there is a deliberate effort to revive Africa's ancestral knowledge using various teaching and learning methods. The ultimate goal is to advance social justice and freedom for the broader African populace. Therefore, when academic literacy instructors and diverse disciplinary educators incorporate ancient, pre-colonial literacies from the African continent into contemporary academic domains, they effectively align with the educational philosophies of scholars like hooks and Butler. These scholars advocate for the liberating potential of creativity, art, imagination, and technologies to emancipate the minds of African and oppressed peoples worldwide.

Despite the benefits of integrating Afrofuturist theory into academic literacies, there remain resilient colonial and apartheid-era teaching, learning, and testing practices that constrain transformation. This thesis argues that the conventional notion of pursuing knowledge solely for its own sake within African disciplines is flawed and potentially harmful to the holistic wellbeing of new entrants to academia. Instead, by embracing Afrofuturist methodological frameworks, particularly when combined with Afrocentric theory, there is a deliberate effort to revive Africa's ancestral knowledge using various teaching and learning methods. The ultimate goal is to advance social justice and freedom for the broader African populace. Therefore, when academic literacy instructors and diverse disciplinary educators incorporate ancient, pre-colonial literacies from the African continent into contemporary academic domains, they effectively align with the educational philosophies of scholars like hooks and Butler. These scholars advocate for the liberating potential of creativity, art, imagination, and technologies to emancipate the minds of African and oppressed peoples worldwide.

To the progressive, Afrocentric, Afrofuturist, or social justice-minded reader, it is understandable to feel overwhelmed or disempowered in the face of centuries of colonial dominance. This is particularly evident in the autonomous, generic academic literacy modules that often disregard the wellbeing and integration of novice scholars' indigenous knowledge systems into distinct disciplines. However, despite these challenges, despair is unwarranted. Instead, let us consider this: the pan-African community is now more aware than ever of the ideologies, tools, and systems used to systematically exploit Africa's natural resources and manipulate human bodies for the benefit of international, neo-colonial, apartheid economies, often labeled as globalism. Furthermore, we have come to realize the central role that academic and disciplinary literacies play in perpetuating socially unjust, neo-apartheid economies from a Higher Education perspective.

These realizations carry profound implications. They signify that academic literacies facilitators are intellectually awakened and prepared to pioneer new paths toward the African Renaissance. They are committed to using mediums and literacies that prioritize the wellbeing of novice scholars and contribute to a more just and equitable society. Critical integration of Afrofuturist and Afrocentric theories with Street's (2006) ideological and autonomous models of literacy, as explored in this chapter, is an effective methodology for decolonizing academic literacies in ways that safeguard novice scholars' wellbeing. The proposed academic literacy model, drawing on Street's (2006) ideological literacy theory which combines identity, culture, and context into literacies, enables academic literacy facilitators to center students' pre-university knowledge systems, multilingualism, and disciplinary affiliations at the core of the curriculum.

In this process, Afrofuturist precepts become vital as they enable students to draw on their ancestral knowledge and literacies in present-day disciplinary spaces, envisioning alternative post-colonial and post-neo-apartheid economic futures. Likewise, Afrocentricity activates as an empowering framework, guiding the integration of identity, culture, and disciplinary context into academic literacies, fostering an integrated approach to safeguarding novice scholars' wellbeing. In doing so, Africans' pre-colonial value of creativity, combined with disciplinary knowledge, safeguards new Higher Education entrants wellbeing against persistent colonial influences and apartheid-era applied linguistics that intentionally separates indigeneity from disciplinarity.

In conclusion, this chapter advocates for a transformative shift in academic literacy, emphasizing emancipation from the coloniality of being (Maldonado-Torres, 2007). By recognizing their significant roles in fostering emancipation, educators are encouraged to explore students' cultures and indigenous epistemologies alongside the established curriculum. This shift signifies a departure from the confines of the traditional autonomous model, urging for a comprehensive, indigenous understanding of the learning journey in post-colonial contexts.

Practical recommendations for implementation include activating multimodality and collaboration, designing culturally responsive curricula, and promoting awareness of indigenous, pan-African epistemologies among educators as outlined in this chapter. These initiatives are designed to not only enhance disciplinary engagement but also crucially safeguard and promote the wellbeing of new entrants to Africa's and global universities. Through these practical methods, educators can weave Afrofuturist and Afrocentric principles into the very fabric of disciplinary learning experiences, fostering a narrative centered on students' cultural identities and holistic wellbeing as discussed in this chapter.

The call for further research is paramount to understand the enduring impact and feasibility of an Afrofuturistic and Afrocentric pedagogy, specifically addressing persistent tensions between pre-colonial and colonial epistemes in academic literacy development. These investigations aim to understand the nuanced influence of Afrofuturist and Afrocentric paradigms on students' academic growth, cultural identities, and overall wellbeing over the long term. Comparative studies are also encouraged to provide insights into the efficacy of this contextual approach versus traditional autonomous literacy models.

Examining the challenges and successes of institutional implementation can offer valuable insights for policymakers and educational leaders in global universities, emphasizing the necessity of embracing emancipatory teaching, learning, and assessment practices rooted in Afrofuturist and Afrocentric principles. Ultimately, the overarching goal of the discourse in this chapter is to elevate academic literacy conversations to prioritize the holistic wellbeing of new university students, anchored in the innovative frameworks of Afrofuturism and Afrocentrism, and emancipation from the coloniality of being. Embracing new academic literacy paradigms ensures that educational models not only transmit knowledge but also cultivate environments conducive to the flourishing of the African Renaissance within the rich tapestry of Afrofuturist and Afrocentric conceptual paradigms.

References

Asante, M. K. (1991). The Afrocentric idea in education. *The Journal of Negro Education*, *60*(2), 170–180. https://doi.org/10.2307/2295608

Butler, O. E. (1993). *Parable of the sower*. Four Walls Eight Windows.

Duffy, D., Jennings, J., Okorafor, N., & Butler, O. E. (2017). *Kindred: A graphic novel adaptation*. Abrams Comicarts.

Hamilton, E. C. (2017). Afrofuturism and the technologies of survival. *African Arts*, *50*(4), 18–23. https://doi.org/10.1162/AFAR_a_00371

Holbert, N., Dando, M., & Correa, I. (2020). Afrofuturism as critical constructionist design: Building futures from the past and present. *Learning, Media and Technology*, *45*(4), 328–344. https://doi.org/10.1080/17439884.2020.1754237

hooks, bell (1989). Choosing the margin as a space for radical openness. *The Journal of Cinema and Media*, *36*, 15–23.

Howell, E., Barlow, W., & Dyches, J. (2021). Disciplinary literacy: Successes and challenges of professional development. *Journal of Language and Literacy Education*, *17*(1), 1–26.

Hubbard, K. (2021). Disciplinary literacies in STEM: What do undergraduates read, how do they read it, and can we teach scientific reading more effectively? *Higher Education Pedagogies*, *6*(1), 41–65. https://doi.org/10.1080/23752696.2021.1882326

Larson, J. (1996). Challenging autonomous models of literacy: Street's call to action. *Linguistics and Education*, *8*(4), 439–445. https://doi.org/10.1016/S0898-5898(96)90020-0

Luiz, J. M. (1998). The evolution and fall of the South African apartheid state: A political economy perspective. *Ufahamu: A Journal of African Studies*, *26*(2–3). https://doi.org/10.5070/F7262-3016619

Maldonado-Torres, N. (2007). On the coloniality of being contributions to the development of a concept. *Cultural Studies*, *21*(2–3), 240–270. https://doi.org/10.1080/09502380601162548

Mattern, C. M. (2023). Wakanda: Opening the high school classroom to Afrofuturism. *Language Arts Journal of Michigan*, *38*(2), 70–80. https://doi.org/10.9707/2168-149X.2389

Mazama, A. (2001). The Afrocentric paradigm: Contours and definitions. *Journal of Black Studies*, *31*(4), 387–405. https://doi.org/10.1177/002193470103100

Na'Puti, R. (2019). Speaking of indigeneity: Navigating genealogies against erasure and #RhetoricSoWhite. *Quarterly Journal of Speech*, *105*(4), 495–501. https://doi.org/10.1080/00335630.2019.1669895

Rabaka, R. (2022). Return to the source: Cabral, fanon, the dialectic of revolutionary Decolonization/Revolutionary re-Africanization, and the African renaissance. *Journal of Black Studies*, *53*(5), 419–440. https://doi.org/10.1177/00219347221077

Reagan, T. G. (1987). The politics of linguistic apartheid: Language policies in black education in South Africa. *The Journal of Negro Education*, *56*(3), 299–312.

Reed, R., & Lohnes, J. (2019). Tripping the Black fantastic at a PWI: Or how Afrofuturist exhibitions in an academic library changed everything. *Alexandria*, *29*(1–2), 116–129. https://doi.org/10.1177/0955749019876383

Samatar, S. (2017). Toward a planetary history of Afrofuturism. *Research in African Literatures*, *48*(4), 175–191. https://doi.org/10.2979/reseafrilite.48.4.12

Seroto, J. (2011). Indigenous education during the pre-colonial period in Southern Africa. *Indilinga – African Journal of Indigenous Knowledge Systems*, *10*(1), 77–88.

Shanahan, T., & Shanahan, C. (2012). What is disciplinary literacy and why does it matter? *Top Language Disorders*, *32*(1), 7–18. https://doi.org/10.1097/TLD.0b013e318244557a

Street, B. (2006). Autonomous and ideological models of literacy: Approaches from new literacy studies. *Media Anthropology Network*, *17*, 1–15.

Waghid, Z., & Ontong, K. (2022). Exploring the phenomenon of Afrofuturism in film in decolonizing the university curriculum: A case study of a South African university. *Citizenship Teaching and Learning*, *17*(1), 27–48.

Womack, Y. L. (2013). Afrofuturism: The world of black sci-fi and fantasy culture. Chicago Review Press. https://doi.org/10.12801/1947-5403.2013.05.02.08

Zunguze, J. (2019). Coping with epistemic trauma. *The Africana Pursuit of New Humanism*, *2*(2), 1–7. https://doi.org/10.25335/PPJ.2.2-10

Chapter 3

Exploring wellbeing in the Arab higher education context

A scoping review

Igor Michaleczek, Weam Ibrahim, and Youmen Chaaban

Introduction

While interest and focus on wellbeing in higher education (HE) is relatively new, it has become a key component of the university life debate (Spratt, 2017; Thorburn, 2018). Due to the relatively recent interest in wellbeing in the public sphere, the number of studies on wellbeing in HE has grown exponentially in the last decade (Hernández-Torrano et al., 2020). However, this surge in research has occurred without a clearly established theoretical basis (Long et al., 2012). Moreover, efforts by researchers to define wellbeing have yet to culminate in a consensus. This growing interest and ongoing discussion surrounding wellbeing within both societal and academic contexts, in addition to the surge in research, have resulted in a very diverse understanding and approach to wellbeing, a diversity that Carter (2016) associated with a chameleon. If, like the chameleon, wellbeing has the ability to adapt and evolve depending on its environment, it should provide researchers with the opportunity to contextualize and appropriate this concept. It remains to be seen whether academics have seized this opportunity while researching and implementing projects presented as part of wellbeing in HE.

Despite variations in the definition of wellbeing, its conceptual framework in research has been based on a particular historical, social, and cultural context, and as such on a particular epistemic and ontological setting. Historically, wellbeing has been linked to psychology and has two main tenants. The first one is a hedonic perspective, which considers wellbeing as the attainment of happiness, and the second one is a eudemonic one, which pursues the realization of oneself and one's full potential (Diener et al., 1999; Douwes et al., 2023; Ryan & Deci, 2001). Furthermore, within the hedonic outlook are subjective theories, such as hedonism, desire fulfillment, and life satisfaction, as well as objective theories, like human-nature fulfillment theory (Thorburn, 2018). By contrast, the eudemonic outlook includes several concepts such as self-actualization and Deci and Ryan's (2000) self-determination theory.

In addition to highlighting the complexity involved in defining the concept of wellbeing, the extensive body of research has also shown the deep interconnections and mutual influences between wellbeing and various educational factors

DOI: 10.4324/9781003491613-3

(Harding et al., 2019). Among these substantial factors of education interrelated with wellbeing are the teacher-student relationship (Spilt et al., 2011), perceived academic competencies and achievement (Elliot & Kobayashi, 2018), as well as satisfaction with university experiences (Harding et al., 2019). Research strives to explore the potential mutual influence that these elements can have, and, as expected consequences, their contribution to the improvement of HE outcomes and a more positive student experience. There is a need to highlight that wellbeing in education has been approached through a subjective, emotional, and cognitive perception of reality (Hascher, 2008, p. 86). Research on wellbeing has been intimately linked to positive psychology and mental health, further reinforcing its association with a determined academic and cultural environment. Ryff's (1989) seminal work investigating psychological wellbeing meaning and its relationship to happiness, shedding light on the close link between wellbeing and positive psychology, has been widely used and referred to in research on wellbeing. Additionally, to highlight the importance of positive psychology in the field of wellbeing development, support, and research, it is relevant to mention its focus on the science of optimal human functioning and flourishing. Seligman and Csíkszentmihályi (2000) also acknowledged the relevance of positive psychology and its capacity to enable happiness, autonomy, self-regulation, optimism, hope, wisdom, talent, and creativity, which are all relevant to the study of wellbeing in HE.

Approached from this angle, one can see the potential contribution of positive psychology to the fulfillment and understanding of happiness, achievement, and realization of individual's full potential. Later research asserted the relevance of measuring subjective wellbeing to gain information about the quality of life in societies leading to reinforcing the role of positive psychology in understanding subjective wellbeing (Diener et al., 2015). Along with the growing importance of positive psychology while approaching wellbeing, mental health has also become a centerpiece in this field. Mental health may focus on difficulties, challenges, and negative aspects of the HE experiences and advocate for the importance of exploring mental health issues and situations to contribute to better wellbeing. This is a quick summary of some of the main components of wellbeing perception in the academic sphere; a summary necessary to comprehend and appreciate the different ongoing themes and conceptual frameworks referred to by academics and their intricate relations with the cultural, intellectual, and social context of the Global North.

These approaches to wellbeing raise several issues. The first and most obvious is the limitation in the design of the conceptual framework to a Global North reference framework. Indeed, more than 50% of research for the past 45 years originated from the USA, and limited research was initiated in other countries than the top ten upper-middle-income countries as listed by the OECD (Hernández-Torrano et al., 2020; McLellan et al., 2022). This predominance in the academic field of a restricted and specific geo-cultural area implies an overrepresentation of specific representation and the silencing of alternative standpoints embedded within a historical, socio-cultural, and political context (McLellan et al., 2022, p. 5). It led to the exportation of Western viewpoints, understanding, and research approaches to other geo-cultural areas, imposing a certain perspective on wellbeing and suppressing others (Summerfield, 2013). This issue is even more acute when the areas receiving these conceptual views of wellbeing have also been subjected to colonization and its ongoing impact. A potential exit from this complex challenge is the broadening of the wellbeing concept to a larger framework more influenced by local socio-cultural contexts and the adoption of wider and more inclusive concepts such as life satisfaction (Derné, 2009). This scoping review aimed to contribute to assessing whether research on wellbeing has adapted to particular socio-cultural context in relation to program adoption, implementation, impact, and sustainability (Barry et al., 2017, p. 437). Examining the current body of research on wellbeing in the Arab region, including how these studies approach the appropriation and influence of wellbeing concept formulation, as well as the development and validation of measurement tools, should be relevant to this analysis.

The second major challenge in current academic research on wellbeing involves narrowing down the research to only certain aspects of wellbeing for quantitative analysis. This segmented approach undermines the effectiveness of program implementation and evaluation (Danker et al., 2019; Svane et al., 2019). Initially recognized as a multifaceted concept, wellbeing encompasses a multiplicity of components (Hossain et al., 2023), highlighting the interrelatedness of hedonic and eudaimonic dimensions as complementary, not separate perspectives. Taking into consideration the tendency of research on wellbeing to compartmentalize independent components is not benign, as this reality is also influenced by academic and theoretical approaches rooted in the Western world. However, this prevalent practice of isolating wellbeing into discrete elements does not align or fully capture the essence of wellbeing in global contexts where individuals are seen in harmony with their communities and local environments.

This leads us to the last issue relevant to this study and the understanding of wellbeing academic research in a different setting than the Global North. The overpowering epistemic approach to research marginalizes the significance of being, relegating it to an insignificant aspect of investigation. Focusing solely on epistemology, this approach detaches knowledge from its historical and cultural context, effectively neutralizing it and leading to the possibility of imposing a hegemonic accepted Western view of education and conception of the world. The relevance of local ontology allows countering the "reduction of education of wellbeing to curriculum as a technical enterprise, to the perpetuation of socially-constructed knowledge guised as transcendent knowledge" (Dewar, 2016, p. 22). This is the risk of relying on measuring tools and conceptual frameworks initiated in an ontological setting different from the one the study is conducted in, leading to the imposition of a foreign model.

Scoping review context

The present scoping review study focused on the Arab countries, which included the Arabian Gulf (Bahrain, Kuwait, Oman, Qatar, Saudi Arabia, and the United Arab Emirate), North African (Algeria, Egypt, Libya, Morocco, Sudan, and Tunisia), and the Levantine countries (Jordan, Lebanon, Palestine, and Syria). This wide region is very diverse in its economic, social, political, economic performance, and standards of living situation. The Arab region represents 6.5% of the world population and covers a rich and diverse landscape with key resources. It links three continents and is at the heart of important trade routes while holding 50–60% of world oil and gas reserves. The Arab region also has an ancient and rich human history and has seen the birth of the three major religions, Christianity, Judaism, and Islam. It is also an important geo-political area attracting the attention and focus of key world powers. HE has a very long tradition in the region, as three of the oldest universities in the world were established in Morocco, Iran, and Egypt. These institutions have been the cradle of many discoveries and academic innovations. However, the number of HE institutions was limited after the Second World War. This number drastically increased in the last decades of the twentieth century with the population of students more than doubling and the number of HE institutions tripling, despite being based on foreign models. It also saw an increase in investments with efforts to improve quality in HE institutions and attract Western university branches. The academic research landscape in the Arab region is characterized by a diverse array of topics and challenges, reflecting both regional specificities and global interconnectedness. HE in the region has encountered numerous challenges. These include lack of professional opportunities for new graduates (Rashidi et al., 2021), poor quality of public institutions in some of the Arab countries (Assaad et al., 2016), and issues related to educational standards for quality assurance and accreditation (Hassan, 2013).

Numerous studies have focused on overall wellbeing in the Arab region, uncovering widespread dissatisfaction with life conditions among various populations. This dissatisfaction has been associated with "feelings of unworthiness, collective low self-esteem, a sense of powerlessness, loss of agency, as well as low trust in institutions and, in some instances, one another" within the general population (Tiliouine, 2022, p. 15). In his research, Tiliouine explored five key factors affecting wellbeing: health, education, income and standard of living, social stability or chaos, and subjective wellbeing and happiness. Despite an overall dissatisfaction among certain populations in the region, it is important to note significant disparities between the different countries of the region. The Gulf nations, in particular, enjoy a considerably better situation. There has been a notable enhancement in health services and overall health conditions across the region. School enrollment rates have seen substantial improvement, though there's a wide gap between countries at the extremes, such as Yemen and Sudan. Adult literacy rates have also increased. Economic conditions vary significantly, with high-income countries like Qatar, Kuwait, and other Gulf states faring much better than North African and other Middle Eastern nations. Therefore, wellbeing is not uniform across the Arab region, making broad generalizations impossible. This diversity suggests that research on wellbeing in HE should consider these disparities to provide a more nuanced understanding of the region.

Numerous reviews have examined wellbeing in HE outside the Arab region, ranging from Dodd et al. (2021)'s scoping review on student wellbeing in the UK to systematic reviews that either directly address wellbeing or topics closely related to it. These studies are more common and tend to specialize in particular aspects of HE. As a dearth of systematic or scoping reviews on wellbeing in HE exists in the Arab region, our study aimed to fill this gap by investigating research and published articles on wellbeing and HE specifically within this region.

The present research explored academic publications in the Arab region that have investigated wellbeing in HE. This research was guided by the following questions:

1 What are the trends within the research on wellbeing in HE in the Arab region?
2 What are the common themes emerging from the identified research?

Methodology

According to Mak and Thomas (2022), a scoping review is "a type of knowledge synthesis that uses a systematic and iterative approach to identify and synthesize an existing or emerging body of literature on a given topic" (p. 565). The main reason for conducting a scoping review is to map extant literature and determine possible gaps on a topic (Gutierrez-Bucheli et al., 2022). Arksey and O'Malley (2005) point out that a scoping review with a vast number of research articles affects the feasibility of the review while a small number of research articles produces narrow results. Following Mak and Thomas (2022), researchers should consider (1) whether the research questions can be addressed using a scoping review, (2) whether a scoping review on the topic has already been conducted, and (3) if there is sufficient literature to warrant a scoping review. The second step includes identifying keywords, inclusion and exclusion criteria, selecting relevant databases, and completing the search in the relevant databases. The next step involves selecting the number of studies that can be included based on their validity to the scoping review. Afterward, researchers look for patterns, trends, and gaps in the literature that may be present, and any other significant information that would be of value to the scoping review. Finally, conclusions are drawn in regard to the research questions based on the studies identified (Bragge et al., 2011).

Research design

In this scoping review, the goal was to define and conceptualize wellbeing by having a scoping view of existing literature in the Arab region, including the Arabian

Gulf (Bahrain, Kuwait, Oman, Qatar, Saudi Arabia, and the United Arab Emirate), North African (Algeria, Egypt, Libya, Morocco, Sudan, and Tunisia), and the Levantine countries (Jordan, Lebanon, Palestine, and Syria). The Preferred Reporting Items for Systematic Reviews and Meta-Analyses (PRISMA) guidelines were used to develop a protocol for this study. The framework that is set by PRISMA allowed us to organize the existing literature and determine which published research meets the inclusion criteria of this scoping review.

Identifying relevant studies

As shown in Figure 3.1, the search and selection of the appropriate studies for this scoping review were completed using multiple databases, including EBSCO, Scopus, and Web of Science. The search was completed for English databases using the following terms: "wellbeing" OR "well being" OR "well-being" AND "higher

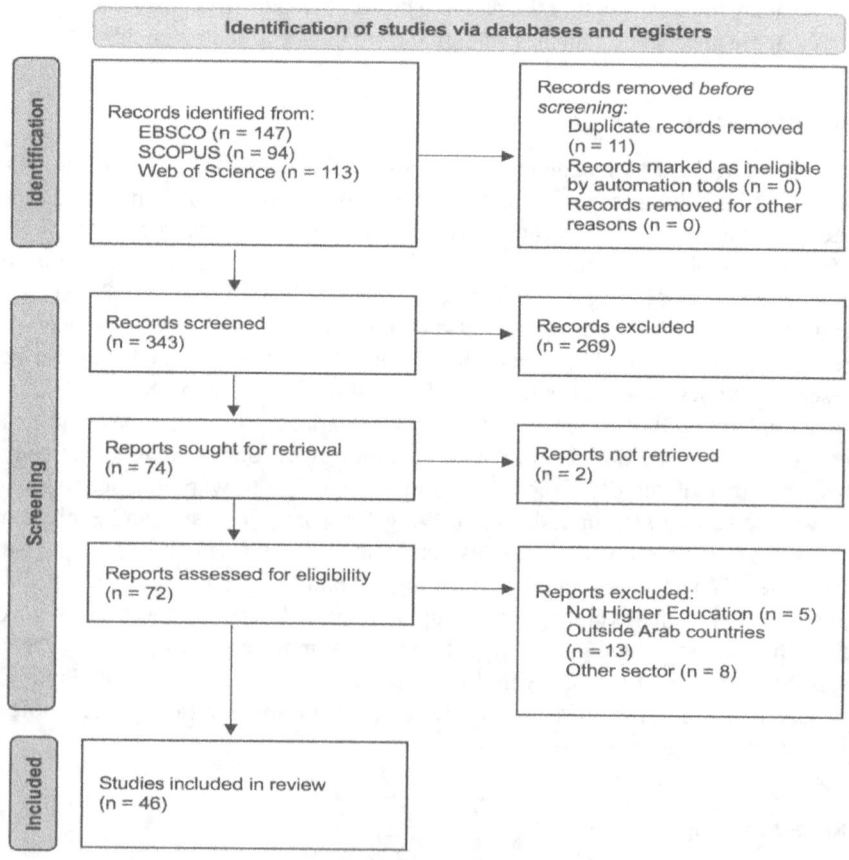

Figure 3.1 PRISMA Flow Diagram of Selected Papers

education," OR "university students." The search was also limited to publications between the years of 2018 and 2023 which were peer-reviewed articles or chapters and filtered to include results from Arab countries. The initial search resulted in 354 studies, as shown in Figure 3.1. EBSCO, Scopus, and Web of Science yielded 147, 94, and 113 results, respectively.

Screening and inclusion criteria

The eligibility criteria for this scoping review were determined before the initial search was completed. The inclusion criteria, included articles and book chapters published between the years 2018 and 2023, were limited to HE in the Arab region. We excluded any studies that involved primary education, schools, children, or K–12 students. The yielded results from the three separate databases were pasted into a single Excel sheet where 11 duplicates were removed, leaving 343 research articles. A total of 269 records were eliminated based on screening the title, keywords, and abstract, which left 74 research articles for retrieval. Only 72 of those 74 were retrieved, and only 46 remained that fit the inclusion criteria after removing studies that were not on HE, the Arab region, or other sectors.

Eligibility

We completed the selection process in which the eligibility criteria were determined. We ranked each research study on a 3-point rubric system using the title, abstract, and keywords. The studies that were ranked as 1 were kept and met all of the eligibility criteria. Studies that were ranked as 2 required further discussion, while those ranked as 3 were automatically deemed irrelevant to the review. The research studies which were ranked as 2 were read completely to determine whether they fit the inclusion criteria or not. In total, 46 research articles were considered relevant to the scoping review, having met all the inclusion criteria, and were focused on the Arab region between 2018 and 2023.

Inclusion

A total of 46 studies were found to meet the inclusion criteria of language, geographical location, and period, and were further scrutinized. The research studies were read and analyzed for key themes and ideas according to the research questions. The details of each research study can be found in Appendix 1.

Findings

The present study identified interesting and insightful findings when looking at the academic research on wellbeing and HE in the Arab region. These findings are organized in different parts.

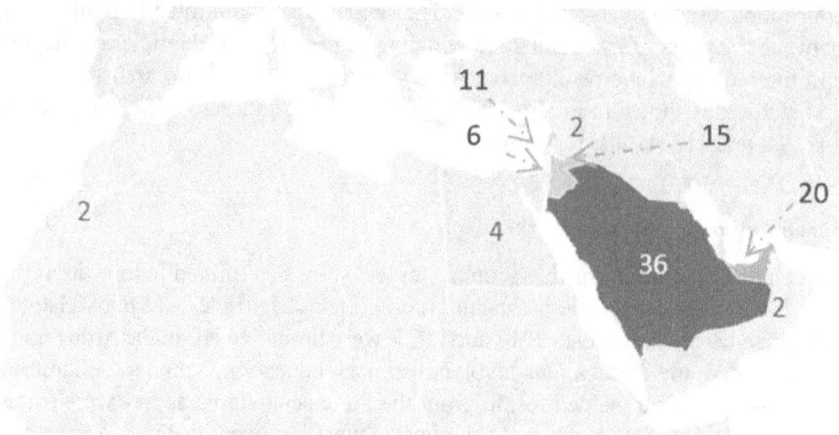

Figure 3.2 Repartition of research on wellbeing by country across the Arab region (in percentage)

Geographical repartition

According to Figure 3.2, the studies on wellbeing in the Arab region were mainly conducted in the Gulf region with two countries initiating more than 50% of them, namely Saudi Arabia (36%) and the United Arab Emirates (20%). In the Middle East, Jordan (15%) and Lebanon (11%) represented the next two main clusters of research production. Several research were conducted internationally, with two involving many countries (studies 4 and 7), or studies involving two to three countries within the Arab region (studies 11 and 35) or between an Arab country and other non-Arab countries (studies 18, 20, and 21).

Year of publication

Publication in the Arab region has seen a gradual increase since 2021, according to Figure 3.3 the highest number of publications was in 2022, and this number remained relatively high despite the slight decrease in 2023.

Emerging themes

Theme 1: Emphasizing the socio-cultural context of the Arab region

The analysis of the studies revealed a multidimensional understanding of wellbeing in HE within the Arab region. These studies, predominantly correlational in nature, offered a broad perspective on the various factors influencing university student's psychological wellbeing.

The primary significance of these correlational studies lies in their ability to uncover associations between variables that are rooted in the unique socio-cultural

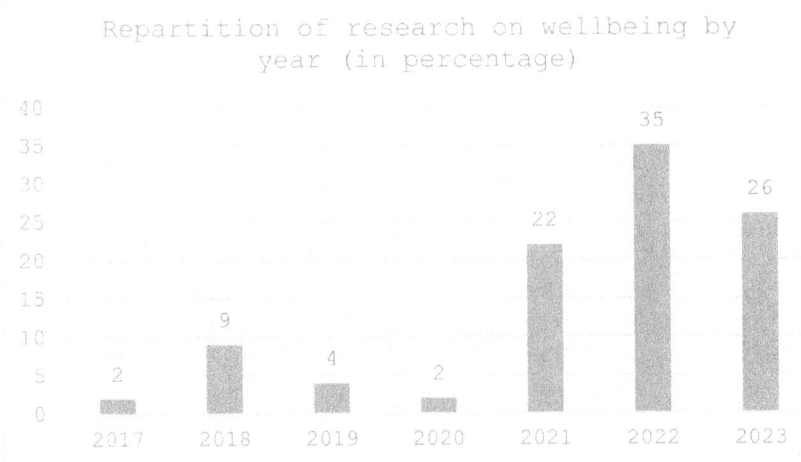

Figure 3.3 Year of Publication of Selected Articles

context of the Arab region. This thematic focus emerges from a series of studies that investigate how aspects of national identity, cultural values, and social belonging interact with and influence the wellbeing of university students in the culturally diverse and socially complex region like the Arab. For instance, the study on Emirati women highlights the positive impact of national identity and in-group preference on psychological wellbeing (Study 1). This underscores the idea that in cultures where communal and collective identities are prominent, the sense of belonging and identification with a group can be a crucial determinant of an individual's mental health. Another study that emphasizes the importance of cultural congruence is Study 4, which is concerned with the concept of honor. These findings suggest that wellbeing in the Arab region is deeply intertwined with cultural values, and any interventions need to be aligned with these cultural contexts.

The Arab region, characterized by its unique socio-political dynamics and history of conflict, presents a compelling context for studies focused on trauma and PTSD. This necessity is evident in research like the cross-sectional study on the mental health of university students in the aftermath of the Beirut port explosion (Study 16), a traumatic event with far-reaching psychological impacts. These circumstances have created an environment where understanding and addressing the effects of trauma on mental health has become important. The study on Syrian university students in Deir ez-Zor further illuminates this need (Study 32). It shows the high prevalence of PTSD among students, a direct consequence of the prolonged conflict in Syria. These examples highlight the critical importance of trauma-focused research in the Arab region, aimed at understanding the extent of mental health challenges and developing effective interventions to support the affected populations.

Also in the Arab region, as religious and spiritual beliefs are deeply embedded in the cultural fabric, the emphasis on these aspects in research on wellbeing is also a common theme. This is exemplified by studies such as the comparative analysis of religious struggles among a multinational Muslim sample from Palestine, Turkey, and Malaysia (Study 18). In this study, the nuanced exploration of how religious struggles correlate with mental health outcomes like satisfaction with life and generalized anxiety highlights the role religion plays in the everyday lives of individuals in this region. Another pertinent example is the Jordanian study on the relationship between spiritual wellbeing, social support, and life satisfaction among university students (Study 10). This research underscores the interplay between spiritual wellbeing and mental health, illustrating how spiritual beliefs and practices are integral to the overall wellbeing of individuals in the Arab region. These studies not only reflect the cultural specificities of the Arab region but also underscore the importance of incorporating religious and spiritual dimensions into mental health research and interventions to ensure they are culturally congruent and effective.

Theme 2: Adopting data collection tools developed in other contexts

The two studies focusing on the validation of data collection tools in the Arab context, specifically the adaptation of the Positive Mental Health (PMH) scale and the Life Skills Scale (A-LSS) for Arabic-speaking populations, highlighted an important methodological concern in wellbeing research, that is, the need for culturally relevant and validated measurement tools. Despite the importance of the studies noted above in the emphasis on the specificities of the socio-cultural context of the Arab region, there remains a prominent pattern among researchers in adopting data collection tools that were developed in Western contexts without regional validation.

For instance, Study 2 on procrastination, negative emotional symptoms, and mental wellbeing employed instruments like the Irrational Procrastination Scale (IPS), the Depression Anxiety Stress Scales (DASS-21), and the Mental Health Continuum-Short Form (MHC-SF). While these tools are widely recognized and used in Western contexts, their application in the Arab region without prior validation brings forth critical questions about their appropriateness and accuracy in capturing the region's unique socio-cultural dynamics.

Furthermore, Study 19 provides an illustrative example of the use of Western-based data collection tools in an Omani context. In this study, researchers used tools like the Brief Resilience Scale, World Health Organization Well-Being Index, and Rosenberg Self-Esteem Scale to assess resilience, wellbeing, and self-esteem among Omani university students. The point to be made here is that the concept of resilience, as understood and measured by the Brief Resilience Scale, might have different connotations in an Omani context, influenced by cultural values, social norms, and environmental factors unique to the region. Similarly, the constructs of wellbeing and self-esteem, as measured by the WHO Well-Being Index and

Rosenberg Self-Esteem Scale, respectively, could manifest differently in Oman due to cultural and societal differences.

A last example serving as an illustration of the utilization of Western-based data collection tools in a Lebanese context is Study 23. In this research, tools like the Well-being Index Scale, Lebanese Anxiety Scale, Patient Health Questionnaire, and Freiburg Mindfulness Inventory were employed to assess various psychological constructs among Lebanese university students. The use of these instruments, particularly the Freiburg Mindfulness Inventory and the Well-being Index Scale, which have origins in Western psychological research, brings into focus the issue of cultural and contextual applicability. Mindfulness, as conceptualized and measured by the Freiburg Mindfulness Inventory, may have different cultural interpretations and implications in Lebanon compared to Western settings. Cultural factors, such as religious practices, societal norms, and everyday stressors specific to the Lebanese context, can influence how mindfulness is understood, practiced, and experienced.

Theme 3: Using the higher education context as a pseudo-context for research on wellbeing

The analysis of the studies that met the criteria of inclusion provided the opportunity to contrast the studies that were conducted before or after the COVID-19 pandemic and those which were conducted during this timeframe. The contrast between these studies was particularly evident in terms of their focus on students' academics and learning experiences. Pre-pandemic studies, as seen in the examples previously discussed, often treated the HE context as a backdrop for exploring various psychological constructs among university students, without a direct emphasis on academic performance. However, the studies conducted during the COVID-19 pandemic reveal a shift in focus, underscoring a more direct relationship between students' mental health or wellbeing and their academic experiences.

For instance, Study 23 that examined mental health, learning behavior, and perceived fatigue among university students during the pandemic directly addressed the challenges posed by the rapid transition to online education in the UAE. This study delved into the consequences of such a drastic change on students' psychological wellbeing and academic performance, highlighting the intertwined nature of these aspects under pandemic conditions. Study 43 that assessed the impact of the transition from onsite to online education on students' learning and psychological wellbeing at King Faisal University, KSA, further illustrates this theme. It specifically investigated how the shift to online learning influenced students' academic performance and psychological state, emphasizing the direct link between educational methods and mental health during the pandemic.

These studies conducted during COVID-19 highlight a clear recognition of the direct impact of the pandemic on the academic life and mental health of students. They underscore the necessity to consider educational methodologies and environments as integral factors influencing students' psychological wellbeing, especially in the circumstances of a global health crisis. The contrast with pre- or post-pandemic research revealed the choice of the HE context as a pseudo-context for research and practices on wellbeing and mental health, without necessarily investigating the educational context per se as an important factor in the relationship between the various factors examined and university students' wellbeing or mental health.

Theme 4: Promoting wellbeing interventions in HE in the Arab region

The analysis of the experimental design studies as a subgroup revealed insightful patterns regarding the impact of interventions on student wellbeing and the role of socio-cultural context in these outcomes.

First, the mixed results in these studies, with two reporting negative findings, suggest that interventions do not uniformly lead to positive outcomes. For instance, in Study 33, the intervention did not significantly improve all aspects of wellbeing. The researchers' discussion of these findings in relation to the socio-cultural context emphasizes the importance of contextual factors in the success of wellbeing interventions. The socio-cultural nuances, such as cultural perceptions of wellbeing and mental health, played a role in how students perceive and benefit from these interventions.

Second, the five studies that reported positive outcomes and recommended similar interventions in HE underscore the potential benefits of these programs. These studies, like Study 3, demonstrated the effectiveness of wellbeing interventions in enhancing certain aspects of student life, advocating for their broader implementation. This pattern suggests a growing recognition of the importance of holistic approaches to student development in HE, encompassing not just academic but also psychological and emotional wellbeing.

Last, the presence of a qualitative study among these predominantly quantitative studies brings a unique perspective. Study 40 utilized a qualitative approach to explore students' experiences in a positive psychology course. This approach allowed for a deeper understanding of the students' personal and emotional journeys, which might not have been captured through quantitative methods. It also points to the value of incorporating qualitative research in educational settings to gain a more nuanced understanding of the impacts of interventions on students' wellbeing.

Discussion and conclusion

This scoping review mapped the research on wellbeing in HE within the Arab world. It raises interesting and informative aspects regarding academic publication among researchers in the region. One of the first major findings emerging from this research is the unbalanced repartition of academic publications in the geographical area, with the overwhelming domination of Saudi and Emirati universities. These two countries have published more than 50% of the research, which demonstrates both the strength and the ascendency of their institutions in representing the reality of the region in the Arab academic world. This dominance raises questions about the diversity of perspectives and experiences being represented in the literature, suggesting that the viewpoints and research findings might disproportionately reflect the socio-economic and cultural contexts of these two nations, potentially overlooking the nuanced realities and challenges faced by other countries in the Arab region.

The second major discovery highlights the critical role of incorporating local contexts into both the implementation of interventions and the research on wellbeing in HE. Integrating the local context has been accepted as being key to gaining positive outcomes for wellbeing (Furst et al., 2020). This local context includes economic, social, or cultural dimensions, as these three facets were alluded to in some of the identified studies as influencing wellbeing. Understanding the difference in health outcomes and health situations between different economic, geographic, and social milieus, similarly to Patton et al.'s (2016) Lancet report on adolescent health, underscores the necessity to recognize local health needs to better support the target population. This scoping review confirms this imperative and the aspiration for a socio-cultural contextual relevance of both research and implementation of programs related to wellbeing in the Arab region. The importance of these contextual factors has been further reinforced by several research (e.g., Diener et al., 1999), which stress the importance of taking individual and contextual factors into consideration when conducting wellbeing research. Among these various factors, culture has been presented in some of the selected research (Studies 4, 27, and 30) as a key aspect and aspiration while approaching the conceptual and practical adoption of wellbeing. Cultural multidimensional values and aspects can influence attitudes toward specific wellbeing services (Choi et al., 2023).

Recent research also highlights the importance of understanding "historical and cultural perspectives in cross-cultural contexts for the development and implementation of culturally responsive services" (Maleku et al., 2021, p. 376). This diversity necessitates a culturally sensitive approach to apprehending and promoting wellbeing in HE. While these studies do not establish causation, they provide valuable insights into potential factors that could be targeted in interventions to enhance student wellbeing. They further highlight the need for culturally attuned wellbeing services and interventions that respect and integrate the cultural identities and values of students. This theme, therefore, not only contributes to the academic understanding of wellbeing in a specific regional context but also has practical implications for developing effective support systems in educational settings.

The third main finding of this study is the reliance on data collection tools exported from different socio-cultural settings in the majority of research and services related to wellbeing. Several studies included in this review have adopted scales borrowed from Western contexts. Some, but not all, have attempted to adapt and validate the scales to the local context. However, this adaptation process is complex and necessitates taking into consideration local cultural dimensions (Hernández-Torrano et al., 2021). Cultural differences can significantly impact how concepts are understood, experienced, and expressed. Culture has multidimensional effects on wellbeing (Diener et al., 2003), and as such various components linked to cultural specificity may influence both the perception and evaluation of wellbeing and its scales. Constructs like wellbeing, stress, and even life skills may have different connotations and determinants in the Arab region compared to Western societies. For instance, factors like collectivism, religious beliefs, and socio-political dynamics in the Arab region might influence these constructs differently. Secondly, language nuances and translation issues can lead to misinterpretation of questions or responses, impacting the reliability and validity of the data collected. This is particularly crucial in regions such as the Arab world, where multiple dialects and linguistic subtleties exist. The need to either validate existing tools or develop new ones that are contextually relevant in this region cannot be overstated. The translation of these tools into Arabic and their adaptation to local dialects and idiomatic expressions are vital to ensure comprehension and accuracy. Misinterpretation due to language differences can lead to skewed results, limiting the utility of the findings for local mental health interventions. Validating tools ensure that they accurately measure the intended constructs within the cultural, social, political, and economic contexts of the region. It also ensures that interventions based on these assessments are appropriate and effective.

Furthermore, developing new tools specific to the Arab region could capture the unique aspects of its diverse cultures more accurately while leading to the culturally relevant appropriation of the wellbeing conceptual framework. It would involve incorporating local values, beliefs, and experiences right from the conceptualization stage, leading to more culturally sensitive research and practice. One cannot ignore the cultural difference between emotional experience and perception (Kitayama et al., 2000). In light of these considerations, it becomes evident that the advancement of research and practice on wellbeing in the Arab region depends significantly on the use of measurement tools that are either validated for or developed within its specific socio-cultural context. It is interesting to see, that despite existing reflection and recognition of the cultural relativism in working on wellbeing and the manifest variability inherent to differences in values and behavior inherent to cultural identities (Chirkov et al., 2003), research in the Arab region remains highly dependent on Western-based tools and concepts. It is also relevant to note that despite the asserted interest and reference to the importance of local culture in the identified research, many still refer to and rely on Western-based scales and frameworks. This may denote an intellectual and psychological dichotomy that needs to be addressed to move forward in academic independence. Accepting and adopting this cultural relativism, here we may prefer the concept of cultural enhancement while acknowledging this academic and conceptual tension would not only heighten the scientific rigor of research conducted in the region but also ensure that the resulting knowledge and interventions are culturally relevant and effective.

The fourth main finding exposes the contrast between studies conducted during the COVID-19 pandemic and those before or after, underscoring the need in educational research to deeply integrate and prioritize the examination of the interplay between students' wellbeing and their academic experiences (Huckins et al., 2020). This approach is essential because the educational context provides unique challenges and stressors that significantly impact students' wellbeing and, consequently, their academic performance. The pandemic has highlighted how changes in educational environments, methodologies, and the overall academic experience can profoundly affect students' wellbeing (Cao et al., 2020; Sahu, 2020). Therefore, future research that merges educational and psychological constructs must not only use the educational context as a pseudo-context but rather place it at the center of the investigation. Such studies should be designed with a keen understanding of the educational context, considering factors like teaching methods, academic pressure, institutional support, and student-teacher dynamics. Integrating insights from educational studies will help researchers appreciate the nuances of the educational context, ensuring that their findings are not only contextually relevant but also practically applicable in addressing the specific wellbeing needs of students within educational settings. This approach will enrich the field of psychology, leading to more effective strategies for promoting student wellbeing and academic success.

The last main finding of this scoping review highlights the need to promote wellbeing intervention in HE in the Arab region. This study suggests that while wellbeing interventions can be beneficial, their success is contingent upon various factors, including the socio-cultural context and the specific needs and perceptions of the student population, corroborating with previous studies (Furst et al., 2020; Maulana et al., 2020). These studies showed a growing awareness among researchers of the need to tailor wellbeing interventions to the specific socio-cultural and educational contexts of students. They also highlighted the importance of diverse research methodologies, including both quantitative and qualitative approaches, to fully understand the multifaceted nature of student wellbeing in HE. However, the majority of identified research in this study remains quantitative, which may make it more challenging to integrate the local socio-cultural dimension, especially when the data collection tools used are not necessarily adapted. These findings suggest that future research should continue to explore contextually relevant interventions and consider the unique academic environments and cultural backgrounds of students to optimize the effectiveness of wellbeing initiatives in HE settings.

In conclusion, this scoping review brings to the literature interesting facts about academic research in wellbeing, both specifically in the Arab region and more generally in the academic field. It exposes the importance of contextualizing wellbeing research in agreement with local social, economic, and cultural particularities. Wellbeing intervention and conceptualization need to be reviewed through Arab cultural and historical perspectives. Importing the wellbeing concept as it is presently the case, based on a hegemonic and foreign framework, is both an opportunity and a challenge. It is an opportunity for local academics to discuss, confront, and reshape imported perspectives on wellbeing, and a challenge for them to ignite and demonstrate their ability to affirm their socio-cultural setting within the academic agenda in the Arab region. The present research underscores the perceived need within the region to develop and extend wellbeing programs and interventions, linked to the imperative to relate this concept to the epistemic and ontological reality of the region, and calls for academics to embrace intellectual emancipation. This could be done through multicultural collaboration within the Arab region embracing the differences and commonalities of its different countries.

References

Arksey, H., & O'Malley, L. (2005). Scoping studies: Towards a methodological framework. *International Journal of Social Research Methodology*, *8*(1), 19–32. https://doi.org/10.1080/1364557032000119616

Assaad, R., Badawy, E., & Krafft, C. (2016). Pedagogy, accountability, and perceptions of quality by type of higher education in Egypt and Jordan. *Comparative Education Review*, *60*(4), 746–775. https://doi.org/10.1086/688421.

Barry, M. M., Clarke, A. M., & Dowling, K. (2017). Promoting social and emotional wellbeing in schools. *Health Education*, *117*(5), 434–451. https://doi.org/10.1108/HE-11-2016-0057

Bragge, P., Clavisi, O., & Turner, T. (2011). The global evidence mapping initiative: Scoping research in broad topic areas. *BMC Medical Research Methodology*, *11*(92), 2–12. https://doi.org/10.1186/1471-2288-11-92

Cao, W., Fang, Z., Hou, G., Han, M., Xu, X., Dong, J., & Zheng, J. (2020). The psychological impact of the covid-19 epidemic on college students in china. *Psychiatry Research*, *287*, 112934. https://doi.org/10.1016/j.psychres.2020.112934

Carter, S. (2016) Holding it together: an explanatory framework for maintaining subjective well-being (SWB) in principals. [Thesis (PhD/Research)].

Chirkov, V., Ryan, R. M., Kim, Y., & Kaplan, U. (2003). Differentiating autonomy from individualism and independence: A self-determination theory perspective on internalization of cultural orientations and well-being. *Journal of Personality and Social Psychology*, *84*(1), 97–110. https://doi.org/10.1037/0022-3514.84.1.97

Choi, N., Li, X., Crossley, R., Gibbs, J., & López-Harder, J. (2023). Mental health and attitudes toward seeking counseling in Mexican Americans: Exploring values and social class. *The Counseling Psychologist*, *51*(4), 560–589. https://doi.org/10.1177/00110000231160766

Danker, J., Strnadová, I., & Cumming, T. M. (2019). Picture my well-being: Listening to the voices of students with autism spectrum disorder, *Research in Developmental Disabilities*, *89*(April), 130–140. https://doi.org/10.1016/j.ridd.2019.04.005

Deci, E. L., & Ryan, R. M. (2000). The "what" and "why" of goal pursuits: Human needs and the self-determination of behaviour. *Psychological Inquiry*, *11*, 227–268. https://doi.org/10.1207/S15327965PLI1104_01

Derné, S. (2009). Well-being, lessons from India. In G. Mathews, & C. Izqierdo (Eds.), *Pursuits of happiness: Well-being in anthropological perspective* (pp. 127–146). Berghahn Books.

Dewar, M. D. (2016). *Education and well-being: An ontological inquiry*. Springer.
Diener, E., Oishi, S., & Lucas, R. E. (2003). Personality, culture, and subjective well-being: Emotional and cognitive evaluations of life. *Annual Review of Psychology, 54*(1), 403–425. https://doi.org/10.1146/annurev.psych.54.101601.145056
Diener, E., Oishi, S., & Lucas, R. E. (2015). National accounts of subjective well-being. *American Psychologist, 70*(3), 234–242. https://doi.org/10.1037/a0038899
Diener, E., Suh, E. M., Lucas, R. E., & Smith, H. L. (1999). Subjective well-being: Three decades of progress. *Psychological Bulletin, 125*(2), 276–302. https://doi.org/10.1037/0033-2909.125.2.276
Dodd, A., Priestley, M., Tyrrell, K., Cygan, S., Newell, C., & Byrom, N. (2021). University student well-being in the United Kingdom: A scoping review of its conceptualisation and measurement. *Journal of Mental Health, 30*(3), 375–387. https://doi.org/10.1080/09638237.2021.1875419
Douwes, R., Metselaar, J., Pijnenborg, G. H. M., & Boonstra, N. (2023). Well-being of students in higher education: The importance of a student perspective. *Cogent Education, 10*(1), 2190697. https://doi.org/10.1080/2331186X.2023.2190697.
Elliot, D. L., & Kobayashi, S. (2018). How can PhD supervisors play a role in bridging academic cultures? *Teaching in Higher Education, 24*(8), 911–929. https://doi.org/10.1080/13562517.2018.1517305
Furst, M. A., Bagheri, N., & Salvador-Carulla, L. (2020). An ecosystems approach to mental health services research. *BJPsych International, 18*(1), 23–25. https://doi.org/10.1192/bji.2020.24
Gutierrez-Bucheli, L., Reid, A., & Kidman, G. (2022). Scoping reviews: Their development and application in environmental and sustainability education research. *Environmental Education Research, 28*(5), 645–673.
Harding, S., Morris, R. W., Gunnell, D., Ford, T., Hollingworth, W., Tilling, K., & Kidger, J. (2019). Is teachers' mental health and wellbeing associated with students' mental health and wellbeing? *Journal of Affective Disorders, 242*, 180–187. https://doi.org/10.1016/j.jad.2018.08.080
Hascher, T. (2008). Quantitative and qualitative research approaches to assess student well-being. *International Journal of Educational Research, 47*(2), 84–96. https://doi.org/10.1016/j.ijer.2007.11.016
Hassan, K. E. (2013). Quality assurance in higher education in 20 Arab economies. *Higher Education Management and Policy, 24*(2), 73–84. https://doi.org/10.1787/hemp-24-5k3w5pdwjg9t
Hernández-Torrano, D., Ibrayeva, L., Muratkyzy, A., Lim, N., Nurtayev, Y. R., Almukhambetova, A., & Sparks, J. (2021). Validation of a Kazakhstani version of the mental health continuum—Short form. *Frontiers in Psychology, 12*. https://doi.org/10.3389/fpsyg.2021.754236
Hernández-Torrano, D., Ibrayeva, L., Sparks, J., Lim, N., Clementi, A., Almukhambetova, A., & Muratkyzy, A. (2020). Mental health and well-being of university students: A biblio-metric mapping of the literature. *Frontiers in Psychology, 11*(1226). https://doi.org/10.3389/fpsyg.2020.01226.
Hossain, S., O'Neill, S., & Strnadová, I. (2023). What constitutes student well-being: A scoping review of students' perspectives. *Child Indicators Research, 16*(2), 447–483.
Huckins, J. F., DaSilva, A. W., Wang, W., Hedlund, E., Rogers, C., Nepal, S., Wu Jialing, O.M., Murphy E. I., Meyer M. L., Wagner D. D., Holtzheimer P. E., & Campbell, A. T. (2020). Mental health and behavior during the early phases of the covid-19 pandemic: A longitudinal mobile smartphone and ecological momentary assessment study in college students. *Journal of Educational Research, 47*(2), 84–96. https://doi.org/10.2196/20185.

Kitayama, S., Markus, H. R., & Kurokawa, M. (2000). Culture, emotion, and well-being: Good feelings in Japan and the United States. *Cognition & Emotion, 14*(1), 93–124. https://doi.org/10.1080/026999300379003

Long, R. F., Huebner, E. S., Wedell, D. S., & Hills, K. J. (2012). Measuring school related subjective well-being in adolescents. *American Journal of Orthopsychiatry Mental Health and Social Justice, 82*(1), 50–60.

Mak, S., & Thomas, A. (2022). Steps for conducting a scoping review. *Journal of Graduate Medical Education, 14*(5), 565–567. https://doi.org/10.4300/JGME-D-22-00621.1

Maleku, A., Soukenik, E., Haran, H., Kirsch, J., & Pyakurel, S. (2021). Conceptualizing mental health through Bhutanese refugee lens: Findings from a mixed methods study. *Community Mental Health Journal, 58*(2), 376–393. https://doi.org/10.1007/s10597-021-00835-4

Maulana, H., Khawaja, N. G., & Obst, P. L. (2020). An Indonesian model of well-being: The integration of universal and cultural factors. *PsyCh Journal, 10*(1), 141–154. https://doi.org/10.1002/pchj.402

McLellan, R., Faucher, C., & Simovska, V. (Eds.). (2022). *Wellbeing and schooling: Cross cultural and cross disciplinary perspectives.* Springer.

Patton, G. C., Sawyer, S., Santelli, J., Ross, D. A., Afifi, R., Allen, N. B., Arora, M., Azzopardi, P., Baldwin, W., Bonell, C., & Kakuma, R (2016). Our future: A lancet commission on adolescent health and wellbeing. *The Lancet, 387*(10036), 2423–2478. https://doi.org/10.1016/s0140-6736(16)00579-1

Rashidi, F. A., Diab-Bahman, R., & Al-Enzi, D. A. (2021). The impact of socio-economic factors on human capital investments a comparative study of the Arab region. *Journal of Education and Human Development, 10*(1). https://doi.org/10.15640/jehd.v10n1a12

Ryan, R. M., & Deci, E. L. (2001). On happiness and human potentials: A review of research on hedonic and eudaimonic well-being. *Annual Review of Psychology, 52*(1), 141. https://doi.org/10.1146/annurev.psych.52.1.141

Ryff, C. D. (1989). Happiness is everything, or is it? Explorations on the meaning of psychological well-being. *Journal of Personality and Social Psychology, 57*(6), 1069–1081. https://doi.org/10.1037/0022-3514.57.6.1069

Sahu, P. K. (2020). Closure of universities due to coronavirus disease 2019 (covid-19): Impact on education and mental health of students and academic staff. *Cureus.* https://doi.org/10.7759/cureus.7541

Seligman, M. E. P., & Csíkszentmihályi, M. (2000). Positive psychology: An introduction. *American Psychologist, 55*(1), 5–14. https://doi.org/10.1037/0003-066x.55.1.5

Spilt, J. L., Koomen, H. M., & Thijs, J. (2011). Teacher wellbeing: The importance of teacher–student relationships. *Educational Psychology Review, 23*(4), 457–477. https://doi.org/10.1007/s10648-011-9170-y

Spratt, J. (2017). *Wellbeing, equity and education. A critical analysis of policy discourses of wellbeing in schools.* Springer.

Summerfield, D. (2013). "Global mental health" is an oxymoron and medical imperialism. *BMJ, 346,* f3509. https://doi.org/10.1136/bmj.f3509 https://doi.org/10.1136/bmj.f3509

Svane, D., Evans, N (Snowy), & Carter, M.-A. (2019). Wicked wellbeing: Examining the disconnect between the rhetoric and reality of wellbeing interventions in schools. *Australian Journal of Education, 63*(2), 209–231. https://doi.org/10.1177/0004944119843144

Thorburn, M. (2018). Personal well-being and curriculum planning: A critical comparative review of theory, policy and practice coherence. *Educational Review, 72*(6), 785–799. https://doi.org/10.1080/00131911.2018.1552660

Tiliouine, H. (2022). The missing link to improving wellbeing in ARAB populations: The restoration of human dignity. *Middle East Journal of Positive Psychology, 8,* 6–17.

Appendix 1 List of studies

	Authors	Title	Country	Year	Methodology
1	Grey, Ian; Thomas, Justin	National Identity, Implicit In-Group Evaluation, and Psychological Well-Being Among Emirati Women	UAE	2019	Quantitative
2	Dardara, Elsaeed A.; Al-Makhalid, Khalid A.	Procrastination, Negative Emotional Symptoms, and Mental Well-Being among college students in Saudi Arabia	Saudi Arabia	2022	Quantitative
3	Alhaj-Mahmoud, Ferial M.; Ahmad, Somia A.	Psychological well-being program efficacy on meaning-in-life in a sample of University of Jeddah students	Saudi Arabia	2021	Experimental
4	Kirchner-Haeusler, Alexander; Schoenbrodt, Felix D.; Uskul, Ayse K.; Vignoles, Vivian L.; Rodriguez-Bailon, Rosa; Castillo, Vanessa A.; Cross, Susan E.; Gezici-Yalcin, Meral; Harb, Charles; Husnu, Shenel; Ishii, Keiko; Karamaouna, Panagiota; Kafetsios, Konstantinos; Kateri, Evangelia; Matamoros-Lima, Juan; Miniesy, Rania; Na, Jinkyung; Ozkan, Zafer; Pagliaro, Stefano; Psaltis, Charis; Rabie, Dina; Teresi, Manuel; Uchida, Yukiko	Proximal and distal honor fit and subjective well-being in the Mediterranean region	International (Mediterranean countries)	2022	Quantitative
5	Mahasneha, Ahmad M.	The Relationship between Subjective Well-being and Social Support among Jordanian University Students	Jordan	2022	Quantitative
6	Al Sultan, Adam A.; Alharbi, Abdulmajeed A.; Mahmoud, Somaya S.; Elsharkasy, Ahmed S.	The Mediating Role of Psychological Capital Between Academic Stress and Well-Being Among University Students	Saudi Arabia	2023	Quantitative

(Continued)

Appendix 1 (Continued)

	Authors	Title	Country	Year	Methodology
7	Krys, Kuba; Haas, Brian W.; Igou, Eric Raymond; Kosiarczyk, Aleksandra; Kocimska-Bortnowska, Agata; Kwiatkowska, Anna; Lun, Vivian Miu-Chi; Maricchiolo, Fridanna; Park, Joonha; Solcova, Iva Polackova; Sirlopu, David; Uchida, Yukiko; Vauclair, Christin-Melanie; Vignoles, Vivian L.; Zelenski, John M.; Adamovic, Mladen; Akotia, Charity S.; Albert, Isabelle; Appoh, Lily; Mira, D. M. Arevalo; Baltin, Arno; Denoux, Patrick; Dominguez-Espinosa, Alejandra; Esteves, Carla Sofia; Gamsakhurdia, Vladimer; Fulop, Marta; Gardarsdottir, Ragna B.; Gavreliuc, Alin; Boer, Diana; Igbokwe, David O.; Isik, Idil; Kascakova, Natalia; Kracmarova, Lucie Kluzova; Kosakowska-Berezecka, Natasza; Kostoula, Olga; Kronberger, Nicole; Lee, J. Hannah; Liu, Xinhui; Luzniak-Piecha, Magdalena; Malyonova, Arina; Barrientos, Pablo Eduardo; Mohoric, Tamara; Mosca, Oriana; Murdock, Elke; Mustaffa, Nur Fariza; Nader, Martin; Nadi, Azar; Okvitawanli, Ayu; van Osch, Yvette; Pavlopoulos, Vassilis; Pavlovic, Zoran; Rizwan, Muhammad; Romashov, Vladyslav; Roysamb, Espen; Sargautyte, Ruta; Schwarz, Beate; Selim, Heyla A.; Serdarevich, Ursula; Stogianni, Maria; Sun, Chien-Ru; Teyssier, Julien; van Tilburg, Wijnand A. P.; Torres, Claudio; Xing, Cai; Bond, Michael Harris	Introduction to a Culturally Sensitive Measure of Well-Being: Combining Life Satisfaction and Interdependent Happiness Across 49 Different Cultures	International (World, 49 countries)	2022	Quantitative

Exploring wellbeing in the Arab higher education context 47

	Authors	Title	Country	Year	Type
8	Mahmid, Fayez; Bdier, Dana; Chou, Priscilla	The association between problematic Internet use, eating disorder behaviors, and well-being among Palestinian university students	Palestine	2021	Quantitative
9	Balay-odao, Ejercito Mangawa; Cruz, Jonas Preposi; Bajet, Junel Bryan; Alquwez, Nahed; Mesde, Jennifer; Otaibi, Khalaf Al; Alsolais, Abdulellah; Danglipen, Cherryl	Influence of student nurses' perceived caring behavior of their instructors on their psychological well-being: a cross-sectional study	Saudi Arabia	2022	Quantitative
10	Alorani, Omar Ismael; Alradaydeh, Mu'taz Fuad	Spiritual well-being, perceived social support, and life satisfaction among university students	Jordan	2017	Quantitative
11	Al-Sabbah, Saher; Darwish, Amani; Fares, Najwan; Barnes, James; Almomani, Jehad Ali	Biopsychosocial factors linked with overall well-being of students and educators during the COVID-19 pandemic	Jordan / UAE	2021	COVID
12	AlAhmari, Fatimah Saeed; Aloqail, Alaa; Almansour, Shahad; Bagha, Mohammad	State of well-being among residents in a tertiary center in Riyadh, Saudi Arabia	Saudi	2023	Experimental
13	Mosleh, Sultan M.; Shudifat, Raed M.; Dalky, Heyam F.; Almalik, Mona M.; Alnajar, Malek K.	Mental health, learning behaviour and perceived fatigue among university students during the COVID-19 outbreak: a cross-sectional multicentric study in the UAE	UAE	2022	COVID
14	Albaqawi, Hamdan Mohammad; Nageeb, Shaimaa Mohamed	The Relationship between Psychological Well-being, Academic Engagement, and Self-Regulated Learning among Student Nurses	Saudi Arabia	2022	Quantitative
15	Maddah, Diana; Saab, Youssra; Safadi, Hani; Farraj, Nermine Abi; Hassan, Zeinab; Turner, Sophia; Echeverri, Lina; Alami, Nael H.; Kababian-Khasholian, Tamar; Salameh, Pascale	The first life skills intervention to enhance well-being amongst university students in the Arab world: 'Khotwa' pilot study	Lebanon	2021	Experimental

(Continued)

Appendix 1 (Continued)

	Authors	Title	Country	Year	Methodology
16	Bouclaous, Carmel; Fadlallah, Najat; El Helou, Mohamad Othman; Dadaczynski, Kevin	University students' experience of the Beirut port explosion: associations with subjective well-being and subjective symptoms of mental strain	Lebanon	2023	Quantitative
17	Mohammed, Bakheeta AbdEl-Aziz; Mohammed, Ikram Ibraheem; Ahmed, Hossam Khalifa; El-Naser, Amera Azzet Abd	Effect of educational program on the psychological challenges of electronic learning among university nursing students: a quasi-Experimental study	Egypt	2023	COVID
18	Abu-Raiya, Hisham; Ayten, Ali; Agbaria, Qutaiba; Tekke, Mustafa	Relationships between Religious Struggles and Well-Being among a Multinational Muslim Sample: A Comparative Analysis	Palestine / Türkiye / Malaysia	2018	Quantitative
19	Al Omari, Omar; Al Yahyaei, Asma; Wynaden, Dianne; Damra, Jalal; Aljezawi, Maen; Al Qaderi, Mohammad; Al Ruqaishi, Huda; Abu Shahrour, Loai; ALBashtawy, Mohammed	Correlates of resilience among university students in Oman: a cross-sectional study	Oman	2023	Quantitative
20	Moussa, Mona Merhej; Elphinstone, Brad; Thomas, Justin; HerArab, Ehab W.; Barbato, Mariapaola; Whitehead, Richard; Bates, Glen	Nonattachment as a Mediator of the Mindfulness-Well-being Relationship: Comparing Emirati and Australian Students	UAE / Australia	2022	Quantitative
21	Alblwi, Abdulaziz; McAlaney, John; Altuwairiqi, Majid; Stefanidis, Angelos; Phalp, Keith; Ali, Raian	Procrastination on Social Networks: Triggers and Countermeasures	Saudi Arabia / UK	2020	Quantitative
22	Almubaddel, Abdulmohsen	Psychometric properties of a Saudi Arabian version of the Positive Mental Health (PMH) scale	Saudi Arabia	2022	Quantitative
23	Bitar, Zeinab; Rogoza, Radoslaw; Hallit, Souheil; Obeid, Sahar	Mindfulness among Lebanese university students and its indirect effect between mental health and wellbeing	Lebanon	2023	Quantitative

#	Authors	Title	Country	Year	Method
24	Qanash, Sultan; Al-Husayni, Faisal; Falata, Haneen; Halawani, Ohud; Jahra, Enas; Murshed, Boshra; Alhejaili, Faris; Ghabashi, Ala'a; Alhashmi, Hashem	Effect of Electronic Device Addiction on Sleep Quality and Academic Performance Among Health Care Students: Cross-sectional Study	Saudi Arabia	2021	Quantitative
25	El-Ashry, Ayman Mohamed; Atta, Mohamed Hussein Ramadan; Alsenany, Samira Ahmed; Abdelaliem, Sally Mohammed Farghaly; Khedr, Mahmoud Abdelwahab	The Effect of Distress Tolerance Training on Problematic Internet Use and Psychological Wellbeing Among Faculty Nursing Students: A Randomized Control Trial	Saudi Arabia	2023	Quantitative
26	Alshehri, Abdullah; Alshehri, Badr; Alghadir, Omar; Basamh, Abdullah; Alzeer, Meshari; Alshehri, Mohammed; Nasr, Sameh	The prevalence of depressive and anxiety symptoms among first-year and fifth-year medical students during the COVID-19 pandemic: a cross-sectional study	Saudi Arabia	2022	COVID
27	Lambert, L.; Passmore, H-A; Joshanloo, M.	A Positive Psychology Intervention Program in a Culturally-Diverse University: Boosting Happiness and Reducing Fear	UAE	2019	Experimental
28	Maddah, Diana; Hallit, Souheil; Kabbara, Wissam; Akel, Marwan; Bowen, Keith; Hasan, Zeinab; Khasholian, Tamar Kabakian; Alami, Nael H.; Salameh, Pascale	Validation of the first Arabic version of the life skills scale among university students	Lebanon	2023	Quantitative
29	Bergenfeld, Irina; Cislaghi, Beniamino; Yount, Kathryn M.; Essaid, Aida A.; Sajdi, Jude; Abu Taleb, Rand; Morrow, Grace L.; D'Souza, Janice S.; Spencer, Rachael A.; Clark, Cari Jo	Diagnosing Norms Surrounding Sexual Harassment at a Jordanian University	Jordan	2021	Quantitative
30	Lambert, L.; Draper, Z. A.; Warren, M. A.; Joshanloo, M.; Chiao, En-Ling; Schwam, A.; Arora, T.	Conceptions of Happiness Matter: Relationships between Fear and Fragility of Happiness and Mental and Physical Wellbeing	UAE	2022	Quantitative

(Continued)

Appendix 1 (Continued)

	Authors	Title	Country	Year	Methodology
31	Sanchez-Ruiz, Maria-Jose; Tadros, Natalie; Khalaf, Tatiana; Ego, Veronica; Eisenbeck, Nikolett; Carreno, David F.; Nassar, Elma	Trait Emotional Intelligence and Wellbeing During the Pandemic: The Mediating Role of Meaning-Centered Coping	WOS	2021	COVID
32	Yousef, Latifeh; Ebrahim, Omar; AlNahr, Mohammad Hareth; Mohsen, Fatema; Ibrahim, Nazir; Sawaf, Bisher	War-related trauma and post-traumatic stress disorder prevalence among Syrian university students	Syria	2021	Quantitative
33	Lambert, Louise; Warren, Meg A.; Schwam, Allison; Warren, Michael T.	Positive psychology interventions in the United Arab Emirates: boosting wellbeing - and changing culture?	UAE	2021	Experimental
34	Samad, Sarminah; Nilashi, Mehrbakhsh; Ibrahim, Othman	The impact of social networking sites on students' social wellbeing and academic performance	Malaysia	2023	Quantitative
35	Asi, Yara M.; Unruh, Lynn; Liu, Xinliang	Conflict and well-being: a comparative study of health-related quality of life, stress, and insecurity of university students in the West Bank and Jordan.	Jordan / Palestine	2018	Quantitative
36	Hamididin R.M.; El Keshky M.E.S.	Making life better for female students with motor disabilities: Success in Saudi Arabia with a Selective Counselling Program	Saudi Arabia	2018	Experimental
37	Lambert L.; Draper Z.A.; Warren M.A.; Mendoza-Lepe R.	Assessing a Happiness and Wellbeing Course in the United Arab Emirates: It is What They Want, but is it What They Need?	UAE	2022	Experimental
38	Darawsheh N.	The Impact of Cyber Bullying on the Psychological Well-being of University Students: A Study in Jordanian Universities	Jordan	2023	Quantitative
39	Aboelmaged M.; Ali I.; Hashem G.	Mobile apps use for wellness and fitness and university students' subjective wellbeing	Egypt	2021	COVID

	Authors	Title	Country	Year	Type
40	Shrivastava A.; Azhar H.; Hyland L.	A Personal Journey of Studying Positive Psychology: Reflections of Undergraduate Students in the United Arab Emirates	UAE	2022	Experimental
41	Ibrahim A.M.; Teleb A.A.; Abdelmagid A.S.; Azam M.R.; Abdel Alim E.F.	Academic Subjective Well-being Among Students at College of Education in King Khalid University in the Light of Some Demographic Variables	Saudi Arabia	2022	Quantitative
42	Soliman M.; Rasheed A.; Hady H.A.; Jdaitawi M.; Khamees A.; Abdelsalam R.	The impact of mobile phone fitness applications on the level of physical fitness and psychological well-being during covid-19: The case of university students	Saudi Arabia	2022	COVID
43	Irshad S.; Al-Saeed O.; Begum N.	Impact of Transition from Onsite to Online Education on Students Learning and Psychological Well-being: A Cross-sectional Study of King Faisal University, KSA	Saudi Arabia	2023	COVID
44	Sabaoui I.; Lotfi S.; Zerdani I.; Talbi M.	Desynchronized daily activity rhythms and gender related psychological well-being of Moroccan university students during the quarantine-isolation	Morocco	2023	COVID
45	Mabrouk F.; Abdulrahim H.; Gangwani S.; Alsmari E.	A Comparative Analysis of Student Satisfaction and Motivation, Academic Performance and Subjective Well-Being Before and During Covid-19 Pandemic	Saudi Arabia	2023	COVID
46	Alkhatib M.A.H.	Investigate the relationship between psychological well-being, self-efficacy and positive thinking at prince Sattam Bin Abdulaziz University	Saudi Arabia	2020	Quantitative

Chapter 4

Student wellbeing in the Pacific Islands

Challenges and opportunities for enhancing academic success

Annie Crookes

Introduction

The Pacific context: the Oceania and Pacific island nations overview

The Pacific Oceania Region includes Australia and New Zealand alongside the many smaller island countries that constitute Melanesia, Micronesia, and Polynesia. Many of these smaller nations have been impacted by European colonization leading to enduring cultural and political ties with Western nations. As a result, some of these islands continue to be jurisdictions of other nations (e.g., American Samoa and Guam, French Polynesia, and New Caledonia). However, others gained independence and now form the cooperative of Pacific Island Countries (PICs): Niue, Palau, Papua New Guinea, Republic of Marshall Islands, Samoa, Solomon Islands, Tonga, Tuvalu, and Vanuatu Kiribati, Nauru Cook Islands, Federated States of Micronesia, Fiji.

Although the independent nations have relatively small populations, they cover a geographic area equating to 15% of the Earth's surface.[1] Papua New Guinea is the most populated country with over 10 million people followed by Fiji as the second largest, with only 900,000 people. Meanwhile, Tuvalu and Nauru have populations of around 11,000 each. These populations are located across a large number of remote islands. For example, Fiji comprises over 330 islands spread across 18,300 square kilometers and Kiribati has a population of around 130,000 spread out over 33 million square kilometers of ocean. This geographic spread and remoteness mean that each country, and the region as a whole, has a very diverse culture. Additionally, the Pacific region is one of the most linguistically diverse regions in the world with 18.5% of the world's languages originating from the Pacific (Sato & Bradshaw, 2017). Importantly, the historical colonization introduced (and imposed) social values, religions, and cultures onto the Pacific nations. For example, Indian-ethnic Fijians, brought over by the British as indentured labor, now make up 37.5% of the total population. Furthermore, PICs are now strongly Christian-affiliated countries and religious faith is a defining feature of their modern socio-cultural and political environment (Ernst & Anisi, 2016; Fountain & Troughton, 2019).

DOI: 10.4324/9781003491613-4

The Pacific context: mental health and wellbeing challenges

With a history of political and social changes, the low- and middle-income PICs are challenged by a number of health, mental health, and socio-cultural issues. For example, several of these countries rank among the highest globally for Non-Communicable Diseases (NCDs) and obesity (Global Obesity Observatory, n.d.; WHO, 2018). In addition, several studies have indicated the relatively high rates of mental health issues with depression, suicide, alcohol, and substance abuse all found to be rapidly rising in these countries (Mathieu et al., 2021). While chronic health issues and low life expectancy (around 69 years; UNFPA, 2014) necessarily impact the psychological distress and wellbeing of the broader population, there are also several specific socio-cultural problems facing these populations. For example, low economic opportunities, urbanization, and loss of traditional community structures are recognized as negatively impacting mental health in the region (Ali et al., 2020). PICs also have some of the highest rates of domestic violence and violence against girls and women globally, with estimates that 60–80% of the female population in Pacific islands will experience this during their lifetime (UN WOMEN Pacific, 2011). Critically, these economic and social challenges are compounded by the effects of climate change. That is, ongoing natural disasters, forced migration due to land erosion, loss of food sources because of land and ocean destruction, and the loss of cultural heritage and identity impact the psychosocial issues (Gibson et al., 2020; Patrick et al., 2023; Tiatia et al., 2023).

Given this extremely challenged environment, coupled with a stigma around discussions of distress and mental health, as well as a lack of investment and specialist resources, the estimated treatment gap is generally thought to be at least 90% for those needing help (Ali et al., 2020; Chang, 2011; Charlson et al., 2015 among others). The impact of this lack of support systems can be seen in rates of suicide, where PICs have some of the highest rates of suicide within the western Pacific and several have population rates far above the global average (WHO, 2021). A review of literature on suicide in the PICs reported that particularly Samoa, Kiribati, and Solomon Islands had the highest rates of suicidal ideation and attempts among young people. Mathieu and colleagues (2021) state that young people are particularly vulnerable to suicidal ideation and behaviors. They argue that the ongoing social changes and loss of traditional social structures in these countries have potentially led to a deterioration in traditional support mechanisms for young people during their early development and transitions to adulthood.

The PICs report growing concerns about the use of alcohol and drugs, particularly among young people. The use of alcohol varies across the PICs (Kessaram et al., 2016) due to differences in cost and availability. That is, while some countries have relatively low consumption of alcohol, others such as Tokelau, Nauru, and Cook Islands report much higher alcohol use (up to 60% of male adults). Furthermore, Police data suggests an exponential growth in the number of arrests for drug offenses in the past 15 years (UNODC, 2020) and authorities have acknowledged the use of PICs as stopovers in the trafficking of cocaine and methamphetamine to

Australian and New Zealand markets (see Gounder, 2022). This is likely driving an increase in the availability and abuse of these substances among young people. For example, the use of methamphetamine in many PICs was recorded as having higher lifetime use among secondary school students than seen in neighboring Australia and New Zealand (UNODC, 2012).

The Pacific context: conceptualizing mental health and wellbeing

In order to effectively promote mental health and wellbeing among the Pacific populations, it is important to understand Indigenous Pacific conceptualizations of these phenomena. Indeed, how wellbeing is experienced and what is perceived to drive wellbeing and happiness are known to differ across populations. Joshanloo and others (2021) describe distinctions in wellbeing between individualist and collectivist populations globally. First, the value given to positive emotional experiences when evaluating subjective wellbeing (SWB) differs across world regions. For example, positive emotion is found to be far more highly valued in American populations than in East Asian and Arab populations (Joshanloo et al., 2021). Second, the role of self-enhancement and autonomy, which are common to many models of wellbeing and human flourishing (e.g., PERMA model by Seligman, 2018; Self-determination Theory by Deci & Ryan, 2008), may be weighed against the cultural norms of humility and maintaining communal harmony for individuals from collectivist cultures. This may mean that individual achievements, agency, and self-esteem are less directly related to personal wellbeing and may be superseded by feeling equal and in harmony with the community. In the context of university students, this balance between agency and social harmony may suggest that a student's appraisal of their successful transition into studies must also incorporate an appraisal of other things happening in their family at the time. Finally, Joshanloo and colleagues (2021) discuss the importance of the holistic context of wellbeing in collectivist cultures. Wellbeing is a product of all aspects of life at any given time including family and community connectedness, spirituality, and a personal history. In many ways, this broader, multi-factored wellbeing mindset is found to support resilience against individual events that may occur because they can be accepted within the more holistic balance of forces.

The research on Pacific Oceania peoples' wellbeing supports a fundamentally holistic understanding and experience. For example, the Fonafale model (Pulotu-Endemann, 1995) is a widely acknowledged conceptualization of health and wellbeing in Pacific Islander and Pasifika (more specifically Polynesian and Māori) populations. This model describes both physical health and psychological wellbeing as being the product of a system that includes not only the family and the community but also an active and spiritual connection to one's cultural history and land. This model uses the metaphor of a house (see Figure 4.1) to represent the different components of wellbeing and indicate their necessary interdependence. For example, an individual's overall health and wellbeing are built from the foundation of the family (broadly defined), but this must also be 'sheltered' by cultural identity,

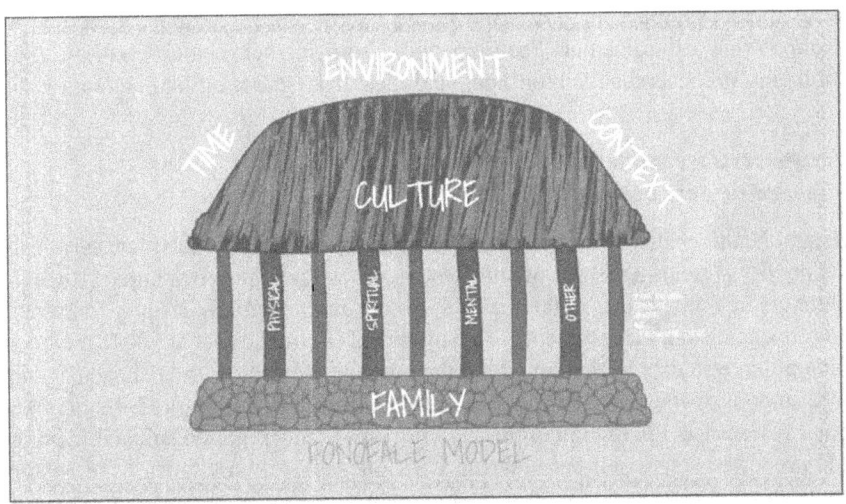

Figure 4.1 The Fonafale Model

values, and traditions (sense of belonging, meaning). However, this foundation and sheltering roof must also be connected by 'pillars' of physical, spiritual, mental, and other factors (accomplishment, engagement, positive emotion). Moreover, it is these multiple pillars between the foundation (family) and roof (cultural values) which provide the strength and resilience of the building (individuals' health and wellbeing). More recently, Manuela and Sibley (2014) present a hierarchical structure of Pacific wellbeing in which an individual's SWB is driven by their Pacific identity and cultural connectedness, perceived social and familial wellbeing, and religious embeddedness.

Furthermore, Pasifika worldviews and cultural concepts around relationships and wellbeing have been explored within the context of school systems in New Zealand. For example, the Teu Le Va project (Anae et al., 2010) explored ways in which Pasifika worldviews could and should be embedded into educational policies and practices to strengthen outcomes for Pacific students. A second example is the Tapasa Cultural Competency Framework (https://tapasa.tki.org.nz/), which provides resources for schoolteachers who work with Pacific community learners. This framework is designed around the Pasifika worldviews, values, and cultural stories, indicating how these can be translated into practice in the classroom. Finally, Reynolds (2016) described the way in which the Samoan concept of 'Va', which points to the nature of the relational space between people, is an active ingredient in successful student-teacher relationships for Pasifika students. That is, for Pasifika people, 'Va' requires the need to foster an inherent sense of connectedness to allow the exchange of information within the learning and academic context. The teacher should be concerned about and nurture the wellbeing of the students as an act of humanity and an act of community (see discussion in Reynolds, 2016).

What these examples suggest is the strong interdependence for Pasifika (and by extrapolation all Indigenous Pacific peoples) students between their culture, how wellbeing is conceptualized for them, and their academic learning outcomes.

Pacific tertiary students and mental health: a review of past literature

Mental health challenges among college students are a rising global concern. University life presents a number of unique stressors and pressures that impact students, putting some at risk of mental health disorders and potentially leading to burnout and low academic achievement for many others (Portoghese et al., 2018). Indeed, several large studies have highlighted the growing mental health crisis among college students, even prior to the COVID-19 pandemic. For example, Eisenberg and other researchers (2018) found the 11% of respondents reported suicidal ideation, 21% reported active self-harm across US Colleges, and only half of the 34% of students who underwent a mental health diagnosis reported receiving any form of formal support. Specific challenging factors were reported by students, including balancing studies and work or personal responsibilities, financial pressures, and high academic demands (Hamaideh, 2011; Stallman & Hurst, 2016) as well as inter-personal relationships and long-distance travel to reach classes (Amanya et al., 2016; Reddy et al., 2018). Importantly, students experiencing distress and mental illness are at high risk of withdrawal from studies (Lipson & Eisenberg, 2018).

Similar student mental health crises are reported within the Pacific Oceania region. For example, surveys of tertiary students in Australia found rates of psychological distress as high as 65%, and 35% of respondents reported thoughts of self-harm (Browne et al., 2017; Rickwood et al., 2017). Moreover, studies of student outcomes in New Zealand have consistently shown that compared to their white European peers, Indigenous Pacific and Pasifika students are underrepresented in higher education (Sopoaga et al., 2018; Theodore et al., 2018) and have comparatively worse mental health and lower completion rates. For example, Theodore and colleagues (2018) reported that only 58% of Pasifika students completed a degree within five years of enrollment, compared to 74% of all students in New Zealand. Of course, lower academic achievement in the population will be associated with the previously discussed broader socio-economic challenges in Pacific communities. However, these systemic factors will be compounded by the particular stressors of university study and the process of transition into the new learning (and for many, living) environment.

Anae and other researchers (2002) asked Indigenous Pacific students in New Zealand about the factors they think impact their success at university the most. Some of the reported influences were individual such as the students' time management and study skills and the strength of their study goals. These skills reflect the alignment of prior educational experiences with tertiary studies. Individual factors also include personal traits, such as being self-confident and assertive (Theodore et al., 2018). These traits are important as they facilitate students in their class participation and ability to request guidance from tutors, but are traits likely to differ across cultures. Second, students reported external factors such as the amount and form of support from family and community. The external factors also included the design and provision of support services by the institution itself. That is, the specific support needs, understanding of how to use support, and familiarity with service protocols may differ for students from different educational and cultural backgrounds (see discussions in Fredericks et al., 2023; Sopoaga et al., 2018). Therefore, designing support and predicting success for Pacific student populations require consideration of how this group is impacted by the intersections of culture, social challenges, and university stressors.

Various models have been developed to understand the particular processes of transition a student must navigate and to understand the interplay between the different helping and hindering factors. For example, Gale and Parker (2014) describe different forms of transition itself. First, the transition can be seen as '*Induction*', the process of orientation to the university. The student learns to navigate the procedures and expectations of the institution and successful transition is defined by the institution through quantitative outcomes of knowledge and behavior. The second transition theme is '*Development*', a life stage marked by qualitative changes in the student. This comes through internalizing the socio-cultural norms of the institution and beginning to identify with your chosen field. Finally, the transition may be '*Becoming*', a wholly subjective, bottom-up process of the educational systems being enmeshed with the student's life. Recognizing this typology may help to understand when institutional support does not match the processes of transition students undergo. For example, institutions predominantly design first-year experiences as *Inductions* with the expectation that students will successfully transition as a product of 'having enough information' and 'knowing what to do'. However, as Gale and Parker (2014) suggest, successful transition may also require support toward personal growth and change (Gosai et al., 2023). This would entail mentoring programs, visible role models, and career-oriented experiences. Furthermore, Gale and Parker (2014) argue that students specifically from marginalized groups may need to experience transition as *Becoming*. This is because tertiary education has not historically been part of these communities. Also, because these are groups who have multiple, collective elements making up their identities which need to now incorporate the identity of 'student'. In this way, the transition of *Becoming* for minority and marginalized student groups (i.e., incorporating *studentness* into their established self) needs to come through malleable forms of study and acquiring knowledge, culturally inclusive curricula, and spaces for education to feel collaborative and student-led.

Perhaps the most comprehensive model of tertiary education transition was developed by Tinto (1975, see Figure 4.2). This model begins with the background and personal attributes of a student referring to what provides a level of commitment to goals and to the institution. During the first year, the student has experiences relating to their own intellectual development, achievements, and social interactions with peers and staff members. This in turn impacts the level of

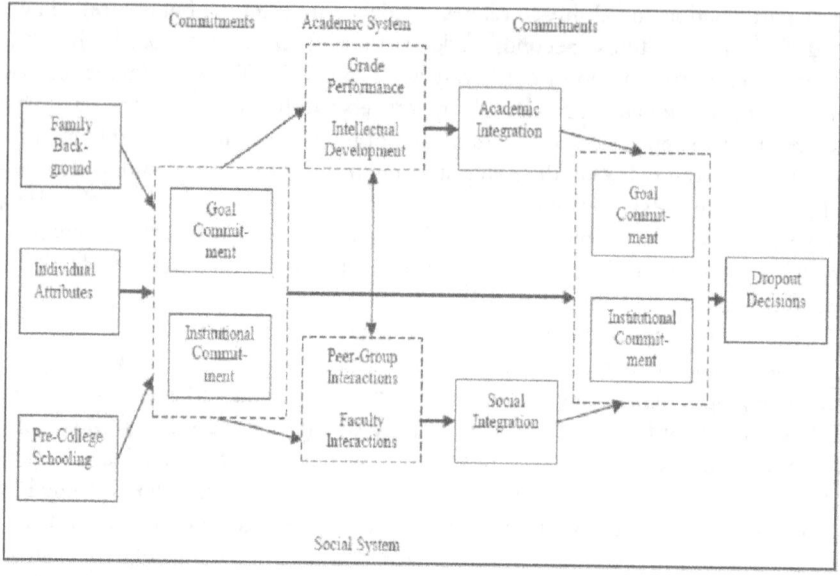

Figure 4.2 Tinto's Model of Student Transition (1975)

academic and social integration, which will either be enough to reinforce the student's goals and commitment or lead to decisions to withdraw. Recently, Sopoaga et al. (2018) created an updated, culturally sensitive model based on discussions with Pacific and Māori first-year students in New Zealand. This Pacific-transition model was labeled '*Folauga*' (The Journey) and uses the metaphor of an outrigger canoe. Here, Tinto's model remains as the boat 'hull' but is given additional protection and balance from the outrigger float of culture and identity, which are attached through the crossbeams of spiritual and physical health, and social and mental wellbeing. In many ways, this reflects Gale and Parker's (2014) suggestion that a more holistic and culturally inclusive approach to transition may be critical for some student groups.

Finally, it is important to pay particular attention to the ubiquitous role that the family plays in the general wellbeing and academic success of Pacific students. Indeed, the most common factor differentiating the needs of Pacific students from their European peers is the enmeshed and prioritized role of the (extended) family in the students' life (Chu et al., 2013; Mayeda et al., 2014; Sopoaga et al., 2018; Theodore et al., 2018; Zepke et al., 2011). As one author describes it: '*in Western society, Knowledge is power (but) in Pacific culture a strong family and community is power*' (Ravulo, 2015, p. 8). That is, for Pacific students, learning itself is not a product of the teaching strategy but fundamentally grown from the pillars of the family, the community, cultural capital, collaboration, and support (Chu et al., 2013). For a Pacific student to be successful academically, all of these elements need to be aligned within the study environment. On the one hand, the strong sense of family provides a positive source of support and motivation for Pacific University students (Gosai et al., 2023; Mayeda et al., 2014; Perrot, 2015; Theodore et al., 2018) and students often mention the value their degree will bring to the family and the community (Theodore et al., 2018). However, this is also a source of stress as the pressure to succeed becomes an obligation to the family and the community (Sopoaga et al., 2018; Theodore et al., 2018). Furthermore, the family is reported as a hindrance, for students are often obligated to travel and attend family events or expected to suspend studies in order to financially support the family or care for a family member (Benseman et al., 2006; Chu et al., 2010; Theodore et al., 2018).

A family-related factor often discussed in the Oceania student literature is the lack of family awareness about academic studies particularly at the tertiary level (Anae et al., 2002; Gosai et al., 2023; Meyeda et al., 2014; Perrot, 2015; Sopoaga et al., 2018; Theodore et al., 2018). This factor creates university stress in several ways. For example, stress comes from being among the first generations to attend tertiary education and provides the springboard to new opportunities for the family and immediate community adding to the pressure to succeed. Furthermore, Pacific students begin their studies without the accumulated knowledge from relevant role models and the shared experiences of university study passed on from the family (Mayeda et al., 2014). Finally, the lack of shared experiences and knowledge about tertiary education may lead to conflict where the family misunderstands the practical protocols and requirements of university study, the policies and expectations around class and library attendance, course assignments, and deadlines (Anae et al., 2002; Mayeda et al., 2014). They may also misunderstand the differences in grading standards and protocols between the Institution and the community school system (Sopoaga et al., 2018). This may be heightened for Pacific students attending international universities or institutions associated with internationally standardized systems.

Pacific tertiary students' mental health: the first Pacific islands student health and wellbeing survey

As has been described, populations in the PICs are faced with many socio-economic challenges that may impact their mental health throughout life. Yet, except for the developed nations of New Zealand and Australia, little research exists on student health and mental health across the smaller PICs. The University of the South Pacific (USP) is the largest tertiary institution in the Pacific with students at 15 campuses across 12 PICs. This provides an ideal platform to collect data on mental health and wellbeing from a range of Pacific students across different Island nations. In addition, USP students represent Pacific Islanders living in an Indigenous regional setting, as opposed to living as ethnic minorities and international students in otherwise 'Western' and developed nations. Accordingly, a cross-campus university survey was undertaken as the first comprehensive assessment of health and wellbeing measures from a regional Pacific Islands university student sample. The primary aim was to provide some basic indicators of current student wellbeing and explore trends in health behaviors across the Pacific Islands.

The survey was completed over two data collection cycles using an online survey. The first took place in 2020–2021 (reported in Crookes, 2021) and included a dataset of 7.89% of the total study population from 15 campuses (although predominantly Fijian students). The survey covered a range of measures on weight perceptions, diet and exercise behaviors, substance use, mental health, and academic stressors. Briefly, the findings from this first cycle indicated relatively high SWB across the whole sample, with scores on loneliness, anxiety, and depression symptoms being comparatively lower than reported in other student surveys (Eisenberg et al., 2018). Tobacco and alcohol use was also comparatively low relative to Western college student samples. At the same time, one-quarter of students reported having considered suicide during their lifetime. This was particularly among females and younger age groups. In addition, among those who did consume alcohol, the common pattern of drinking was that of binge-drinking with five or more consecutive drinks. This first dataset also showed high levels of stress related to academic studies. The Pacific students rated themselves as lacking competence in their ability to manage their studies and stay motivated.

The second student survey took place from August 2022 to March 2023 and is summarized in more detail below. This second implementation included additional questions about exposure to suicidal behaviors, the use of different substances among students, academic and test-specific anxiety, and students' perception of support services currently provided by USP.

Survey procedures and student sample

The student health and wellbeing survey was developed from a range of scales and measures based on established national student surveys in the literature. The 2022 survey had a total of 56 questions across five sections: demographics, physical health, mental health, subjective wellbeing, and academic stress. The physical health section asked students to rate their perceived weight and to report their consumption of fruits, vegetables, fast food, and their weekly exercise behaviors. This section also assessed tobacco and alcohol use (lifetime and current) and two items asking about marijuana and other drugs (self-report and perceived drug use among peers). The mental health section included single items assessing loneliness, sleep disturbance, and self-harm (Pereira et al., 2019) and the Kessler-6 item scale for anxiety and depression (Kessler et al., 2002). Suicidal ideation was measured using yes/no response items of lifetime and past year ideation, and exposure to suicide of others. This section also included an assessment of attitudes toward mental health help-seeking (Hammer et al., 2018). Subjective wellbeing included two items on life satisfaction and happiness using a 1–10 rating scale. Finally, the academic stress section included the text anxiety inventory (Stöber, 2004), the educational self-efficacy scale (Imperial College London, n.d.), and the university stress scale (Stallman & Hurst, 2016). Alongside these health and wellbeing measures, students were asked about their perception of the university support services currently provided for their health, mental health, and academic stress.

A link to the online survey was disseminated to all enrolled USP students through university emails, local campus coordinators, and targeted advertisements on social media during the 8-month survey period. Students were offered compensation for their participation in the form of a series of cash prize draws specific to each campus. A total of 2498 students responded to the survey (10.07% of the total student body). However, 420 surveys were removed due to voluntary withdrawal or invalid responses. The final dataset was 2078 respondents (8.38% of the total student body). This was predominantly students from the three Fiji campuses (including the largest, main university campus in Suva, Fiji) with 972 respondents located at the (smaller) regional campuses. The dataset is summarized as a single Pacific Islands Student sample unless otherwise specified.

Respondents in the final dataset were predominantly female (68.43%) from the youngest age group 18–24 years (67.4%), with the majority identifying themselves as heterosexual (85.5%); bisexual (9%); and gay/queer (3.4%). Most of the sample identified themselves as Indigenous Pacific Islanders (62.3%) with 30.4% Fijian of Indian descent. The remaining students were of Chinese descent (1.7%), European descent (2.9%), and other origins (2.6%). Most were taking a bachelor's level program (77.7%) and 27.43% reported working either part-time or full-time alongside their studies. A further 3.5% engaged in regular unpaid work. In total, 11.8% of the respondents reported having a paid job alongside studying full-time. Overall, at the time of conducting this study, 24.95% of the students were married and 28% had children.

Results

Substance use

The use of tobacco, alcohol, and marijuana among the student sample was low, with only 5% of students reporting currently using tobacco and 10.32% consuming alcohol at least once a week. Of those who did consume alcohol (even irregularly), many reported binge drinking in the past month (59.53% of alcohol consumers) with 7.76% reporting binge drinking at least once a week and 3.53% several times in an average week. When asked about the use of (illegal) marijuana, 13.69% reported a lifetime use and 3.85% reported using it in the past 6 months. However, when asked about their observations and perceptions of drug use among their peers at USP (as an indirect but less sensitive indicator of student drug use), the students reported perceived use of substances by students to be higher (average reported percentage of 21.43%).

Mental health and stress measures

Respondents were asked to rate how frequently they experienced loneliness and sleeping problems on a 1–6 Likert scale (never to always). Results revealed an average of the responses being 3.13 and 3.34, respectively indicating a 'sometimes' response. Similarly, items asking how often depression symptoms had occurred in the last month showed an average score of 2.79, again falling between 'a little time' and 'some of the time'. On the other hand, nearly half (47.4%) of the sample reported needing professional help for emotional distress at some point in their life, and 36.2% reported considering suicide, of which 64.6% had considered in the past year. Moreover, 46.4% of the students reported a suicide attempt or death among their immediate family and friends. This was particularly high in Vanuatu and Solomon Islands students/respondents. Over half (63.9%) of students said they have actively concealed distress from their family and friends for fear of social stigma.

When asked about academic stressors, examples reported as occurring most frequently include academic demands, finances, study/life balance, and parental expectations. In addition, Test Anxiety was measured specifically on a 1–4 scale, with students' scores being generally above mid-level (total mean= 2.83; 2.73 Male, 2.87 female, 2.74 non-binary). In particular, respondents reported experiencing worry about test outcomes and grades (overall mean= 3.74). Despite the self-reported anxiety, students in this cohort still rated themselves as generally confident that they can complete the assigned course work (mean= 3.38 on a 1–5 confidence scale; 3.50 males, 3.32 females, 3.86 non-binary).

Subjective health and wellbeing

Pacific students reported overall wellbeing in the mid-range with average responses of 5.79 (life satisfaction) and 6.58 (current happiness) on 1–10 scales. However, 43.8% of the students rated themselves at 5 or below on overall life satisfaction and 33.5% for happiness. Wellbeing, as it relates to physical health, also showed that while about half the sample perceived their weight as about right (48.29%) another 40.62% reported being slightly or very overweight (7.4%). This was particularly high in the sample from Cook Islands and Tuvalu, where the majority of campus respondents said they were very overweight. In terms of diet, most students reported consuming only one to two servings of fruit and vegetables per day (70.20%) and 18.67% reported zero fruit and vegetables on an average day. Furthermore, 24% of students reported zero sessions of intentional exercise in an average week. Finally, there was a significant (though small) association between students' perceived weight and their scores on depression and academic confidence. That is, students who rated themselves as more overweight were also more likely to score higher on depression items and to be less confident in their academic studies.

Perceptions of university support

Students held very positive attitudes toward help-seeking for mental health, with almost all students rating the use of services as highly important, useful, and healthy. When asked about their awareness of and perceptions of current university support services, they were generally aware of services they could access for academic support, such as the library, peer mentoring system, and student learning support unit (69.6%); they were also aware that there was a counseling service to support mental health (70.7%) and programs to support their health, including free gym sessions and health awareness campaigns (66.4%). The majority also felt that the university was not doing enough to support their academic stress (76% responding no), or their mental health and wellbeing (65% responding no).

Key findings

The USP student health and wellbeing survey is the first cross-national exploration of the student population from across the PICs with two datasets collected. Taken together, the findings suggest some positive indicators of Pacific student wellbeing in comparison to what is being reported globally. That is, in both datasets, the self-reported scores on depression items, loneliness, and substance use were comparatively low. In addition, students rated themselves as generally above the midpoint on current life satisfaction and happiness. These findings may reflect cultural norms to present happiness and resilience rather than express personal distress (see Crookes & Warren, 2022) or to perceive one's own distress as not problematic or significant (e.g., as noted in Mason et al., 2022). Indeed, most students in both datasets indicated that they have actively concealed mental health issues from others for fear of stigma.

However, both datasets indicate a clear subset of students who are highly vulnerable and experience current distress. For example, one quarter (2021) and over one-third (2022) of the sample reported suicidal ideation, with the majority reporting this within the last year. In addition, nearly half of the students had experienced a suicide attempt or death among their close family and friends. This strongly supports published studies showing very high rates of suicide across the Pacific region (Mathieu et al., 2021). Given that exposure to both suicide attempts and deaths is shown to be a risk factor for suicidal behavior (Hill et al., 2020), this indicates a much larger portion of the sample may be vulnerable. Furthermore, where students reported consumption of alcohol, this was commonly in the form of heavy 'binge' drinking which has been associated with depression, anxiety, and poor quality of life (Lee et al., 2020). So again, while the overall portion of students in the Pacific engaged in this behavior is lower than seen globally, it suggests those who do are significantly vulnerable.

Findings regarding academic stress and confidence were somewhat mixed across the two datasets. The overall level of reported daily stress related to academic studies was higher in the 2021 dataset than in 2022. This is likely due to the immediate impact of COVID-19 in the former and a more settled return to studies in the latter. However, in both years the stressors reported to be most frequent encompassed academic demands, finances, and study/life balance. This makes sense given that at least one-quarter of the (predominantly undergraduate, 18–24-year-old) students were balancing studies against employment and/or childcare. When asked about any other sources of stress, students often reported conflict in relationships and lack of support from family as a significant impact on their studies. In addition, many mentioned the stress of balancing the obligations of family, church, and community groups, as well as the impact of unforeseen events such as family deaths and funerals. Finally, stress was often related to chronic health (their own or their child's) issues and factors such as lack of work opportunities and travel distances to access campus resources, classes, or the necessary internet connectivity. These responses strongly align with the range of socio-environmental factors indicated in models of Pacific student success (Anae et al., 2002; Sopoaga et al., 2018).

Finally, students positively rated the importance of university services in supporting health and wellbeing. When asked what the university should be doing, they reported such things as ensuring the availability of a mental health specialist at each campus, online counseling access, and having a wider team of mental health professional services available. They also mentioned the importance of student involvement in support service decision-making and development. Some of the ideas they suggested for service development included peer-led support groups, incorporating a mental health course into the first-year curriculum, and a more proactive and direct awareness and promotion of identifying stress and accessing the university services. In addition, several students commented on the role of academic staff and course tutors in building relationships with students, checking in with students on general wellbeing as well as course and assignments, and being a point of contact for mental health help-seeking.

Recommendations for supporting the wellbeing of Pacific students

This chapter has provided an overview of the mental health context of PICs and the specific challenges faced by students globally and by Indigenous Pacific and Pasifika students. In addition, data was presented from the first systematic survey of health and wellbeing among students in the PICs. This final section will bring together these discussions to review recommendations for university support programs as they relate to the wellbeing of Indigenous Pacific students.

As a starting point, Chu and colleagues (2013) describe three themes for Pacific student support. The first, 'Appreciative pedagogy' includes designing collective learning experiences where possible. One suggestion is to create collective over competitive course outcomes (Mayeda et al., 2014). That is, using competency outcomes as opposed to numerical grades, or embedding social outputs into the grading system such that students can achieve learning more as a class not as individuals. The second theme is related to the nature of the teacher-student relationships as respectful and nurturing and recognizes and appreciates the value of the Pacific culture (Chu et al., 2013; Mayeda et al., 2014; Sopoaga et al., 2018). Finally, Chu and others (2013) describe the institutions' role in proactively engaging with Pacific communities (beyond enrolled students), showing strong leadership, and ensuring there are relevant Pacific role models for Pacific students. The inclusion of Pacific role models could be in the form of ensuring diversity in teaching staff, promoting Pacific post-graduates, or using former students as career mentors or guest speakers to undergraduate groups. These suggestions together indicate that it is not enough for an institution to set up cultural student clubs and delegate support to them; rather, Pacific students need to see the institution (as a whole) engaging in a commitment to valuing Pacific communities and culture.

Decentralize campus mental health services

As noted in the USP student data, there is a substantial subset of Pacific students who experience significant distress and are vulnerable to harmful and suicidal behavior. Furthermore, concealing distress and not seeking help was common. As well as ensuring formal mental health services and referral pathways are available, institutions must recognize and overcome the cultural norms surrounding help-seeking and accessing services. For example, Toombs and Gorman (2011) found that Aboriginal and Torres Strait Islander students felt uncomfortable using university mental health services, despite being positive about them, preferring to seek help from friends and family. Similarly, Mason et al. (2022) suggest that students in New Zealand would not use the university counseling services because they did not feel their problems were significant enough (despite indicators of anxiety, stress, and suicidal ideation among the sample). This suggests students may need a wider range of gateways to help them explore their mental health needs and have a number of support steps prior to entering formal counseling or treatment referral.

First, universities could design programs in which students nominated as 'mental health mentors' are given basic training in non-specialist listening and mental health literacy skills and supervised to run mental health discussions with students to explore their wellbeing and needs (cf. the resources from the Mental Health Talanoa project, Ravulo et al., 2021). In addition, universities should have active partnerships with faith-based organizations and religious counselors in the community who may provide a link between Pacific cultural identity and student wellbeing (Manuela & Sibley, 2014). Partnerships could also mean a bridge between familiar in-community gateways for seeking help, and the professional services available through the institution. Designing support service systems with a more community-centered, non-specialist foundation aligns with the recommended frameworks for national mental health service development within the Pacific (WHO, 2023).

Utilize family as support and motivation

The family was commonly cited as both the biggest help and hindrance factor. A key disadvantage is that students from Pacific backgrounds are often the first in the family to attend tertiary education (Mayeda et al., 2014; Sopoaga et al., 2018). That is, the family may not understand the logistics around studying, attending lectures, and meeting multiple course deadlines and may expect 'perfect' scores without knowing the differences in grading practices between school and university. The SHS found that students are particularly stressed by family pressures and worried about test scores. One suggestion has been to bring the family into the learning context (Chu et al., 2013) by, for example, having the family involved in course presentations or assignments. This would also help families themselves engage and build an awareness of university practices to help them understand their students' needs. It would also provide a platform for growing this experiential capital for younger siblings.

Use connection as the space for learning

As discussed in Teu Le Va and Tapasa projects, the '*Va*' of the student-teacher relationship is a source of wellbeing and not just learning in schools, and several authors have noted the importance of this to Pacific tertiary students as well (Chu et al., 2013; Mayeda et al., 2014; Reynolds, 2016; Theodore et al., 2018). Indeed, the students in the recent USP student survey reported specifically wanting tutors to check in on their general wellbeing alongside asking about course-related work. Given the increasing role of online learning in facilitating access across remote Pacific locations, the need for strong learning relationships could be challenged. However, studies have argued that building these relationships using virtual learning environments can still be successful (Walton et al., 2020). The present author trialed an online peer mentoring component on a large first-year course with Pacific students and this involved signing up for a small-group online meeting with the tutor, focusing on sharing expectations and needs. The groups are then required to set up a messaging platform and check in on each other throughout the semester, reflecting on the role of peer support during a final meeting at the end of the course.

Another concern reported by Mayeda and others (2014) was the practical need for teachers to be accepting (to some extent) of the ways in which Pacific students are pulled in different directions by events affecting their families and communities. Importantly, Pacific students did not equate this to being given concessions as they also preferred teachers to insist on high standards and academic achievement as a form of motivational nurturing (Chu et al., 2013; Mayeda et al., 2014). Instead, teachers' openness to working with some flexibility is seen as a sign of respect for students and their culture. For PICs, this need for flexibility increasingly includes climate disasters. For example, USP regional campuses have, in the last three years alone, experienced multiple cyclones as well as the volcanic eruption affecting Tonga in 2022. Students must deal with significant personal and community loss as well as study center closures, and loss of internet access while the courses themselves may be continuing and they cannot afford to delay studies due to repeating whole semesters.

The pilot of a youth mentoring program to support Māori students in New Zealand provides a good example of the importance of the relationship over and above the provision of resources and investment. Turner-Adams and Webber (2022) describe the outcomes of this program in which students were allocated to a working professional mentor to support them from the last year of high school through the first three years of their degree studies. Feedback indicated two key pitfalls in the scheme for Māori students. First, mentors were chosen based on their career expertise and availability rather than being matched based on cultural background. This led to some reports of conflict between mentees and their assigned mentor due to a lack of cultural understanding particularly around the role of family in the students' priorities. The mentors also tended to expect students to seek out their help when needed, which was consequently interpreted by the students as mentors being disinterested in them. This is similar to the point made by Sopoaga and colleagues (2018), who argue that peer mentoring would be powerful for Pacific students but only if it uses culturally matched role models, and where the mentors are responsible for proactively arranging meetings and guiding students through set outcomes. That is, they must actively build the relationship space as one of nurturing and respect not just as a source of (albeit friendly) guidance.

Embed culture and identity into university courses

As noted in the models of Pasifika and Pacific Islander wellbeing, cultural identity and heritage are active elements that need to be overtly promoted. This is particularly important for Pacific students who may be studying away from home, or where they are joining internationally focused institutions. One suggestion raised by Chu et al. (2013) and others (Fredericks et al., 2023; Sopoaga et al., 2018) is for the institution to set up a 'learning village' as a space for studying within a culturally familiar and shared communal environment. It is important to remember that learning within the Pacific mindset is a product of culture, community, and support, and that the transition of Pacific students during their first year of university is protected by these cultural elements (Sopoaga et al., 2018). Therefore, to understand that the physical space is not just about familiarity for comfort but fundamentally tied to enabling learning as it provides a safe and culturally strengthening experience. A culturally symbolic learning space allows Pacific students to be reminded of their purpose and of the support of their cultural ancestors, and to feel protected when seeking help or struggling with academic tasks.

However, this is not just about the provision of space; it is also about the student experiencing their heritage being valued and respected by the institution. This is critical for Pacific and Indigenous populations that have been impacted (and collectively traumatized) by European colonization and where they are still minorities within their native environments. Theodore and fellow researchers (2018) recommend including or connecting Pacific histories into the curriculum. Of course, not all academic fields of study will lend themselves to culturally informed curriculums (e.g., natural sciences and mathematics). Perhaps in these cases, the Pacific cultural respect could be fostered through different forms of assessment or learning activities that incorporate traditional forms of communication. For example, presenting scientific ideas and concepts as metaphors or through arts, dance, and story-telling.

Another way to embed a sense of Pacific culture into otherwise culturally neutral (or inherently Western) courses could be to enhance student input into the course learning and assessments, that is, to hold discussions between students and teachers

(*Talanoa*) at the start of a course to share expectations and experiences of study. Importantly, such an open forum could allow students to frame some aspects of the course such as specific learning activities, a subset of open course learning outcomes or deadlines. This would also reflect recognized Indigenous research methods, which necessitate participant input into actions that are for and about them (e.g., the Vanua Research Framework: Nabobo-Baba, 2008; Neapi, 2019). Moreover, these sorts of discussions may help build a stronger sense of *Va* and human connection between teachers and students, as described by Reynolds (2016). Finally, it reflects transition as *Becoming* (Gale & Parker, 2014) in which both the student and the learning environment itself shift toward each other.

Summary and conclusion

In summary, the chapter aimed to present and critically review the mental health, wellbeing, and academic outcomes of tertiary students within the Pacific Oceania region. This began with a description of the unique and challenging socio-environmental context Pacific Oceania students are embedded in as part of their Indigenous communities and heritage. Indeed, studies on tertiary institutions in New Zealand consistently indicate lower enrollment, higher withdrawal, and more mental health issues among Pasifika students compared to their white European peers. The chapter went on to present findings from the first cross-national survey of students in the smaller independent PICs which indicated areas of significant distress and mental health risk. Students also noted sources of stress during their studies that aligned to both the socio-economic context of the PICs as well as the culturally specific factors around family and community pressures. This regional overview highlighted the role of university support services in helping students with the academic transition, as a safe space to develop coping and resilience skills, and as a hub for accessing formal mental health services. Importantly, the chapter argued that the development of university support systems (both academic and mental health) needs to be culturally informed, particularly for Pacific student cohorts with little cultural background in formal academic studies. In particular, the fact that wellbeing is experienced as a fundamentally holistic mindset drawing from the individual, their family, and community, as well as their broader identity and cultural history.

Moreover, these discussions provide a background on which several recommendations were made for how best to support Pacific students. Importantly, it has been noted that universities need to go beyond compartmentalizing cultural sensitivity and student support services, and instead, Pacific students should feel their identity is acknowledged and valued by the institution at all levels. This can be done through decentralizing support services, so it is embedded and connected to the students and their communities rather than as a segregated university department. Second, the role of family as a priority for Pacific students needs to be recognized and adapted to but should also be seen as a resource for academic motivation and drive. Third, consideration should be given to the training of course faculty and tutors in building rapport and relational space as part of learning. Finally, the chapter recommended ways in which culture could be embedded into curriculum and assessment.

Taken together the chapter provided an insight into how cultural identity and heritage fundamentally impact the transition processes and academic outcomes of Pacific students, and by extension any student cohorts from non-Western, highly communal contexts. It also explores how this cultural context can be used as an opportunity and resource in developing more effective support services both for student mental health and wellbeing, as well as academic learning and outcomes.

Note

1 https://www.worldbank.org/en/country/pacificislands

References

Ali, S., Williams, O., Chang, O., Shidhaye, R., Hunter, E., & Charlson, F. (2020). Mental health in the Pacific: Urgency warning and opportunity. *Asia Pacific Viewpoint*, *61*(3), 537–550.

Amanya, S. B., Nakitende, J., & Ngabirano, T. D. (2016). A cross sectional study of stress and its sources among health professional students at Makerere University, Uganda. *Nursing Open*, *5*, 70–76.

Anae, M., Airini, A., & al, K. (2010). *Teu le Va - relationships across research and policy: A collective approach to knowledge generation and policy development for action towards Pasifika education success*. Ministry of Education.

Anae, M., Anderson, H., Benseman, J., & Coxon, E. (2002). *Pacific peoples and tertiary education: Issues of participation*. Ministry of Education.

Benseman, J., Coxon, E., Anderson, H., & Anae, M. (2006). Retaining non-traditional students: Lessons learnt from Pasifika students in New Zealand. *Higher Education Research and Development*, *25*, 147–162.

Browne, V., Munro, J., & Cass, J. (2017). The mental health of Australian University Students. *Journal of the Australian and New Zealand Student Services Association*, *50*, 51–62.

Chang, O. (2011). Mental health care in Fiji. *Asia-Pacific Psychiatry*, *3*, 73–75. https://doi.org/10.1111/j.1758-5872.2011.00105.x

Charlson, F. J., Diminic, S., & Whiteford, H. A. (2015). The rising tide of mental disorders in the Pacific Region. *Asia and the Pacific Policy Studies*, *2*, 280–292. https://doi.org/10.1002/app5.93

Chu, C. M., Abella, I. S., & Paurini, S. (2013). *Educational practices that benefit pacific learners in tertiary education*. Ako Aotearoa, National Centre for Tertiary Teaching Excellence.

Chu, H. C., Hwang, G. J., Tsai, C. C., & Tseng, J. C. (2010). A two-tier test approach to developing location-aware mobile learning systems for natural science courses. Computers & Education, 55(4), 1618–1627. https://doi.org/10.1016/j.compedu.2010.07.004

Crookes, A. (2021). Student health and well-being in the Pacific: Findings from a diverse regional population. *Journal of Pacific Studies*, *41*(1). https://doi.org/10.33318/jpacs.2021.41(1)-7

Crookes, A. E., & Warren, M. A. (2022). Authorship and building psychological research in low and middle income countries: a view from the Pacific Island Nation of Fiji. *South African Journal of Psychology, 52*(2), 154–160. https://doi.org/10.1177/00812463211073371

Deci, E. L., & Ryan, R. M. (2008). Self-determination theory: A macrotheory of human motivation, development, and health. *Canadian Psychology, 49*(3), 182–185. https://doi.org/10.1037/a0012801

Eisenberg, D., Lipson, S. K., Ceglarek, P., Kern, A., & Phillips, M. (2018). College student mental health: The national landscape. In D. Cimini, & E. M. Rivero (Eds.), *Promoting behavioral health and reducing risk among college students: A comprehensive approach* (pp. 75–86). Routledge.

Ernst, M., & Anisi, A. (2016). The historical development of Christianity in Oceania. In L. Sannah, & M. J. McClymond (Eds.), *The Wiley Blackwell companion to world Christianity* (pp. 588–604). John Wiley and Sons.

Fountain, P., & Troughton, G. (2019). Christianity and development in the Pacific: An introduction. *Sites a Journal of Social Anthropology and Cultural Studies, 16*(1), 1–23. http://dx.doi.org/10.11157/sites-id435

Fredericks, B., Barney, K., Bunda, T., Hausia, K., Martin, A., Elston, J., & Bernardino, B. (2023). The importance of Indigenous centres/units for Aboriginal and Torres Strait Islander students: Ensuring connection and belonging to support university completion. *Higher Education Research & Development*, 1–14. DOI: 10.1080/07294360.2023.2258825

Gale, T., & Parker, S. (2014). Navigating change: A typology of student transition in higher education. *Studies in Higher Education, 39*(5), 734–753. https://doi.org/10.1080/03075079.2012.721351

Gibson, K. E., Barnett, J., Haslam, N., & Kaplan, I. (2020). The mental health impacts of climate change: Findings from a Pacific Island atoll nation. *Journal of Anxiety Disorders, 73*, e102237.

Global Obesity Observatory (n.d.). Ranking (% Obesity by Country). Available online: https://data.worldobesity.org/rankings/ (accessed on 2 April 2023).

Gosai, S. S., Tuibeqa, A. T., & Prasad, A. (2023). Exploring the transition challenges of first year college of Business students in Fiji. *International Journal of Education Research, 117*, e102131. doi.org/10.1016/j.ijer.2022.102131

Gounder, S. (2022). Are we losing the battle: Fiji's efforts against illicit drugs. Pacific dynamics. *Journal of Interdisciplinary Research, 6*(2), 202–221. doi.org/10.1016/j.ijer.2022.102131

Hamaideh, S. H. (2011). Stressors and reactions to stressors among university students. *International Journal of Social Psychiatry, 57*, 69–80. doi: 10.1177/0020764010348442

Hammer, J. H., Parent, M. C., & Spiker, D. A. (2018). Mental Help Seeking Attitudes Scale (MHSAS): Development, reliability, validity, and comparison with the ATSSPH-SF and IASMHS-PO. *Journal of Counseling Psychology, 65*, 74–85. doi: 10.1037/cou0000248

Hill, N. T. M., Robinson, J., Pirkis, J., Andriessen, K., Krysinska, K., Payne, A., Boland, A., Clarke, A., Milner, A., Witt, K., & Krohn, S. (2020) Association of suicidal behavior with exposure to suicide and suicide attempt: A systematic review and multilevel meta-analysis. *PLoS Medicine, 17*(3): e1003074. https://doi.org/10.1371/journal.pmed.1003074

Imperial College London (n.d.). The Educational Self-Efficacy Scale. Downloaded from https://www.imperial.ac.uk/media/imperial-college/staff/education-development-unit/public/Educational-self-efficacy-scale.pdf

Joshanloo, M., Jovanovic, V., & Park, J. (2021). Differential relationships of hedonic and eudaimonic well-being with self-control and long-term orientation. *Japanese Psychological Research, 63*(1), 47–57.

Kessaram, T., McKenzie, J., Girin, N., Roth, A., Vivili, P., Williams, G., & Hoy, D. (2016). Alcohol use in the Pacific region: Results from the STEPwise approach to surveillance, global school-based health survey and youth risk behavior surveillance system. *Drug and Alcohol Review, 35*, 412–423. DOI: 10.1111/dar.12328

Kessler, R. C., Andrews, G., Colpe, L. J., Hiripi, E., Mroczek, D. K., Normand, S. L. T., Walters, E. E., & Zaslavsky, A. M. (2002). Short screening scales to monitor population prevalence's and trends in non-specific psychological distress. *Psychological Medicine*, 32, 959–956.

Lee, Y. Y., Wang, P., Abdon, E., Chang, S., Shafie, S., Sambasivam, R., Tan, K. B., Heng, D., Vaingankar, J., Chong, S. A., & Subramaniam, M. (2020). Prevalence of binge drinking and its association with mental health conditions and quality of life in Singapore. *Addictive Behaviors*, 100, e106114. doi.org/10.1016/j.addbeh.2019.106114

Lipson, S., & Eisenberg, D. (2018). Mental health and academic attitudes and expectations in university populations: Results from the healthy minds study. *Journal of Mental Health*, 1–9.

Manuela, S., & Sibley, C. G. (2014). Exploring the hierarchical structure of pacific identity and wellbeing. *Social Indicators Research*, 118, 969–985. DOI 10.1007/s11205-013-0472-y

Mason, A., Johnstone, G., Riordan, B. C., Lie, C., Rapsey, C., Treharne, G. J., Jang, K., Collings, S. C., & Scarf, D. (2022). Understanding Aotearoa New Zealand university students intentions to seek help if experiencing mental distress: A comparison of naturalistic and interventional findings. *International Journal of Environmental Research and Public Health*, 19, 15836, https://doi.org/10.3390/ijerph192315836

Mathieu, S., deLeo, D., Koo, Y. W., Leske, S., Goodfellow, B., & Kolves, K. (2021). Suicide and suicide attempts in the Pacific Islands: A systematic literature review. *The Lancet Regional Health – Western Pacific*, 17, e100283.

Mayeda, D. T., Keil, M., Dutton, H. D., & Ofamo'oni, F. H. (2014). "You've gotta set a precedent": Māori and Pacific voices on student success in higher education. *AlterNative*, 10(2), 165–179.https://doi.org/10.1177/117718011401000206

Nabobo-Baba, U. (2008). Decolonising framings in Pacific research: Indigenous Fijian Vanua research framework as an organic response. *AlterNative*, 4(2), 140–154.

Patrick, R., Snell, T., Gunasiri, H., Garad, R., Meadows, G., & Enticott, J. (2023). Prevalence and determinants of mental health related to climate change in Australia. *Australia New Zealand Journal of Psychiatry*, 57(5), 710–724. doi: 10.1177/00048674221107872.

Pereira, S., Reay, K., Bottell, J., Walker, L., Dzikiti, C., Platt, C., & Goodrham, C. (2019). University Student Mental Health Survey 2018. *The Insight Network and Dig-In*. https://assets.website-files.com/602d05d13b303dec233e5ce3/60305923a557c3641f1a7808_Mental%20Health%20Report%202019%20(2020).pdf

Perrot, A. R. D. (2015). *Overcoming Challenges: Pacific students' experiences of being resilient through tertiary education* (Unpublished master's thesis). Victoria University of Wellington, Wellington, New Zealand.

Portoghese, I., Leiter, M.P., Maslach, C., Galletta, M., Porru, F., D'Aloja, E., Finco, G. & Campagna, M. (2018). Measuring burnout among university students: factorial validity, invariance, and latent profiles of the Italian version of the Maslach Burnout Inventory Student Survey (MBI-SS). (2018). Measuring burnout among university students: factorial validity, invariance, and latent profiles of the Italian version of the Maslach Burnout Inventory Student Survey (MBI-SS). *Frontiers in psychology*, 9, 2105. https://doi.org/10.3389/fpsyg.2018.02105

Pulotu-Endemann, K. (1995). The Fonofale model of health. *Published in: Strategic directions for mental health services for pacific island people*. Ministry of Health. https://d3n8a8pro7vhmx.cloudfront.net/actionpoint/pages/437/attachments/original/1534408956/Fonofalemodelexplanation.pdf?1534408956

Ravulo, J. (2015). *Pacific communities in Australia*. University of Western Sydney. https://doi.org/10.13140/RG.2.2.18439.65442.

Ravulo, J., Winterstein, U., & Said, S. J. (2021). *Mental Health Talanoa Research and Resources: Collaborative community engagement enhancing mental health and wellbeing across pacific communities*. University of Wollongong. https://doi.org/10.13140/RG.2.2.14707.66087

Reddy, K. J., Menon, K. R., & Thattil, A. (2018). Academic stress and its sources among university students. *Biomedical and Pharmacology Journal, 11*(1), 531–537.

Reynolds, M. (2016). Relating to Va: Re-viewing the concept of relationships in Pasifika education in Aotearoa New Zealand. *AlterNative, 12*(2), 190–202.

Rickwood, D., Telford, N., O'Sullivan, S., Crisp, D., & Magyar, R. (2017). *National Tertiary Student Wellbeing Survey 2016.* Headspace National Youth Mental Health Foundation. https://headspace.org.au/assets/Uploads/headspace-NUS-Publication-Digital.pdf

Sato, H., & Bradshaw, J. (2017). *Languages of the Pacific Islands: Introductory readings.* CreateSpace Independent Publishing. ISBN: 154423922X, 9781544239224

Seligman, M. (2018). PERMA and the building blocks of well-being. *The Journal of Positive Psychology.* https://doi.org/10.1080/17439760.2018.1437466.

Sopoaga, F., Van Der Meer, J., Shyamala, N., Wilkinson, T., & Jutel, S. (2018). Mental health and wellbeing of Pacific students starting university in New Zealand. *Pacific Health Dialog, 21*(2), 71–79. https://doi.org/10.26635/phd.2018.916.

Stallman, H. M., & Hurst, C. P. (2016). The university stress scale: Measuring domains and extent of stress in university students. *Australian Psychologist, 51*(2), 128–134.

Stöber, J. (2004). Dimensions of test anxiety: Relations to ways of coping with pre-exam anxiety and uncertainty. *Anxiety, Stress & Coping, 17*(3), 213–226. https://doi.org/10.1080/10615800412331292615

Theodore, R., Taumoepeau, M., Tustin, K., Gollop, M., Unasa, C., Kokaua, J., Taylor, N., Ramrakha, S., Hunter, J., & Poulton, R. (2018). Pacific university graduates in New Zealand: What helps and hinders completion. *AlterNative, 14*(2), 138–146.

Tiatia, J., Langridge, F., Newport, C., Underhill-Sem, Y., & Woodward, A. (2023). Climate change, mental health and wellbeing: Privileging Pacific peoples' perspectives-phase one. *Climate and Development, 15*(8), 655–666. https://doi.org/10.1080/17565529.2022.2145171

Tinto, V. (1975). Dropout from higher education: A theoretical synthesis of recent research. *Review of Educational Research, 45*(1), 89–125. https://doi.org/10.3102/00346543045001089.

Toombs, M., & Gorman, D. (2011). Mental health and indigenous university students. *Aboriginal and Islander Health Worker Journal, 35*(4), 22–24. ISSN 1037-3403

Tucker-Masters, L., & Tiatia-Seath, J. (2017). Reviewing the literature on anxiety and depression in Pacific youth: A fresh perspective. *The New Zealand Medical Student Journal, 25*, 24–28.

Turner-Adams, H., & Webber, M. (2022). Stakeholders' perceptions of a New Zealand Youth Mentoring Programme assisting high-achieving, underprivileged students to attend university. *New Zealand Journal of Psychology, 51*(2), 26–34.

UN Women Pacific (2011). *Ending Violence against Women and Girls: Literature review and annotated bibliography.* Available online: https://asiapacific.unwomen.org/en/digital-library/publications/2011/7/ending-violence-against-women-and-girls (Accessed 5 January 2024).

United Nations Office on Drugs and Crime (UNODC) (2012). *Regional Trends Pacific Island States and Territories.* Available online: https://www.unodc.org/roseap/uploads/archive/documents/2012/12/ats-2012/section/2012_Regional_ATS_Report_Pacific.pdf (accessed 5 January 2024).

United Nations Office on Drugs and Crime (UNODC) (2020). *Regional Overview Asia and Oceania.* Available online: https://www.unodc.org/documents/scientific/Regional_Overview_Asia_and_Oceania.pdf (accessed 5 January 2024).

United Nations Population Fund Pacific Sub-regional Office (UNFPA) (2014). *Population and Development Profiles: Pacific Island Countries.* Available online: https://pacific.unfpa.org/en/publications (accessed 5 January 2024)

Walton, P., Byrne, R., Clark, N., Pidgeon, M., Arnouse, M., & Hamilton, K. (2020). Online Indigenous university student supports, barriers and learning preferences. *International Journal of E-Learning and Distance Education, 35*(2), 1–45.

World Health Organization (2018). *Non-communicable Diseases Country Profiles 2018*. World Health Organization, 223p. Available online: https://apps.who.int/iris/handle/10665/274512 (accessed on 2 April 2023).

World Health Organisation (2021). *Suicide worldwide in 2019: Global health estimates*. World Health Organization. License: CC BY-NC-SA 3.0 IGO.

World Health Organisation (2023). *Regional framework for the future of mental health in the Western Pacific*. Available online: https://www.who.int/publications/i/item/9789290620075

Zepke, N., Leach, L., & Butler, P. (2011). Non-institutional influences and student perceptions of success. *Studies in Higher Education, 36*(2), 227–242. https://doi.org/10.1080/03075070903545074

Chapter 5

The science of wellbeing and success in higher education

Applying positive psychology and PERMA+4 across cultures

Stewart I. Donaldson and Jana Koci

Introduction

In the wake of the global pandemic, universities across the globe were scrambling to find ways to deal with dramatic declines in student health and wellbeing (see Brown et al., 2023). For example, in the United States alone, a recent 2023 survey of more than 95,000 students revealed that 44 percent reported symptoms of depression, 37 percent said they experienced anxiety, and 15 percent said they have seriously considered suicide – the highest rates in the survey's 15-year history (Flannery, 2023). More examples of this mental health crisis can be found in other recent studies from various parts of the world (see Koci, 2023; Koci & Donaldson, 2022; Moussa & Wael, 2022; Waters & Loton, 2021).

Koci and Donaldson (2024) have highlighted that higher education has changed dramatically during the last few years, which has resulted in a massive growth of mental health challenges among students. Faculty and staff at universities across the globe now recognize the need to help students to thrive, not only to survive (Waters & Loton, 2021). Colleges and universities have great potential and a responsibility to promote the wellbeing of all of their students. The fields of positive psychology and positive education have now matured to the point that they can offer evidence-informed approaches to help with these challenges (Donaldson et al., 2023).

Koci and Donaldson (2024) provide students with information, motivation, and skills to build their own unique wellbeing, and to help diverse colleges and universities produce more wellbeing and academic success across a variety of national cultures. This new work is based on 25 years of peer-reviewed research inspired by the development of the science and practice of positive psychology (Donaldson et al., 2023). The purpose of this chapter is to introduce the evidence-based framework of PERMA+4, and to illustrate how positive psychology and PERMA+4 can be used to care for student wellbeing and positive functioning on a regular basis across cultures.

The science and practice of positive psychology

At the turn of the century, the late Mihaly Csikszentmihalyi and Martin Seligman provided a clear vision for how to develop a body of empirical evidence that would contribute to the understanding of what makes individuals, students, teachers, teams, leaders, communities, universities, and organizations flourish. They also encouraged the next generation of psychological scientists to spend at least some of their professional time joining them in the development of "a science of positive subjective experience, positive individual traits, and positive institutions that would promise to improve quality of life and prevent the pathologies that arise when life is barren and meaningless" (Seligman & Csikszentmihalyi, 2000, p. 5). The hope was this new science would take hold in the early 21st century and provide societies across the world with a rigorous evidence-based framework, focused on helping all people thrive regardless of their background, region, cultural beliefs, and traditions (Donaldson et al., 2020).

Donaldson et al. (2015) took stock of the first 15 years of the peer-reviewed literature linked to the vision for a science of positive psychology in their widely cited article "Happiness, excellence, and optimal human functioning revisited: Examining the Peer-reviewed Literature linked to positive psychology." They found the call was clearly answered with more than 1,300 peer-reviewed publications on positive psychology topics, and with more than 750 of these articles including empirical tests of positive psychology theories, principles, and interventions. It was found that wellbeing and positive functioning schools, work, and life in general were some of the most heavily investigated topics. Other popular topics included character strengths, hope, gratitude, resilience, and growth. Collectively these scientific findings revealed that the science of positive psychology had become a growing sub-area within the broader discipline of psychology and was using the scientific methods of psychology to better understand wellbeing, excellence, and optimal human functioning.

This review was recently updated and expanded as an entry in the third edition of the *Encyclopedia of Mental Health* describing the state of the field and some of its main findings related to wellbeing and positive functioning (Donaldson et al., 2023). Simply stated, some of the main findings included:

> More than two decades of peer-reviewed science supports the practice of positive psychology.
> PERMA+4 provides an evidenced-based framework for guiding the assessment, development, and management of well-being and positive functioning.
> Causal evidence supports that Positive Psychology Interventions (PPI) work on average, and work well under specific conditions.
> The science and practice of positive psychology continues to grow and is being taught at universities and through professional associations across the world.
> (Donaldson et al., 2023, p. 79)

Perhaps even more encouraging was while the very early days of positive psychology were lived mostly in the United States, Kim et al. (2018) in their seminal review "The International Landscape of Positive Psychology Research: A Systematic Review" showed that the science of positive psychology quickly became focused on contextually sensitive and culturally responsive perspectives in various regions throughout the world. It is now estimated that the majority of scholarly contributions to positive psychology are being carried out outside the United States. The science and practice of psychology have clearly become cross-cultural and are focused on improving wellbeing and positive functioning in many parts of the world.

Associations and education

An important indicator of the growth of the field is the number and range of professional associations and educational opportunities that have developed in different regions of the world. In 2024, there are now a wide range of positive psychology university courses, degrees, and national and regional professional associations that have been developed, and many explore contextually sensitive and culturally responsive approaches to fostering the growth and wellbeing of the diverse global student body of higher education (Donaldson et al., 2023; Kim et al., 2018; Rao et al., 2015). For example, one of the largest professional associations that support university education and research efforts globally is the International Association of Positive Psychology (IPPA). IPPA was established in 2007 with the mission of:

- To advance the scientific study and ethical application of positive psychology.
- To facilitate collaboration among researchers, teachers, students, and practitioners of positive psychology around the world and across academic disciplines.
- To share the findings of positive psychology with the broadest possible international audience.

Other thriving positive psychology professional associations and universities providing education across Europe, Asia, the Americas, Oceania, and Africa are listed in Table 5.1.

Wellbeing and positive functioning

The science of positive psychology has accumulated more than 25 years of rigorous peer-reviewed science to understand the link between wellbeing and positive functioning across the globe, including career and academic success. A vast number of scientific studies have revealed the link is robust across many cultures (see Donaldson et al., 2015; Kansky & Diener, 2020; Kim et al., 2018). For example, The US Surgeon General makes this link clear in his 2022 National Report on "Workplace Mental Health & Well-being." This reports underscores the importance of working and learning environments, and their influence on wellbeing, and how negative environments not only impact the health and wellbeing of people themselves, wellbeing can affect productivity and performance. The report emphasizes that when people feel anxious or depressed, then the quality, pace, and performance of their work tends to decline.

Table 5.1 Illustrative sample of associations and degree programs by continent

	Associations	Courses and Degrees
Europe	European Network for Positive Psychology German-Speaking Association of Positive Psychology (German speaking areas) German Society for Positive Psychology Research French and Francophone Positive Psychology Association (Francophone areas) Czech Positive Psychology Centre Hellenic Association of Positive Psychology Italian Society of Positive Psychology Polish Positive Psychology Association Portuguese Association for Studies and Intervention in Positive Psychology Spanish Society for Positive Psychology (SEPP) Swiss Positive Psychology Association Turkish Positive Psychology Association	Oslo Summer School (Norway) Aarhus University (Denmark) Universiteit Twente; Maastricht University (the Netherlands) Universidade de Lisboa (Portugal) IE University (Spain) University of East London; City University of London; University of Glasgow; Middlesex University London; Anglia Ruskin University; Buckinghamshire New University (UK)
Asia	Asian Center for Applied Positive Psychology Global Chinese Positive Psychology Association National Positive Psychology Association, India Japan Positive Psychology Association Informal groups in South Korea	Lebanese American University (Lebanon) The Chinese University of Hong Kong; Hong Kong Shue Yan University (Hong Kong) Jerusalem University (Israel) School of Positive Psychology (Singapore)
Americas	Associação de Psicologia Positiva da América Latina (Latin America) Western Positive Psychology Association Canadian Positive Psychology Association Informal groups in Mexico and Brazil	Instituto Chileno de Psicologia Positiva (Chile) Universidad Iberoamericana (Mexico) TechMillenio University (Mexico) Claremont Graduate University; University of Pennsylvania; University of Utah; Harvard University; Stanford University; University of California Los Angeles (UCLA) Extension; University of Michigan, Case Western Reserve University, University of Missouri (US)

(Continued)

Table 5.1 (Continued)

	Associations	Courses and Degrees
Oceania	New Zealand Association of Positive Psychology	University of Sydney; University of Melbourne; RMIT University; TAFE South Australia
Africa		North-West University (South Africa)
International/ Global		International Positive Psychology Association

Source: Republished with permission from Kim et al. (2018).

In a recent large meta-analytic study, Moscoso and Salgado (2021) analyzed the relationship between wellbeing and work performance with a database of 34 independent samples (N = 5352) using supervisory performance ratings and 38 independent samples (N = 12086) using self-reports of job performance. They found a substantial correlation with both supervisor ratings and self-reports across all the wellbeing measures used. This study provides a robust body of evidence to support the phrase "feel well, do well." In other words, feeling well or experiencing high levels of wellbeing appears to be an essential ingredient in being able to perform well at work and school.

In other research, Lester et al. (2021) found that wellbeing measures predicted awards for outstanding performance in a sample of 908,096 US Army soldiers over a four-year follow-up period. Each wellbeing variable in their large-scale study predicted future awards for both women and men, for enlisted soldiers as well as officers, for several ethnicities, for varying levels of education, and for controlling for a number of other potential explanatory variables. Comparing the soldiers' highest vs. lowest in wellbeing predicted an almost fourfold greater award recognition in the high group.

In the third recent analysis (Walsh et al., 2023), the common belief that working hard to be successful will lead to wellbeing and happiness was debunked. Walsh et al. (2023) revisited and updated the evidence across cross-sectional, longitudinal, and experimental studies, suggesting that wellbeing causes success rather than the other way around. They concluded:

> Cross-sectional, longitudinal, and experimental studies persuasively and robustly show that relative to their less happy peers, happy people experience superior success on a host of outcomes, including job satisfaction, performance, productivity, work engagement, burnout, supervisor evaluations, income, negotiations, and creativity. Rather than pressuring employees to act happy – an approach that has previously led to both legal problems and backlash – organizations may foster greater worker well-being by measuring it, building thriving corporate cultures, and deploying positive activities in the workplace.

The same strong link found between wellbeing and positive functioning, as measured by work performance and career success, has been repeatedly found in schools and higher education settings as well (see Koci & Donaldson, 2024; Waters, 2011). That is, many studies and systematic reviews in the field of "Positive Education" – the science of positive psychology applied in educational settings – have confirmed student wellbeing is a strong predictor of academic performance and success across cultural contexts (Gaffaney & Donaldson, 2024). In recent large-scale reviews of positive psychology focused on education programs, the evidence strongly supports that wellbeing and academic success can be significantly improved in educational settings (Francis et al., 2021; Kumar & Mohideen, 2021; Schiavon et al., 2020; Waters, 2011; Waters & Loton, 2019).

For example, Kumar and Mohideen (2021) highlighted that strengths-based positive schooling interventions consistently produce promising positive outcomes in a range of student wellbeing measures. Francis et al. (2021) found online positive psychology interventions (PPIs) provide a more equitable method for young people to access wellbeing education at school than more traditional face-to-face programs. Waters and Loton (2019) reviewed 75 peer-reviewed studies (total student N = 35,888) from North America, Europe, the United Kingdom, Asia, Australia, and New Zealand and further confirmed the strong link between student wellbeing and academic success. In the next section, we will explore a successful evidence-informed framework based in the science of positive psychology for building student wellbeing and academic success across cultures.

PERMA+4 building blocks of wellbeing and positive functioning

The science of positive psychology has led to the development of an evidence-informed framework to guide efforts designed to help students to consistently care for and develop their wellbeing and positive functioning. This framework is known as PERMA+4 (; Donaldson et al., 2021, 2022). The original PERMA model was developed as part of Seligman's (2002) theory of authentic happiness.

Seligman (2011) stated that wellbeing can actively be developed through pursuing five measurable elements, which he called PERMA (see also Donaldson et al., 2022):

1 Positive emotions. Experiencing happiness, joy, love, gratitude, etc. in the here and now
2 Engagement. Being highly absorbed, emersed or experiencing flow while engaged in activities of one's life
3 Relationships. Having the ability to establish and maintain positive, mutually beneficial relationships with others characterized by experiences of love and appreciation
4 Meaning. The experience of being connected to something larger than the self or serving a bigger purpose.
5 Accomplishment. Experiencing a sense of mastery over a particular domain of interest or achieving important or challenging life/work goals.

More than two decade's worth of empirical research now underpins the relationship between the individual elements of PERMA and other forms of wellbeing. However, Seligman (2008) encouraged the scientific community to search for additional building blocks which may enhance or strengthen the PERMA framework. This call inspired Donaldson (2019) and Donaldson et al. (2020) to conduct an extensive systematic literature review, meta-analysis, and a range of qualitative assessments in order to determine if and how the framework could be extended. They discovered four additional building blocks that explained additional variance in wellbeing and positive functioning:

1. Physical Health. Operationalized as a combination of high levels of biological, functional, and psychological health assets.
2. Mindset. Adopting a growth mindset characterized by an optimistic, future-oriented view of life, where challenges or setbacks are seen as opportunities to grow. This may also be a function of psychological capital, perseverance, or grit.
3. Work Environment. The quality of the physical work environment (which includes spatiotemporal elements, such as access to natural light, fresh air, physical safety, and a positive psychological climate) aligned to the preferences of the individual.
4. Economic Security. Perceptions of financial security and stability required to satisfy individual needs (see Figure 5.1).

Koci and Donaldson (2024) provide much more detail on the components of each building block and provide strategies and activities for students and faculty to care for the PERMA+4 building blocks. For example, the components of physical health include adequate body movement, optimal nutrition, high-quality sleep, regular relaxation, proper breathing, and good body posture. The components of

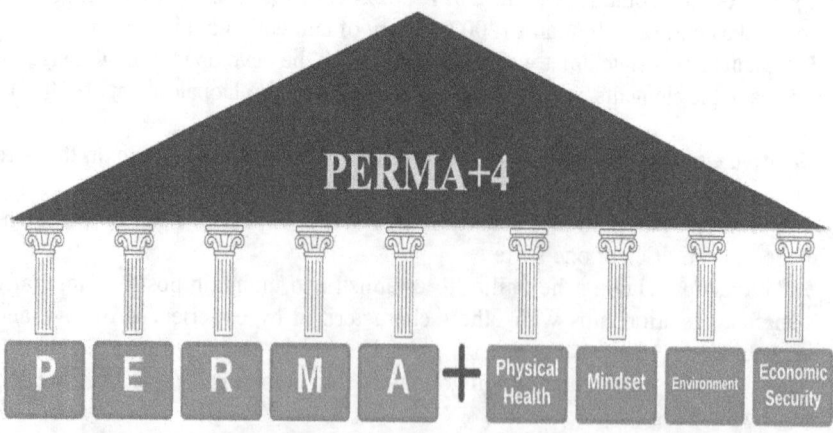

Figure 5.1 PERMA+4 Building Blocks of Wellbeing and Positive Functioning

mindset include hope, efficacy, resiliency, optimism, future orientation, and growth mindset. The environment building block includes developing high-quality living, school, family, work, community, and online environments. Economic security includes income, savings, investments, expense management, financial literacy, and managing health-care costs. The first five PERMA building blocks and how to care for each are also described in practical detail.

The empirical evidence supporting the individual elements or building blocks, as well as the higher order constructs of PERMA and PERMA+4, as predictors of wellbeing and positive functioning across settings (e.g., schools, universities, workplaces) and cultures is strong, and very useful for guiding the designs of future contextually sensitive and culturally responsive programs and interventions in various regions throughout the world.

In an effort to understand the details of the most efficacious PPIs as tested by the most rigorous experimental designs to date, Donaldson et al. (2021) analyzed the findings from 25 meta-analyzes, 42 review papers, and the high-quality randomized controlled trials (RCT) of PPIs designed to generate wellbeing that were included within those studies. They found that on average PPIs do work to generate wellbeing and work very well under certain conditions. They encouraged program designers to use the casual evidence they found to guide their work and to emulate the designs of most efficacious PPIs. They provided specific encouragement and guidance on how to do this across cultures, especially in non-WEIRD (Western, Educated, Industrial, Rich, and Democratic) countries. Finally, they identified five components that can be used in the design of future culturally responsive PERMA+4 programs and interventions to build student wellbeing and positive functioning across cultures.

The five components for designing PPIs emphasized by Donaldson and colleagues include (1) developing an awareness and understanding of topics and oneself, (2) practicing simple skills and exercises that can be incorporated into daily life, (3) practicing reflection after exercises to encourage sense-making and reinforcement of new skills, (4) clarifying understanding with experts and relate to peers to amplify effects and reinforce accountability, and (5) setting goals and creating a plan to practice new skills in daily life to encourage long-term sustainability. Each of these steps is believed to be important for creating lasting lifestyle change. Each component, its objective, and a description are summarized in Table 5.2.

Enhancing student wellbeing care across cultures

University and college students themselves seek wellbeing support like never before and the mental health of students has become one of the top priorities in higher education (Koci, 2022, 2023; Koci & Donaldson, 2022; Koci & Koptikova, 2022a, 2022b; Tansey et al., 2018; Weiss et al., 2024). Not only do students want to feel well, but they also want to study well and experience success in higher education. The evidence for the relationship between students' academic success and their

Table 5.2 Five components that can be incorporated into PPI design

PPI Component	Objective	Description
Learn	Knowledge and awareness	Develop an awareness and understanding of topics and oneself.
Practice	Behavioral skills	Practice simple skills and exercises that can be incorporated into daily life.
Reflect	Sense-making and reinforcement	Practice reflection after exercises to encourage sense-making and reinforcement of new skills.
Relate	Engagement and accountability	Clarify understanding with experts and relate to peers to amplify effects and reinforce accountability.
Plan	Sustainability	Set goals and create a plan to practice new skills in daily life to encourage long-term sustainability.

wellbeing in higher education settings across cultures continues to mount (for example, see Antaramian, 2017; Arslan, 2020; Gaffaney & Donaldson, 2024; Koci, 2023; Koci & Donaldson, 2024; Morris, 2022; Moussa & Wael, 2022; Pascoe et al., 2020; Weiss et al., 2024). By assessing and building student wellbeing in everyday school life, we can ensure that students feel good about their educational experience and perform well in their studies.

As we discussed above, the growing field of positive education science (Waters & Loton, 2021), an approach that brings together the science of positive psychology with best-practice teaching and learning to build student wellbeing around the world, has demonstrated much success. The findings from positive education research can help us develop and promote culturally responsive wellbeing initiatives in diverse colleges and universities.

We encourage you to ask the question what can be done in everyday life to improve student wellbeing at your college or university? Answers from 2,776 Australian students were analyzed and fell into seven different categories (Baik et al., 2019). Students most often recommended that when building student wellbeing, teachers and lecturers should strive to be more approachable and to understand diverse student circumstances. They should try to be more empathetic and communicate better, to be more explicit about their expectations and clearer in presenting information (e.g., in classes). Students would appreciate teachers to initiate interactions and take time to get to know them. These students also reported that teachers should increase engagement via using diverse activities in education and to show individual support, such as by providing individual feedback. Large number of students also provided recommendations related to student services and student support. Students suggested increasing awareness and use of student services (e.g., counseling, academic skills, and student advising services) and they also recommended improving the quality of the services (e.g., availability and range). Classes on course planning and guidance on post-graduate career options would be appreciated by students as well. Students also strongly recommended that educators try to understand that students have responsibilities beyond academic life. They would appreciate community and relationships among peers to be supported. Students also called for wellbeing education and opportunities to practice activities supporting wellbeing, such as to have "mental health days" and to have space on campus to relax and play.

There were similarities found in a recent Eastern European study assessing student wellbeing using student self-assessment among 80 different areas of their lives. Research among 600 students from 17 different schools of Charles University in Prague (Koci, 2023) has identified areas of students' lives that they generally feel need some improvement and growth. Using the 0–10 Cantril ladder (0 = worst; 10 = best), students scaled at the lowest: satisfactory investments; good body posture; enjoyment of what they do at school; faith and spirituality; engagement in school activities; regular relaxation; meaning in school activities; ability to focus; satisfactory savings and good income. On the contrary, respondents felt confident about and rated the best their high-quality relationships with animals and pets; taking responsibility for their actions; high-quality relationships with significant other(s); serving others with no expectation of getting anything back; high-quality relationship with nature; access to quality health care; shared positivity and enjoyed seeing other people being happy; engagement in their hobbies; responsibility and recognition and enjoyment of others' achievements. These examples illustrate that understanding the local context and culture is important when providing culturally responsive wellbeing care for diverse college and university students.

Conclusion

Positive psychology practices and interventions guided by the PERMA+4 framework and the available peer-reviewed scientific evidence hold great promise for improving wellbeing and success in higher education, especially when implemented in a contextually sensitive and culturally responsive manner. This proactive evidence-based approach to promoting student wellbeing in higher education promises to improve the quality of a students' educational experience as well as prevent pathologies such as anxiety and depression that occur when a student life is stressful, barren, and meaningless. Koci and Donaldson (2024) have recently provided a wide range of practical tools and exercises to help colleges and universities foster the wellbeing and academic success of their students, and to create culturally sensitive learning environments where all students can flourish.

This chapter underscores the significant role of positive psychology, through the application of the PERMA+4 framework, in enhancing the wellbeing and academic success of students across diverse cultural backgrounds. The integration of positive emotions, engagement, relationships, meaning, and accomplishment, alongside physical health, a positive mindset, a conducive environment, and economic security, offers a holistic blueprint for addressing the multifaceted dimensions of student wellbeing. Beyond theoretical contributions, this chapter reviews actionable strategies and tools that empower colleges and universities to cultivate environments where students can thrive emotionally, socially, and academically. This includes fostering a positive psychological climate, enhancing students' engagement with their educational journey, and ensuring access to resources that support physical health and economic stability. Moreover, this chapter highlights the importance of a global perspective in the application of PPIs, acknowledging the diverse cultural contexts in which students operate. This global perspective is essential for the development of culturally responsive practices that recognize and respect the unique experiences and needs of students from various backgrounds.

In conclusion, this chapter promoted taking initiatives to embed positive psychology at the heart of higher education. The culturally attuned approach not only holds the promise of mitigating the current mental health crisis but also of reimagining an educational system where student wellbeing is as important as academic achievement. As higher education continues to evolve, incorporating the principles of positive psychology through the PERMA+4 framework emerges as a critical pathway toward nurturing well-rounded, resilient, and successful individuals in an increasingly complex and challenging world.

References

Antaramian, S. (2017). The importance of very high life satisfaction for students' academic success. *Cogent Education*. https://doi.org/10.1080/2331186X.2017.1307622.

Arslan, G. (2020) Social-emotional health in higher education: A psychometric evaluation with Turkish students. *British Journal of Guidance & Counselling, 50*(5), 1–14.

Baik, C., Larcombe, W., & Brooker, A. (2019). How universities can enhance student mental wellbeing: The student perspective. In *Higher education research & development*. Routledge. https://doi.org/10.1080/07294360.2019.1576596

Brown, A. D., Ross, N., Sangraula, M., Liang, A., & Brandon, A. K. (2023). Transforming mental healthcare in higher education through scalable mental health interventions. *Global Mental Health*. https://doi.org/10.1017/gmh.2023.29

Donaldson, S. I. (2019). *Evaluating employee positive functioning and performance: A positive work and organizations approach* [Doctoral dissertation, Claremont, CA, Claremont Graduate University].

Donaldson, S. I., Cabrera, V., & Gaffaney, J. (2021). Following the science to generate wellbeing: Using the highest quality experimental evidence to design interventions. *Frontiers in Psychology*. https://doi.org/10.3389/fpsyg.2021.739352.

Donaldson, S. I., Chan, L., Villalobos, J., & Chen, C. (2020). The generalizability of HERO across 15 nations: Positive psychological capital (PsyCap) beyond the US and other WEIRD countries. *International Journal of Environmental Research and Public Health, 17*(24), 9432. https://doi.org/10.3390/ijerph17249432

Donaldson, S. I., Csikszentmihalyi, M., & Nakamura, J. (Eds.). (2020). *Positive psychological science: Improving everyday life, well-being, work, education, and societies across the globe*. Routledge Academic. https://doi.org/10.1111/peps.12487

Donaldson, S. I., Dollwet, M., & Rao, M. (2015). Happiness, excellence, and optimal human functioning revisited: Examining the peer-reviewed literature linked to positive psychology. *Journal of Positive Psychology, 9*(6), 1–11. https://doi.org/10.1080/17439760.2014.943801

Donaldson, S. I., Gaffaney, J., & Caberra, V. (2023). The science and practice of positive psychology: From a bold vision to PERMA+4. In Invited for C. Markey & H. S. Friedman (Eds.), *The 3rd edition of the encyclopedia of mental health*. Academic Press.

Donaldson, S. I., Heshmati, S., & Donaldson, S. I. (2021). Global perspectives on positive psychological science. In Aleksandra Kostic & Derek Chadee (Eds.), *Positive psychology: An international perspective*. Wiley.

Donaldson, S. I., Heshmati, S., Young, J. Y., & Donaldson, S. I. (2020). Examining building blocks of wellbeing beyond PERMA and self-report bias. *Journal of Positive Psychology*, 1–8. https://doi.org/10.1080/17439760.2020.1818813

Donaldson, S. I., Van Zyl, L. E., & Donaldson, S. I. (2022). PERMA+4: A framework for work-related well-being, performance and positive organizational psychology 2.0. *Frontiers in Psychology*, 12:817244. https://doi.org/10.3389/fpsyg.2021.817244

Flannery, M. E. (2023). The mental health crisis on college campuses: https://www.nea.org/nea-today/all-news-articles/mental-health-crisis-college-campuses

Francis, J., Vella-Brodrick, D., & Chyuan-Chin, T. (2021). Effectiveness of online, school-based positive psychology interventions to improve mental health and wellbeing: A systematic review. *International Journal of Wellbeing*, 11(4), 44–67. https://doi.org/10.5502/ijw.v11i4.1465

Kansky, J., & Diener, E. (2020). National accounts of well-being for public policy. In S. I. Donaldson, M. Csikszentmihalyi, & J. Nakamura (Eds.), *Positive psychological science: Improving everyday life, well-being, work, education, and societies across the globe*. Routledge Academic.

Kim, H., Doiron, K., Warren, M. A., & Donaldson, S. I. (2018). The international landscape of positive psychology research: A systematic review. *International Journal of Wellbeing*, 8(1), 50–70. https://doi.org/10.5502/ijw.v8i1.651

Koci, J., & Donaldson, S. I. (2022). *Zdraví a mentální well-being studentů distančního vzdělávání*. Charles University. ISBN: 978-80-7603-357-3

Koci, J., & Donaldson, S. I. (2024). *Well-being and success of university students*. Applying PERMA+4. Routledge. ISBN: 9781032457185; https://doi.org/10.4324/9781003378365

Koci, J., & Koptikova, D. (2022a). *Podpora mentálního well-beingu žáků středních škol v době digitalizace – teoretická východiska*. UK PedF. ISBN: 978-80-7603-360-3

Koci, J., & Koptikova, D. (2022b). *Budování mentálního well-beingu žáků středních škol v době digitalizace – jak aplikovat praktická doporučení v praxi*. UK PedF. ISBN: 978-80-7603-361-0.

Kumar, P., & Mohideen, A. (2021). Strengths-based positive schooling interventions: A scoping review. *Contemporary School Psychology*, 25(1), 86–98. https://doi.org/10.1007/s40688-019-00260-1

Lester, P. B., Stewart, E. P., Vie, L. L., Bonett, D. G., Seligman, E. P., & Diener, E. (2021). Happy soldiers are highest performers. *Journal Happiness Studies*, 1–22. https://doi.org/10.1007/s10902-021-00441-x

Morris, K. V. A. (2022). Consumerist views of higher education and links to student wellbeing and achievement: An analysis based on the concept of autonomy as depicted in self-determination theory. *Journal of Further and Higher Education*, 46(6), 836–849. https://doi.org/10.1080/0309877X.2021.2011842

Moscoso, S., & Salgado, J. F. (2021). Meta-analytic examination of a suppressor effect on subjective wellbeing and job performance relationship, *Journal of Work and Organizational Psychology*, 37, 119–131. https://doi.org/10.5093/jwop2021a13

Moussa, N., & Wael, F. A. (2022). Exploring the relationship between students' academic success and happiness levels in the higher education settings during the lockdown period of COVID-19. *Psychological Reports*, 125(2), 986–1010. https://doi.org/10.1177/0033294121994568

Pascoe, M. C., Hetreick, S. E., & Parker, A. G. (2020). The impact of stress on students in secondary school and higher education. *International Journal of Adolescence and Youth, 25*, 104–112. https://doi.org/10.1080/02673843.2019.1596823

Rao, M. A., Donaldson, S. I., & Doiron, K. M. (2015). Positive psychology research in the Middle East and North Africa. *Middle East Journal of Positive Psychology, 1*(1), 60–76.

Schiavon, C. C., Teixeira, L. P., Gurgel, L. G., Magalhães, C. R., & Reppold, C. T. (2020). Positive education: Innovation in educational interventions based on positive psychology. *Psicologia: Teoria e Pesquisa, 36*, e3632. https://doi.org/10.1590/0102.3772e3632

Seligman, M. E. (2002). Positive psychology, positive prevention, and positive therapy. *Handbook of positive psychology, 2*, 3–12.

Seligman, M. E. (2008). Positive health. *Applied psychology, 57*, 3–18.

Seligman, M. E. (2011). *Flourish: A visionary new understanding of happiness and well-being*. Simon and Schuster.

Seligman, M. E., & Csikszentmihalyi, M. (2000). Positive psychology: An introduction. *American Psychological Association, 55*(1), 5.

Tansey, T. N., Smedema, S., Umucu, E., Iwanaga, K., Wu, J. R., Cardoso, E. D. S., & Strauser, D. (2018). Assessing college life adjustment of students with disabilities: Application of the PERMA framework. *Rehabilitation Counseling Bulletin, 61*(3), 131–142. https://doi.org/10.1177/0034355217702136

Walsh, L. C., Boz, S. G., & Lyubomirsky, S. (2023). *Well-being and career success*. American Psychological Association.

Waters, L. (2011). A review of school-based positive psychology interventions. *The Australian Educational and Developmental Psychologist, 28*(2), 75–90. https://doi.org/10.1375/aedp.28.2.75

Waters, L., & Loton, D. (2019). SEARCH: A meta-framework and review of the field of positive education. *International Journal of Applied Positive Psychology, 4*(1–2), 1–46. https://doi.org/10.1007/s41042-019-00017-4

Waters, L., & Loton, D. (2021). Tracing the growth, gaps, and characteristics in positive education science: A long-term, large-scale review of the field. *Frontiers in psychology, 12*, 774967. https://doi.org/10.3389/fpsyg.2021.774967

Weiss, E. L., Donaldson, S. I., & Reece, A. (2024) Well-being as a predictor of academic success in student veterans and factor validation of the PERMA + 4 well-being measurement scale, *Journal of American College Health*. https://doi.org/10.1080/07448481.2023.2299417

Chapter 6

University students' wellbeing

Diversity across contexts

Noor Al-Wattary, Hessa Al-Thani, and Aisha Al-Ahmadi

Introduction

Preparing students to be successful candidates requires broad and holistic educational opportunities that ensure their knowledge of essential professional skills and empower them to enter adulthood with the highest levels of mental health (Noddings, 2005).

Mental wellbeing is a key national outcome and a fundamental part of being a healthy and resilient individual. The concept of mental health cannot be separated from overall health, which was defined by the World Health Organization Constitution of 1946 as a state of complete physical, mental, and social wellbeing and not merely the absence of disease or injury (Kessler & Üstün, 2004). More recent definitions have gone on to describe mental wellbeing as a resource for good living and as an essential asset for an individual's personal resources, as well as inner capacities (Holte et al., 2014). Furthermore, the phrase "there is no health without mental health" clearly represents the importance of mental welding (Adamson, 2007).

Mental health issues can impact any individual, anywhere, and at any stage of life. In relation, the Word Health Organization (WHO) argues that youth and adolescents can be affected by mental disorders (Kessler & Üstün, 2004). These issues of mental wellbeing issues can result in negative consequences on the economic status of countries. To overcome these obstacles, serious commitments to invest in mental wellbeing services and social-emotional interventions are needed.

One of the main sources of wellbeing services can be placed at University settings (Jarden & Roache, 2023). Worldwide, many interventions were conducted with the aim of improving students' wellbeing in higher education. However, the prevailing focus on Westernized conceptions of wellbeing often overlooks the importance of contextualized interventions tailored to specific cultural and educational contexts. As wellbeing is a dynamic and multi-dimensional concept, varying widely across different age groups, cultures, genders, or population groups, there is a need to consider all the related social and contextual factors to design, measure, and implement related interventions.

Approaching the literature reveals different approaches, interventions, and initiatives that aim to empower students with the social, emotional, spiritual, cognitive,

DOI: 10.4324/9781003491613-6

and different non-academic skills to support their mental health and wellbeing. Building on this understanding of wellbeing's diverse interpretations, many studies were conducted to explore factors influencing students' wellbeing. Studies such as those by Baik et al. (2019) and Klapp et al. (2023) shed light on this area of wellbeing. Notably, Baik and colleagues found in their study of around 6500 students at two Australian universities that a staggering 84% exhibited elevated levels of distress, a figure significantly higher than the 29% prevalence in the general Australian population (2019). This research underscores the importance of recognizing and addressing students' struggles and barriers at educational institutions beyond the academic realm. Furthermore, Baik et al. emphasized the necessity of involving students in policy and decision-making processes and providing access to key resources like counseling, career advice, and mental health interventions to enhance wellbeing (2019).

The growing awareness of the importance of student wellbeing has led to the emergence of initiatives and support services that focus on nurturing "hearts as well as minds" worldwide. This approach to students' support is not only about fostering academic performance, as noted by Klapp and others (2023), but also about enhancing positive social relations (Kansky & Diener, 2017; Sandstrom & Dunn, 2014) and improving inner life satisfaction levels (Bashir et al., 2016). This perspective firmly positions wellbeing as a pivotal factor in educational success.

In this context of broadening our understanding of wellbeing, it becomes essential to explore interventions specifically tailored for students. A holistic (that addresses body and soul) approach is paramount in examining students' wellbeing, encompassing various social and emotional forces. This approach draws on the renowned scholar Ibn Hazm, who explored the concept of Hmm (anxiety) in depth, stating that seeking meaning is our way out of the abyss. It is a spiritual endeavor that centers around discovering what makes our lives worth living by working on enriching the spiritual dimension of humans as well as the body and cognitive ones (Coope, 2000).

In this regard, many scholars emphasized the importance of addressing individuals' social, emotional, and spiritual as well as physical and bodily needs. For instance, Baik et al. (2019) outline five key action areas aimed at improving individuals' wellbeing. The first action is focused on preparing engaging curricula and learning experiences that provoke students' thinking. The second action is creating supportive social, physical, and digital environments that address students' various needs. Third, strengthening individual's awareness about their own actions and decisions. The fourth action is focused on improving students' mental health knowledge and their self-regulation skills. And the final action is to ensure access to effective services that work on enriching all dimensions of human wellbeing, social, cognitive (academic profession), spiritual, and emotional. These areas represent a proposed strategy for educational institutions to support their students holistically.

This chapter delves into the impact of a Social Emotional Learning (SEL) intervention, viewed from an Islamic perspective, on five dimensions of wellbeing for students: social, emotional, spiritual, and cognitive (academic profession), and physical. This focus on is crucial for students of all professions, as their wellbeing directly influences their effectiveness in the educational environment and, by extension, the wellbeing of their students.

Literature review

Wellbeing interventions

The implementation of interventions that aim to improve students' wellbeing in higher education is crucial. The objective of these interventions is to target the social, emotional, cognitive, physical, and spiritual aspects of wellbeing that improve students' life satisfaction. These interventions can be defined as SEL interventions that cover the mental, psychological, spiritual, and personal dimensions of individuals (Guerra & Bradshaw, 2008). Within this literature review, we explored different types, approaches, and results of SEL interventions in university settings worldwide. The main conclusion derived from this literature is that most of the research is conducted in Western contexts, which leaves a significant gap in the literature as not enough is known about wellbeing in non-Western settings. Looking at an alternative Middle Eastern example offers an alternative perspective that reflects an Arab and Islamic view on wellbeing interventions in higher education. This view presents the culturally responsive and religious

What is SEL intervention?

Social-emotional interventions are programs designed with the focus on prompting preventive skills that reduce the risk factors of mental health issues and increase the levels of psychological immunity (Kenny & Hage, 2009). This preventive approach can be considered external forces that contribute to building individuals' strengths and increasing their positive inner development (Lerner et al., 2005). As a result, increasing individuals' capacities to understand their own self, manage their emotions, face different life challenges, and maintain positive relations can improve their life satisfaction and wellbeing levels (Kenny & Hage, 2009). Higher levels of life satisfaction and wellbeing can in turn empower individuals to participate effectively in their societies (Lerner, 2001). Thus, higher levels of wellbeing can be directly related to the enhancement and development of social-emotional skills (Guerra & Bradshaw, 2008).

Western interventions

With the aim to improve wellbeing through SEL programs, many interventions were conducted worldwide with the objective of promoting inner students' mental health and wellbeing by focusing on values, creative thinking, positive psychology, and self-regulation skills. In this regard, wellbeing interventions in the literature vary across cultures in terms of delivery approaches, content, objectives, and duration of the programs. Furthermore, different approaches to evaluating SEL interventions have been used to improve students' wellbeing. The focus of this part of the chapter is to explore studies that reported interventions in terms of duration, aim, and approach of evaluation and its impact on students. The majority of those interventions were designed, implemented, and evaluated in the West.

In a longitudinal study, de Vibe et al. (2018) explored the effects of a mindfulness-based intervention over (six years). The experiment was completed on Norwegian aspiring healthcare professionals' students who received a mindfulness course over the span of seven weeks and received a booster session twice every year. de Vibe and colleagues (2018) concluded that students who received this intervention reported higher levels of wellbeing, relaxation, self-compassion, and empathy. Wellbeing was measured using The Five Facet Mindfulness Questionnaire and the Ways of Coping Checklist. At the six-year follow-up, the students in the intervention group reported improved wellbeing levels compared to students in the control group (de Vibe et al., 2018). The length of this experiment is one of a kind and requires replication in order to prove its results again.

In another study, Chelsea Brett and other researchers (2020) focused on improving students' wellbeing through a behavioral intervention that improves mental wellbeing. The study was implemented based on a self-directed behavioral intervention at Yale University School of Public Health. Students were enrolled in a course on "Health Behaviour Change" (Brett et al., 2020). The data was collected through a quasi-experimental longitudinal study and were analyzed after 12 weeks of the experiment. The study revealed that students who were enrolled in the course reported significant improvement in mental wellbeing compared to the students who were not. In other words, "self-directed behaviour change interventions are effective in promoting mental and physical health among graduate student populations" (Brett et al., 2020, p. 350).

Another approach used to improve wellbeing involved focusing on Gratitude, which is a prominent intervention reported in the literature. For instance, Tolcher and colleagues (2022) looked at the possible impact of gratitude interventions on the wellbeing of American college students in the Northwest. In order to investigate the impact of the intervention, two different forms of evaluations were applied: journaling and reflection. Students in the experiment group completed evaluations at pre-intervention and post-intervention assessments after eight weeks that tested different aspects of wellbeing: satisfaction with life, happiness, resilience, depression, anxiety, and stress. The results revealed that all the different groups of students had improved wellbeing and affective functioning while students in the control group reported no improvements in overall wellbeing (Tolcher et al., 2022).

In another study that focused on an inner-strengthening approach, Taylor and others (2022) linked the improvement of wellbeing to the enhancement of self-compassion and self-efficacy through a mindfulness-based intervention. Specifically, the study evaluated the effects of this intervention on improving stress, coping, and psychological skills in relation to wellbeing among college students in

Arizona, USA (2022). The students that participated in the study underwent mindfulness meditations, reflective journaling, and participation in group discussions for a period of eight weeks while the control group in the experiment did not participate in those activities (Taylor et al., 2022, p. 142). The study measured students' perceived stress, mental health, mindfulness, self-compassion, and coping self-efficacy in pre-intervention, during instruction and post-intervention (Taylor et al., 2022). The results revealed that there were significant improvements in self-compassion and coping, which directly contribute to individuals' wellbeing. The findings suggest that the integration of mindfulness-based instruction into classroom instruction and classroom work can greatly improve the wellbeing of college students (Taylor et al., 2022).

Another study conducted by Myers and others (2022) focused on improving students' wellbeing through habits behavioral change is related to psychological satisfaction. Specifically, the study determined "students' reaction and experiences with an intervention based on the principle of salience to reduce psychological attraction and addiction to smartphones" (Myers et al., 2022, p. 330). Therefore, students in the study were instructed to "adjust their smartphone's color settings to 'grayscale mode', turn off social media notifications, remove social media icons from smartphone home screens and place their device away from their beds whilst sleeping for a period of three weeks" (Myers et al., 2022, p. 330). During the study, students were requested to record any noticeable changes to their productivity, wellbeing, and sleep. The results revealed that the physical act of changing the habit of addiction to smartphones led to higher levels of productivity and improvements in both sleep and overall wellbeing. Furthermore, this behavioral change contributed to improving students' face-to-face interactions, social relations, and leisure activities (Myers et al., 2022).

In a similar intervention, Waechter and colleagues (2021) looked at the importance of mandating participation in wellness intervention programs. In the study, medical students in St. George, Grenada, participated in sessions of either yoga, mindfulness, or walking twice weekly for a period of 12 weeks. The results revealed that students who were enrolled in the intervention program reported lower anxiety and stress-related issues (Waechter et al., 2021). The study enforces the importance of mandating wellness intervention programs into university programs in order to maximize student success and thus minimize stress and poor mental health.

In a different approach, with similar objectives, intervention, Singh and Bandyopadhyay (2021) looked at approaches that enhance college students' wellbeing through a psycho-spiritual wellbeing intervention in New Delhi, India (2021). The study comprised 14 module videos that included videos of Indian spiritual leaders and motivational speakers. The effects of the modules were tested through a web-based study as well as two classroom-based studies. The categories of wellbeing that were observed were positive and negative aspects: general wellbeing, mental wellbeing, thriving, peace of mind, harmony in life, resilience, and depression, anxiety, and stress symptoms, respectively (Singh & Bandyopadhyay, 2021).

The results revealed that students showed a significant improvement in general wellbeing, thriving, and peace of mind (Singh & Bandyopadhyay, 2021).

Finally, a Best Possible Self (BPS) intervention conducted on undergraduate students as part of a study proved to have no impact in the long run and the control groups in the experiment outperformed the intervention groups (Duan et al., 2021). Duan and other researchers categorized BPS as one of the leading and most effective positive psychology interventions used and as a future-oriented intervention that requires participants to describe their best possible self (2021). Post-intervention included three writing activities and four different tests at four points in the experiment. The data revealed that the control group outperformed the intervention group, and the intervention did not improve the subjective and psychological wellbeing of the students in the treatment group (Duan et al., 2021). It is worth noting that the data collection period was interrupted by the COVID-19 Pandemic, which could have also impacted the final results of the experiment. A study of this nature outlines the importance of research on implementing classroom interventions to improve wellbeing. In this case, the theory proved that BPS is an effective intervention for improving wellbeing, but the implementation of the said intervention failed to prove the theory.

Interventions in the Arabic and Islamic context

In the Middle East and Arabic context, in which the religion is Islam, and the language is Arabic, few initiatives started to focus on students' positive development and mental wellbeing within the higher education context. Some of those initiatives are limited to a proposed' framework and a suggested design of SEL higher education programs while other interventions are implemented, empirically evaluated, and applied in different educational contexts (Maddah et al., 2021). This significant lack of literature on what can work in the Arabic and Islamic contexts creates room for further research opportunities.

The need for wellbeing in the Arabic context was pointed out by Zuhdi and Syarief's study which explored the approach of constructing the concept of wellbeing among students in an Islamic environment (2023). The study revealed that students and faculty of an Indonesian Islamic University believe that subjective wellbeing is vital in maintaining the needs of students and faculty in higher education. The article also emphasized that some core Islamic values align with hedonic views of wellbeing.

Despite the gap in the literature, very few studies were conducted in Arabic contexts with a focus on Mental-Health or Psychological immunity. For instance, Thamer Makbis & Jabber Khalf (2022) aimed in her study that included 120 students in Iraq to explore what is called (students' psychological immunity) and the role of this immunity in decreasing psychological and physical issues and overcoming stressful situations. In addition, the study proposed a SEL program that aims to support and enrich psychological immunity for students. The study revealed that students' level of psychological immunity is low and there is a need for the construction of preventive interventions and counseling programs that improve students' wellbeing and mental health. However, the research did not mention the steps, procedures, or strategies implementation of the suggested program or the evaluation of the outcomes.

Life Skills interventions are a common form of intervention on wellbeing; however, not many experiments of this nature have been carried out to test the effects of life skills interventions. Diana Maddah and her colleagues (2021) tested the effectiveness of a Life Skills intervention (KHOTWA – Step) in improving Arab university students in Lebanon's overall wellbeing. The Life Skills program was held online and noticeable differences were observed between the control and intervention groups in terms of the life skills acquired, dietary habits, and mental health scores during the three-month follow-up. The intervention group reported a greater increase in the following life skills categories, including self-care, work and study, career and education planning, and goal setting. The study also revealed that students in the intervention group reported a higher rate of healthy eating and decreased their intake of processed foods (Maddah et al., 2021). The study concluded that Life Skills interventions significantly improve mental health and wellbeing and promote healthy lifestyles.

In short, many interventions serve as different methods for improving the wellbeing of students in higher education. The methods that have had positive impacts can be used by educators in their institutions to improve the wellbeing of their students. The methods that failed to positively impact students' wellbeing can be further researched and tweaked in order to be used as methods of improving the wellbeing of students in higher education. The Islamic perspective on wellbeing in higher education is also crucial as it addresses the possible interventions that can be employed in higher education institutions in Islamic countries where faith and spirituality have proven to play an active role in the general wellbeing of people.

Methodology

The College of Education initiated the Education and Well-being Initiative (EWI) as an initiative to promote transformation in teaching and learning by preparing holistic, authentic, resilient, and collaborative learners. The initiative consists of five pillars of wellbeing that are critical to support emerging teachers spiritually, emotionally, intellectually, physically, and socially. In this study, six workshops were implemented at the College of Education. The outcomes of each workshop were evaluated and analyzed to explore the impact of SEL interventions on students' perceived wellbeing in the Arabic and Islamic contexts.

The aim of this study was to explore and evaluate in an in-depth approach the SEL program's impact from the participants' perspectives and the program's dynamics to understand factors that might facilitate or hinder the SEL program's success. In recruiting participants, all College of Education students were invited by email to attend optional social-emotional workshops at the college. A total of 65 female students accepted the invitation to participate for reasons related to local cultural sensitivities and management restrictions, separate workshops were held for female and male students. This study was focused on female students. The outcomes can provide a basis for more future studies that involve girls' and boys' schools at different stages.

A series of six weeks of wellbeing intervention workshops were administered at the College of Education by one faculty member. This faculty has a background in education and wellbeing and experience in social-emotional interventions. The target group was College of Education female students aged 18–25. The workshops were lecture-based, with some activities and discussions related to the different concepts of wellbeing. Each workshop was designed to cover specific areas of mental wellbeing, with all the related resources, worksheets, and activities that support students to perceive, apply, and gain the required knowledge. The workshops were conducted in the 1-hour free time at the college, from 12 to 1:30 pm on Wednesdays. Participation in the study and the workshops was voluntary. Data was collected right after each workshop where students wrote reflective papers to describe their experiences with the workshops and the impact on their wellbeing and emotions. These reflective papers encouraged students to reflect and think of the main outcomes and benefits gained after participating in the SEL program.

The SEL program

The SEL workshops in this program were derived from the Spiritually Focused Assistance (SFA) program. This program was designed by a group of educational and psychological specialists in Qatar in order to improve students' wellbeing through a cognitive and spiritual approach that focuses on the five dimensions of wellbeing; social, emotional, spiritual, physical, and cognitive. Within this study, students' experiences and perceived impact of the implemented workshops were collected by reflective papers. Each workshop covered different subjects related to self-regulation, positive thinking, self-realization, and social relations.

The aim of the implementation and evaluation of the workshops was to establish interventions based on the Arabic and Islamic social context. The program was based on cultural and Islamic religious concepts and was implemented at the College of Education. These concepts suggest that human interaction and actions in this life are the results of the integration of social, spiritual, cognitive, emotional, and physical wellbeing. Each dimension will be discussed based on the findings in light of the existing literature and the best practices of students' support services.

Procedures

The workshop lasted for 2 hours and was conducted during the spring and fall semesters by the College of Education faculty. The target group comprised College of Education female students studying different disciplines.

At the start of each session, students were engaged in an icebreaker and were asked questions in relation to positive feelings, negative feelings, and the impact on their thinking. Then, during each session, students were provided with focused and clear explanations of the concepts of wellbeing, such as emotional management, social relations, self-regulation, and self-realization. Each implemented session was based on the Islamic concepts related to wellbeing, including quotes from the Qur'an and the Hadith. For instance, spiritual education in Islam involves exploring questions of purpose and meaning in life, emphasizing on qualities such as compassion, empathy, and forgiveness. By incorporating these values into education, students may develop inner resilience, enabling them to cope better with challenges. As a result, this exploration can assist students in developing a sense of purpose, which is linked to greater life satisfaction and wellbeing (Appendix A).

Data analysis

A qualitative thematic analysis of the reflective papers was conducted to explore the main themes and categories of the findings. At the end of each workshop, students were asked to reflect on any perceived changes in their wellbeing and any areas of improvement that they witnessed after the program. The reflection papers were examined according to students' perceptions, the meaning of wellbeing, life satisfaction, and happiness, what wellbeing meant to students, and how they understood and defined it in their own words.

In more detail, a deductive approach was applied in the analysis of students' reflective papers. This deductive approach involved thematic analysis in searching for common themes, threads, and categories that extend across the set of reflective papers in relation to the five wellbeing pillars; social, emotional, spiritual, cognitive, and physical. Furthermore, this approach involved capturing themes that emerge directly from the data through the process of reading and interpreting data by way of systematic classification. Sandelowski and Leeman (2012) define themes as a coherent integration of the different components, responses, and patterns of the data set in relation to the research question. Therefore, each theme in the qualitative analyses can be considered a descriptor that organizes a group of related and repeated ideas to unify the different concepts regarding the subject of inquiry.

This theme determination was applied in the analysis of the data in this study to facilitate a comprehensive view by uncovering patterns related to student participants' perspectives. This approach involved careful reading, classifying, comparing, and labeling the data to identify and collapse related patterns and major themes. The deductive analysis approach aimed to capture participants' different experiences, viewpoints, suggestions, and impressions of the SEL program's impact in detail. As a result, four major themes emerged that guided the analysis process: spiritual, cognitive, emotional, and social. These results indicate that there was no specific impact on students' physical wellbeing; therefore, this theme was not covered in the discussion and the findings section.

Findings and discussion

The reflective papers of the 65 students who participated in the workshops were analyzed and categorized based on the thematic analysis into four main dimensions: spiritual, cognitive, emotional, and social. Each theme is presented separately and discussed in the following sections based on the main findings.

Emotional: significantly reduced hopelessness and increased optimism

The majority (50 students) emphasized that participating in the SEL workshops at the College of Education resulted in positive changes to their emotional wellbeing levels. These changes included being more optimistic about the future, having more motivation toward their studies, and feeling more peaceful and satisfied.

Regarding the first dimension, students mentioned that they started to feel more optimistic:

> I felt that I can think differently, I am now more focused on how to achieve the best in my future, at the same time, feeling optimistic about myself.

This was supported by another opinion:

> I used to feel very low, and a deep feeling of failure was always inside my mind, now, and after I had attended these extra-circular workshops, I feel much better in terms of future plans, achievements in my studies and trust in my own abilities.

Another student mentioned the positive effect on depression symptoms or burnout levels:

> The sessions provided me with practical steps on how to manage, understand and realizes my emotions, which leads to my mental health and reduced the feeling of burn out.

Spiritual: Inner peace and inner satisfaction

Students mentioned that one of the main skills that they acquired from the SEL program was the linkage between spiritual beliefs and their own practical life, for instance:

> One of the main results is the relation of the spiritual and religious practices to our daily life, I realized the sessions allowed me to underhand that I need to put my beliefs into practice.

Another student supports this result by indicating, that peace, was the main outcome:

> Everything is better, I feel that I am peaceful from inside, my intentions are changed to the better, my conceptions about important matters in life are changed, I learned that, giving, and continuing, are two major factors for my inner peace and outer achievements.

Life satisfaction was also reported by another student as an outcome of these sessions:

> The spiritual sessions reminded me of the importance of my relationship with God, and the impact on my inner peace and self-sufficiency, most importantly, I realized that satisfaction is moral, not only about materials.

Cognitive: sense of purpose and engagement in learning

Students mentioned that the program improved their capacities and strengths related to learning and engagement. This impact was directly related to developing their curiosity for learning, the importance of having a purpose in life, and the feeling of responsibility for developing their own abilities to achieve the best in their future, and for their bigger society. For instance:

> Now I realize that my learning is not only a task that I need to do, rather it's a future, a responsibility and a goal that I need to achieve for myself and for my country.

Another example:

> I used to view my studies as a burden, that lead me to depressed thinking, now, I feel it's a responsibility to have a specific purpose in life, a purpose that guide my motivation every morning to attend, to achieve and to fulfill the different tasks required from me.

From another view, related to the mental health, many students mentioned the impact of workshops on their motivation levels. Those levels were related mainly to the sense of strengthening the inner feelings by the outer forces. For instance:

> I think one of the major benefits of SEL workshops is to motivate us to think, to achieve and to become better candidates in the future. I feel more responsible of my own, and my country's future.

Another opinion, within the same line, shows:

> Those workshops represent an outer messages to our hearts, to feel more actively motivated in our current and future plans. The real stories and the religious guidelines related to the context made a huge difference to me.

Social: thinking of others and collaborative work

Students mentioned that the workshops fostered a sense of community and connection among them.

> I realized the importance of being part of a supportive community, to have positive bounds, to care for others and support them. It enabled me to develop values of tolerance and respect for diversity.

Another student expressed how her perceptions about others have been changed:

> I realized how people have different personalities, different backgrounds, different challenges and different perceptions about reality. This understanding will support me in my current and future realization, to deal with patience, consideration and empathy

The results of this study revealed different positive outcomes in the light of students' wellbeing. As suggested earlier in this chapter, the aim of social-emotional interventions is to empower students with the skills and knowledge that enable them to face different life challenges. The results indicate that SEL interventions can act as external forces that support students' inner forces and, as a result, improve students' wellbeing. External factors include factors beyond an individual's own control, such as how people deal with others, social norms educational environment, and social support. Internal factors include an individual's own attitude, mindset, perceptions, cognitive thinking, view of the world, and emotions (Rotter, 1990). Each individual has little or no influence on external factors but more control over internal factors (Ajzen, 2002). As a result, external forces such as social support in the educational environment can support students' mental wellbeing and improve their abilities to face life challenges, motivation to achieve the best in their academic and personal life, and maintain positive relations with others. In contrast, when students are emotionally low, their inner motivation, relationships with others, and life achievements will be negatively impacted.

Therefore, when faced with a challenge, individuals first need to determine whether they are dealing with external or internal factors. Then, their reaction will be based on the perceived factors. For instance, when encountering an external challenge, individuals can react or respond to it, and this reaction is related to inner forces to face that specific challenge (Merz & Huxhold, 2010). As suggested by Sandstrom & Dunn, 2014), individuals with stronger inner forces can be more proactive in their daily activities and more positive toward different challenges. In addition, as Kansky and Diener (2017) suggest, people with stronger inner forces have more self-awareness. Therefore, when students reported that these workshops were able to change their way of perceiving their inner abilities, life purpose, and social relations, this may suggest that educational initiations can achieve positive sustainable wellbeing outcomes. Those outcomes can contribute to sustainable development by focusing on enhancing people's different aspects of mental, academic, and personal wellbeing.

The outcomes of this study also shed light on the importance of considering the social and cultural context in the design, implementation, and evaluation forces of SEL interventions. Many universal values, such as honesty, mercy, care, support, and love, can be applied in different contexts; however, some values are more culturally sensitive. Therefore, considering the context, the culture, and the religious practices constitute key success factors in the design and implementation of this program. In the present study, the majority of students indicated that the workshop related them to the spiritual and religious Islamic practices and, as such, had a deep impact on their hearts. They indicated how the integration of these religious practices enabled them to understand their role in this life and to realize the responsibility they have toward their selves and their society. These results indicate the real and valuable impact of integrating religious studies with the higher education curriculum in order to relate students to the different concepts related to their daily lives is documented in the literature. Seligman (2011) emphasized the positive effect of applying and integrating religious practices in educational settings on students, and how students found themselves living and thinking in ways they had not anticipated. He explained this change as an outcome of empowering students with the appropriate interventions that provoke the concepts of life satisfaction, patience, gratitude, and all the related values.

Therefore, integrating religious rules, practices, and values within the educational curriculum in a culturally appropriate approach can be considered another outcome of the SEL interventions that can promote wellbeing within higher education. These results indicate how students started their own personal dialogue about the meaning of existence, their relation with Allah, and the impact of this relation in guiding them in their route through this life. This guidance acted as an outer source to shaping an individual's thinking, building their inner capacities to overcome challenges, and empowering them with the morals and skills needed to have a specific purpose in life. This sense of purpose can facilitate individuals' beliefs of their potential, the value of their contribution to their society, and the sense of belonging to their environment. This sense of purpose supports the inner beliefs about the self, the world, and the relationship with others and, as a result, supports positive development outcomes such as wellbeing and resilience.

Empowering students through morals and values education building is well documented in the literature. For instance, (Diener & Seligman, 2002), argued that everything is better, that is, everything except human morals. As a result, there is a real need to integrate the religious, cultural, and spiritual norms within the educational system in order to reduce the mental and psychological issues that can lead to depression and anxiety. This preventive approach was explored in the previous Arabic and Islamic literature. For instance, in his work on the sustenance of the soul, Abu Zaid Al-Balkhi (849 AD), one of the first Muslim scholars who studied the deep insights and sources of wellbeing, mentioned the importance of acquiring the skills that nourish individuals' inner capacities to be able to cope with different challenges (Shamsuddin & Abd Rahman, 2021). He emphasized the crucial role of a nourished soul, in reaching a nourished, healthy and powerful body. Therefore, within this view, the soul is considered the catalyst that drives the body.

In terms of social relations, the findings help to explain why students conceptualized social connectivity within educational settings from a different lens. The multiple tasks students have to perform when studying at university may require working during outside of classroom hours and during weekends, having less time to sleep, and feeling overwhelmed. This can negatively impact their behavior toward others, leading to some conflicts in their relationships with others. As was noted in a study that examined burnout of public school teachers in Qatar, individuals' emotional exhaustion in terms of feeling overwhelmed and fatigued leads to low levels of mental wellbeing and depersonalization, resulting in "an inappropriate attitude towards others" (Alloh et al., 2019, p. 3). Therefore, supporting students to understand their own self and the importance of maintaining positive social relations by increasing the feeling of supporting, caring, and giving can positively lead students to cognitively realize and view the social relations as one of the key factors that can contribute to their own and that of their society's success.

Most of the concepts taught in this program were covered, derived from, and based on Islamic and Arabic concepts and cultural norms. All that we need as educators is to apply the social-emotional concepts in practice, to relate religious practices to address the everyday challenges. As such, these spiritually and socially based interventions emphasize the need for more initiatives that adopt culturally sensitive approaches. The outcomes of these interventions and initiatives can serve to enhance understanding of effective ways to contribute to the development of society.

Conclusion

The guiding objective of this initiative was to (a) explore the impact of SEL interventions offered in university settings, and (b) highlight the role of socio-cultural aspects on SEL interventions. This initiative sought to increase understanding of wellbeing, expanding on the investigations into wellbeing initiatives globally; these initiatives focus on promoting student wellbeing and prioritizing their care and mental health. By presenting these results, this chapter aims to contribute to the area of social-emotional learning and students' wellbeing. Specifically, this chapter sheds light on a new culturally based pilot intervention, providing suggestions for future interventions. This study revealed that there is a positive change, a difference in students' thinking, and a change in their perceived wellbeing. This impact can be explained in the light of students' feedback, perceptions, and experiences of whether there was a difference in their wellbeing, and why that difference had occurred. In addition, this chapter emphasized the reasons why wellbeing should be taught in university settings. A greater emphasis on wellbeing is synergistic with enhanced learning outcomes and higher wellbeing levels. The positive outcomes of the program might be related to the holistic approach of touching the core values and encouraging students to pay attention to the importance of the nourishment of the hearts as well as minds. Therefore, these results emphasize on the need to implement, evaluate, and explore the effectiveness of similar, context-sensitive interventions that can contribute to the future sustainable development of societies.

References

Adamson, P., 2007. Child poverty in perspective: An overview of child well-being in rich countries. Innocenti Report Card 7. UNICEF.

Ajzen, I. (2002). Perceived behavioral control, self-efficacy, locus of control, and the theory of planned behavior. *Journal of Applied Social Psychology, 32*(4), 665–683.

Alloh, M. M., Hasan, M. A., Du, X., & Romanowski, M. H. (2019). Burnout of primary teachers in Qatar government schools during an era of educational reform. *International Journal of Learning, Teaching and Educational Research, 18*(10), 1–19.

Baik, C., Larcombe, W., & Brooker, A. (2019). How universities can enhance student mental well-being: The student perspective. *Higher Education Research and Development, 38*(4), 674–687. https://doi.org/10.1080/07294360.2019.1576596

Bashir, N., Shafi, H., Yousuf, U., Parveen, S., & Akhter, K. (2016). Spiritual well-being and depression among middle aged people. *The International Journal of Indian Psychology, 3*(2), 36–41.

Brett, C., Wang, K., Lowe, S. R., & White, M. A. (2020). Evaluation and durability of a curriculum-based intervention for promoting mental health among graduate students. *American Journal of Health Education, 51*(6), 350–359. https://doi.org/10.1080/19325037.2020.1822240

Coope, J. A. (2000). With Heart, Tongue, and Limbs: Ibn Hazm on the essence of faith. *Medieval Encounters, 6*(1–3), 101–113.

de Vibe, M., Solhaug, I., Solhaug, I., Rosenvinge, J. H., Tyssen, R., Hanley, A., & Garland, E. (2018). Six-year positive effects of a mindfulness-based intervention on mindfulness, coping and well-being in medical and psychology students; Results from a randomized controlled trial. *PLOS One, 13*(4), e0196053. https://doi.org/10.1371/journal.pone.0196053

Diener, E., & Seligman, M. E. (2002). Very happy people. *Psychological Science, 13*(1), 81–84.

Duan, S., Exter, M., Newby, T., & Fa, B. (2021). No impact? Long-term effects of applying the best possible self-intervention in a real-world undergraduate classroom setting. *International Journal of Community Well-Being, 4*, 581–601.

Guerra, N. G., & Bradshaw, C. P. (2008). Linking the prevention of problem behaviors and positive youth development: Core competencies for positive youth development and risk prevention. *New Directions for Child and Adolescent Development, 2008*(122), 1–17.

Holte, A., Barry, M., Bekkhus, M., & Trommsdorff, G., 2014. Psychology of child well-being. In A. Ben-Arieh, F. Casas, I. Frones, & J. E. Korbin (Eds.), *Handbook of child well-being* (pp. 555–631) Springer.

Jarden, A., & Roache, A. (2023). What is well-being? *International Journal of Environmental Research and Public Health, 20*(6). https://doi.org/10.3390/ijerph20065006

Kansky, J., & Diener, E. (2017). Benefits of well-being: Health, social relationships, work and resilience. *Journal of Positive Psychology and Wellbeing, 1*(2), 129–169.

Kenny, M. E., & Hage, S. M. (2009). The next frontier: Prevention as an instrument of social justice. *The Journal of Primary Prevention, 30*, 1–10. https://doi.org/10.1007/s10935-008-0163-7

Kessler, R. C., & Üstün, T. B. (2004). The world mental health (WMH) survey initiative version of the World Health Organization (WHO) composite international diagnostic interview (CIDI). *International Journal of Methods in Psychiatric Research, 13*(2), 93–121.

Klapp, T., Klapp, A., & Gustafsson, J. (2023). Relations between students' well-being and academic achievement: Evidence from Swedish compulsory school. *European Journal of Psychology of Education*. https://doi.org/10.1007/s10212-023-00690-9

Lerner, R. M. (2001). Promoting promotion in the development of prevention science. *Applied Developmental Science, 5*, 254–257. https://doi.org/10.1207/S1532480XADS0504_06

Lerner, R. M., Lerner, J. V., Almerigi, J. B., Theokas, C., Phelps, E., & Gestsdottir, S., et al. (2005). Positive youth development, participation in community youth development programs, and community contributions of fifth-grade adolescents findings from the first wave of the 4-H study of positive youth development. *The Journal of Early Adolescence, 25*, 17–71. https://doi.org/10.1177/0272431604272461

Maddah, D., Saab, Y., Safadi, H., Abi Farraj, N., Hassan, Z., Turner, S., Echeverri, L., Alami, N. H., Kababian-Khasholian, T., & Salameh, P. (2021). The first life skills intervention to enhance well-being amongst university students in the Arab world: 'Khotwa' pilot study. *Health Psychology Open, 8*(1). https://doi.org/10.1177/20551029211016955

Merz, E. M., & Huxhold, O. (2010). Well-being depends on social relationship characteristics: Comparing different types and providers of support to older adults. *Ageing and Society, 30*(5), 843–857. https://doi.org/10.1017/S0144686X10000061

Myers, E., Drees, E. T., & Cain, J. (2022). An intervention utilizing the salience principle to reduce pharmacy students' psychological attraction to smartphones. *American Journal of Pharmaceutical Education, 86*(4), 330–337.

Noddings, N. (2005). What does it mean to educate the whole child? *Educational Leadership, 63*(1), 8.

Rotter, J. B. (1990). Internal versus external control of reinforcement: A case history of a variable. *American Psychologist, 45*(4), 489.

Sandelowski, M., & Leeman, J. (2012). Writing usable qualitative health research findings. *Qualitative health research, 22*(10), 1404–1413. https://doi.org/10.1177/1049732312450368

Sandstrom, G. M., & Dunn, E. W. (2014). Social interactions and well-being: The surprising power of weak ties. *Personality and Social Psychology Bulletin, 40*(7), 910–922. https://doi.org/10.1177/0146167214529799

Seligman, M. E. (2011). Flourish: A visionary new understanding of happiness and well-being. *Policy, 27*(3), 60–61.

Shamsuddin, A., & Abd Rahman, A. A. (2021). Abū Zayd Al-Balkhī's sustenance of the soul and the development of self-control. *Al-Itqan: Journal of Islamic Sciences and Comparative Studies, 5*(2), 99–115.

Singh, K., & Bandyopadhyay, S. (2021). Enhancing college students well-being: The psycho-spiritual well-being intervention. *Journal of Human Behavior in the Social Environment, 31*(7), 867–888. https://doi.org/10.1080/10911359.2020.1823294

Taylor, S. B., Kennedy, L. A., Lee, C. E., & Waller, E. K. (2022). Common humanity in the classroom: Increasing self-compassion and coping self-efficacy through a mindfulness-based intervention. *Journal of American College Health, 70*(1), 142–149. https://doi.org/10.1080/07448481.2020.1728278

Thamer Makbis, R., & Jabber Khalf, N. (2022). Psychological immunity of orphan female students. *Al-Mustansiriya Journal of Humanities, 1*, 250–258.

Tolcher, T., Cauble, M., & Downs, A. (2022). Evaluating the effects of gratitude interventions on college student well-being. *Journal of American College Health*, 1–5, https://doi.org/10.1080/07448481.2022.2076096

Waechter, R., Stahl, G., Rabie, S., Colak, B., Johnson-Rais, D., Landon, B., Petersen, K., Davari, S., Zaw, T., Mandalaneni, K., & Punch, B. (2021). Mitigating medical student stress and anxiety: Should schools mandate participation in wellness intervention programs? *Medical Teacher, 43*(8), 945–955. https://doi.org/10.1080/0142159X.2021.1902966

Zuhdi, M., & Syarief, K. (2023). Constructing the concept of student well-being within Indonesian Islamic higher education. *Religions, 14*(9). https://doi.org/10.3390/rel14091140

APPENDIX (A)

Examples of this session content were:

- The importance of visualizing life as a beautiful chance given by God to each individual
- The need to face challenges with a positive energy
- Spreading happiness and hope to others is part of getting mercy and blessings from Allah.
- Each individual is promised by Allah to have a happy, blessed, and satisfying life, as long as he/she is doing good for him/herself and others
- Muslims need to be strong from within and outside, to be supportive, to be humble, and to assist anyone in need, in order to achieve real happiness
- Why we are here, the story of existence, the chance to achieve here and in the next life after death

Another session involved an introduction to emotional management skills: the strategies of emotional management (individuals' ability to regulate thoughts, emotions, and behaviors) are given to students as follows:

- Realizing inner feelings
- Speaking with someone close to you
- Write down the negative feelings as an approach to remove them from the memory
- Consult a psychologist
- Read the Qur'an and perform daily prayers
- Support others so you can gain the satisfaction of giving
- Take a break
- Do something that you like to do
- Appreciate all the blessings that you have and you might not realize
- Stop overthinking and focus on improving yourself
- Be proud with your simplest achievements

Chapter 7

Students' wellbeing in online and blended Arabic as second and heritage language courses
Challenges and suggested solutions

Mohamed Mahgoub, Hany Fazza, and Martine Elie

Introduction

According to the World Health Organization (World Health Organization, 2024), 'Well-being is a positive state experienced by individuals and societies ... it is a resource for daily life and is determined by social, economic and environmental conditions.' While wellbeing applies to the health of individuals across their lifespan, student wellbeing has become a national/international construct due to its impact on student performance. Natural events such as the COVID-19 pandemic magnified the significance of wellbeing due to the disruption of various aspects of life, including academic, social, emotional, and psychological welfare. Additionally, they brought heightened awareness to investigating student wellbeing in higher education settings.

In 1948, the WHO introduced the concept of health as 'a state of complete physical, mental and social well-being and not merely the absence of disease or infirmity' (Breslow, 1972). According to Keyes (1998), social wellbeing is the evaluation of one's circumstances and effectiveness in society Furthermore, mental health is a state of wellbeing in which individuals can realize their full potential, manage life's challenges effectively, work productively, contribute to their community, and feel a sense of fulfillment (World Health Organization, 2001). Cognitive engagement can be defined as the level of personal investment that students have in their learning activities. This encompasses a range of factors, including their ability to self-regulate, commitment to mastery learning, and effective studying strategies (Sedeghat et al., 2011).

According to Adams et al. (2000), student wellbeing constitutes psychological, intellectual, emotional, physical, and spiritual aspects (in essence, it is the ability to balance school and life demands and/or expectations. While the concept of student wellbeing is well-researched, there remains a gap in the literature regarding an agreed-upon definition. Research in this area has traditionally focused mainly on wellbeing with limited focus on student-identified wellbeing challenges and proposed solutions. This chapter focuses on students' self-reports of wellbeing while learning Arabic as a foreign or heritage language online within the Arabian Gulf countries. More specifically, the chapter

DOI: 10.4324/9781003491613-7

delves into students' perceived challenges affecting their wellbeing and proposes student solutions.

Literature review and key concepts

The following section briefly reviews the relevant literature regarding four types/aspects of wellbeing and the key concepts underpinning this chapter.

Social wellbeing challenges

Several studies have shown that the transition to online learning has impacted students' wellbeing, posing social, physical, mental, and cognitive challenges for students.

Social presence is a crucial aspect of online learning environments, particularly in teacher-student and student-student interactions (Choo et al., 2020; Garrison et al., 2010). As Reio and Crim (2013) posit, social presence fosters a learning environment where students feel at ease and connected with their instructors and peers. When educators shifted from face-to-face to remote teaching, they faced challenges with online teaching, including a lack of student engagement. According to Hardy et al. (2023), educators frequently encounter challenges in comprehending the needs of their students in situations where communication is restricted, particularly in the absence of nonverbal cues and face-to-face interactions. This limitation can impede educators' ability to provide adequate support and guidance to their students, ultimately impacting academic performance and success.

In a recent study conducted by Biwer and others (2021), the researchers analyzed the effects of emergency remote learning on students' engagement and sense of connectedness with their peers. The study revealed a noticeable decline in students' understanding of connectedness with their peers, indicating that the transition to remote learning significantly impacted students' engagement and relationships with their peers and teaching staff. Moreover, the study highlighted the crucial role of social interaction and connectedness in learning, as students expressed missing personal contact with their teachers and peers. These findings emphasize a decreased sense of community and connectedness in remote learning environments (Biwer et al., 2021).

Studies have shown that incorporating collaborative learning activities like working in pairs or groups can increase students' interest and satisfaction in online learning. Hardy and others (2023) mentioned that educators commonly observe that students who form study groups perform better and have a stronger sense of wellbeing. However, according to Petillion and McNeil (2020), several students have expressed their discontent with the difficulties associated with remote group work, especially when coordinating across different time zones. To facilitate more collaborative learning, instructors can use scaffolding techniques and provide opportunities for study partners and group formation at the beginning of the course (Hardy et al., 2023).

According to recent studies, deactivating video cameras during online classes can negatively impact students' engagement and ability to form opinions about their peers (Castelli & Sarvary, 2021; Maimaiti et al., 2023). When cameras are turned off, students become less engaged and feel less socially present, leading to distractions and ultimately affecting their focus and participation (Maimaiti et al., 2023). Furthermore, the absence of nonverbal cues, such as facial expressions and body language, can hinder students from forming impressions of their classmates and instructors, detracting from the overall learning experience (Maimaiti et al., 2023).

On the other hand, video cameras have been found to foster collaboration, communication, self-regulation, and self-discipline among students (Sederevičiūtė-Pačiauskienė et al., 2022). When cameras are switched off, students may experience a sense of detachment, which can impede their participation and hinder their ability to form opinions about their classmates (Sederevičiūtė-Pačiauskienė et al., 2022). Therefore, it is crucial that students keep their cameras on during online classes to stay engaged and connected with their peers and instructors (Castelli & Sarvary, 2021; Maimaiti et al., 2023; Sederevičiūtė-Pačiauskienė et al., 2022).

Several studies, including Mayer (2012) and Molinari and others (2013), have explored turn-taking patterns in teacher-student talk. However, getting the teacher's permission to speak, time constraints, and other factors can limit engagement and peer collaboration in educational settings. Lin and other researchers (2015) found that teachers' instructional strategies are crucial in students' relational thinking during small-group collaborative discussions. Additionally, turn-taking and teacher control can affect peer collaboration, and the distribution of speaking opportunities can influence engagement and equity in participation (Lin et al., 2015).

In addition to turn-taking and how it limits learners' engagement in Arabic classes, the diglossic nature of Arabic adds to the challenges non-native Arabic language learners have. Regional dialects are commonly used in social interactions and media consumption more than Modern Standard Arabic (MSA), as shown by studies conducted by Al-Kahtany (1997) and Ryding (1991). However, there is a strong institutional preference for MSA in academic and media settings. This creates a diglossic situation – with two variations of the language: high (MSA) and low (dialects) (Ferguson, 1959) – that can be frustrating for non-native Arabic learners, who may require assistance applying what they have learned in the classroom to real-life communication, as Harbi (2022) noted. Moreover, Arabic heritage speakers face a challenge in the Arabic language classroom as the MSA taught in educational institutions differs from the colloquial dialects they may have used at home (Albirini, 2014).

Physical wellbeing challenges

The shift to online learning has brought concerns regarding students' physical wellbeing, with issues such as screen fatigue, eye strain, back pain, and headaches being common. These challenges can hinder students' academic performance and limit their exploration beyond the classroom. Agarwal and others (2022) have delved into the symptoms associated with increased screen time, including dizziness and screen fatigue. Similarly, Syahputri et al. (2020) and Shahriar and Koly (2021) have argued that students suffer from fatigue, headaches, and other physical discomforts due to excessive screen time. Similarly, Sharma and Sharma (2021) have highlighted that sustained use of screens beyond 3 hours a day can have adverse effects on both mental and physical health, leading to issues such as sleep disorders, musculoskeletal discomfort, stress, and eyesight problems.

Mental/emotional/psychological wellbeing challenges

Online learning has been associated with decreased motivation and heightened anxiety. Additionally, students may feel apprehensive about speaking up in class and miss out on opportunities for conversational practice. While specific individuals may find the privacy of virtual learning comforting, others may feel intimidated by the digital environment.

According to Elshami and others (2021), the COVID-19 pandemic caused a sudden shift to online learning, decreasing student motivation. Biwer and others (2021) found that the lack of social interaction and a stimulating atmosphere in virtual learning environments has lowered students' motivation levels. Maksoud (2018) highlighted that students may feel isolated in such settings. According to Damayanti and Listyani (2020), fear of making mistakes, embarrassment, lack of confidence, and fear of judgment can contribute to speaking anxiety in the classroom. For example, academic pressure and the need to perform well in speaking activities can exacerbate anxiety. Pahargyan (2021) highlights that speaking in a foreign language classroom can be particularly challenging due to fear of negative evaluation, worries about fluency and pronunciation, and limited vocabulary knowledge.

While some students may experience anxiety when learning online, others may find it beneficial. Shy or introverted students may feel more comfortable in an online setting, as it offers them a degree of anonymity and freedom from social pressure. This can enable them to participate more actively through written communication, such as chat features, discussion boards, or private messaging platforms, and alleviate any anxiety they may have about speaking in front of a group (Castelli & Sarvary, 2021; Maimaiti et al., 2023).

A prevalent issue concerning learners of MSA is anxiety related to using spoken MSA outside of the classroom. Bahruddin and Febriani (2020) highlighted that students perceived Arabic online learning as less effective due to the lack of instructions given by lecturers, limited internet connection, lack of internal motivation of students, and lack of discussion hours. Febriani (2021) mentioned that COVID-19 has adversely affected learning Arabic, especially online. The challenges faced by both Arabic as a Foreign Language (AFL) students and instructors include limited opportunities for interaction and collaboration, poor internet connectivity, and providing feedback (Febriani, 2021).

In contrast, research conducted by Yaniafari and Rihardini (2021) suggests that engaging in online speaking practice can create a more relaxed environment for students, which may ultimately lead to decreased levels of anxiety. Furthermore, the fear of negative evaluation was identified as a significant cause of anxiety. As a result, incorporating more supportive and non-threatening speaking activities, such as virtual classes or online discussion forums, could prove beneficial in reducing anxiety related to speaking Arabic outside of class.

Cognitive/intellectual wellbeing challenges

When it comes to cognitive and intellectual development, there are several challenges that students and instructors face in online learning environments. Students may need help to concentrate and fully engage with the material. According to Gao and Li's (2022) research, the design of online courses plays a crucial role in capturing and retaining students' attention. Gao noted that strategically incorporating animation can help enhance students' concentration, whereas relying solely on text can lead to quick disengagement. Furthermore, Hollister et al. (2022) found that technical issues, such as unreliable WiFi and poor physical environments, can negatively impact students' online learning experiences. These factors can contribute to difficulties with concentration while learning online. Kofoed and others (2021) reported that students in online classes reported lower levels of concentration than in-person classes, as evidenced by a significant decline in their perception of concentration.

Additionally, due to time constraints and a lack of opportunities for reflection, students may need help to evaluate their learning properly. According to Ariani and Tawali (2021), not having a structured classroom and face-to-face interactions can create challenges when organizing study schedules and dedicating time to language learning activities. This can cause students to feel hurried and stressed, negatively affecting their ability to evaluate their progress. Moreover, the lack of immediate feedback and reduced social interactions in online learning environments can limit opportunities for reflection on language learning. This absence of feedback and interaction may impede students' ability to accurately assess their language skills, as Rahman et al. (2022) noted.

Furthermore, practicing spoken MSA can be difficult for students in their home countries, especially under lockdown conditions. According to Yaniafari and Rihardini (2021), the Arabic online learning system could have been more efficient. This was due to unclear instructions, minimal facilitation, and inadequate monitoring, which resulted in a lack of response from students. Albirini (2014) mentioned that learners might have difficulty practicing and improving their spoken MSA skills due to the prevalence of colloquial dialects in daily interactions and the limited exposure to MSA outside formal educational settings.

Feedback is essential for students' growth, but instructors may need help offering detailed, personalized, and constructive feedback due to time constraints and their lack of being trained to provide it, especially in an online context. Additionally, the sudden transition to online teaching has presented technical obstacles, and educators have had to learn to use new technologies for facilitating the communication between instructors and students such as Learning Management Systems (LMS), such as Moodle, Canvas, Blackboard, and Google Classroom. Moreover, as Paris (2022) observed, unstable home internet connections and technical glitches have compounded the difficulties of providing feedback.

The above brief review illustrates the interconnectedness and intertwining among the four aspects/types of wellbeing and how they influence each other. It also demonstrates the gap in the literature and the scarcity of evidence and information that this chapter attempts to provide regarding the wellbeing challenges university students can face in online and blended learning in the context of MSA. This gap reveals the need for empirical evidence such as that provided in this chapter.

Design, methodology, and context

This section illustrates the mixed method design followed in the current research project. It presents the research questions for the exploratory phase and the subsequent explanatory phase, the theoretical framework based on which the questions in the exploratory phase were developed, and the analysis approach adopted in each phase. Furthermore, it describes the sample and sampling approach and some brief details about the context of the study and ethical approval granted by the Institutional Review Board (IRB).

This chapter is based on a small-scale research project that adopted the mixed-method exploratory-sequential approach (Fetters et al., 2013). First, the research team used an open-ended questionnaire – developed across the lines of the Community of Inquiry (CoI) framework based on Arbaugh and others (2008) and Swan et al. (2008), with a specific focus on social, cognitive, and teaching presences of the CoI Framework (Garrison & Archer, 2000) – and collected qualitative data to answer the following research questions:

RQ1: What challenges do students face when engage in an online Arabic course in an online Arabic course during the COVID-19 lockdown?
RQ2: What solutions do these students propose to improve their engagement in this course?
RQ3: What policy recommendations can be proposed to promote students' engagement in online Arabic courses in the future?

The team conducted a thematic analysis (Braun & Clarke, 2012) of the qualitative data collected through the online open-ended questionnaire completed by 13 students (10 non-native speakers of Arabic at elementary or intermediate proficiency level according to the American Council on the Teaching of Foreign Languages [ACTFL, 2021] plus 3 heritage speakers of Arabic at the advanced level). The analysis focused on identifying the emerging codes and themes that answer the two research questions: (1) What challenges do students face regarding their social, physical, mental/emotional/psychological, and cognitive/intellectual wellbeing?

And (2) What solutions do students propose for achieving their social, physical, mental/emotional/psychological, and cognitive/intellectual wellbeing?

Second, the emerging themes – particularly the challenges faced during Arabic online courses – informed building a questionnaire with a four-point scale; we used this questionnaire with a group of 49 students, 30 of whom were Arabic Heritage Learners (AHL) at the Intermediate level, 10 AHL at the elementary level, plus nine non-native speakers of Arabic at intermediate level (ACTFL, 2021) in the target International Branch Campus (IBC). These students were asked to rank each set of challenges under each type/aspect of wellbeing (social, physical, mental, and cognitive) from the least challenging to the most challenging.

This project adopted a convenience, purposive sampling approach because it targeted a specific small group of MSA learners experiencing wellbeing challenges during and following the COVID-19 pandemic. Participants formed two groups of undergraduate students studying Arabic courses at the target IBC; the first group constituted 13 students who were studying online Arabic courses under COVID-19 lockdown in Spring 2021, and the second group comprised 49 students who studied online courses under COVID-19 and were studying Arabic in face-to-face classes in February 2024 at the target IBC. Ethical approval was granted for this research project by the target IBC IRB.

Key findings and discussion

The following section presents and discusses the key findings based on both (1) the qualitative data collected through the exploratory phase of this project using the open-ended questionnaire and (2) the quantitative data collected during the second phase, in which a closed-ended questionnaire was used. First, the key findings emerging from the participants' narratives are presented and discussed under the four types/aspects of wellbeing: (1) social, (2) physical, (3) mental (emotional/psychological), and (4) cognitive/intellectual wellbeing. This section presents and discusses the challenges our participating students identified and the solutions they proposed for these challenges. Although each aspect/type of wellbeing is presented separately below, these aspects/types are closely interconnected and intertwined and influence each other. For example, the physical aspect impacts the social and psychological aspects. The psychological aspect is affected by the physical effects, the social, and so on. Second, the results and charts based on the quantitative data collected through the closed-ended questionnaire – during phase two – are presented and discussed below; the sections of findings are based on qualitative data.

Social wellbeing

A set of intertwined themes emerged under social wellbeing. Our participating students identified challenges such as insufficient communication, inadequate collaborative learning and peer collaboration, and the inability to socialize in or outside of class, which all contributed to the lack of a sense of community.

Insufficient communication

The participating students described their inability to communicate sufficiently with their peers in online courses and classes. For example, Student # 1 said, 'Hardly anyone talks during online classes.' Student # 10 highlighted that there was not sufficient 'emphasis on speaking' activities. Student # 2 attributed this to 'the language barrier' among students, especially those who are non-native speakers of the Arabic language. Student # 5 highlighted students' fear of making mistakes [errors] when communicating in the Target Language (MSA).

Our participants' experience regarding scarcity of communication – as peers and students in online Arabic classes – concurs with what Damayanti and Listyani (2020) claimed, illustrating the adverse effect of fear of making mistakes when speaking in online classes. Other participants, e.g., Student # 6 blamed the lack of communication on the instructors, saying that they had to 'take turns to speak' and had to 'gain [instructor's] permission to speak' Mayer (2012) and Molinari and others (2013) highlighted how turn-taking influences student-teacher communication. Student # 11 said, 'It gets intimidating speaking in online class' and blamed this on not knowing other students and inability to bond with them. Other students – such as Student # 7 – claimed that they could not communicate with their peers – especially Muslim females – when they 'turned their cameras off' as they were attending online classes from home, and putting the video camera on may have exposed some of their homes' privacy. The same student explained that 'internet ... instability and interruptions' – especially for students locked down in their home countries outside the Qatar-based campus – increased communication challenges during online classes.

To overcome these challenges, our participants suggested that the Arabic course instructors 'encourage students to speak and participate' (Student # 11), that students should not be afraid of making errors, and that instructors should allow and encourage students' errors while communicating in the Arabic language. Another participant proposed that instructors should ask all students to keep their 'cameras on' and be ready to be 'called upon' to participate and engage in class activities (Student # 4). The effective role of keeping video cameras on in online courses has been reiterated by scholars such as Maimaiti and others (2023), Sederevičiūtė-Pačiauskienė and others (2022), and Castelli et al. (2021). To motivate students to talk, Student # 1 suggested that instructors include class participation as part of the course assessment. In addition, participants suggested using Moodle and other digital communication applications, such as WhatsApp, so that students could add their contributions whenever they had internet access.

Lack of peer collaboration

Students underscored the lack of peer collaboration. They claimed that instructors provided too much input in an instructor-led and fronted teaching manner (c.f. Lin et al., 2015). To improve students' collaborative learning, Student # 11 suggested that the instructors encourage students to speak and participate through role plays, and Student # 7 stated that 'students turn their cameras on,' especially during pair and group work so that students know each other and feel comfortable to learn collaboratively. The same student emphasized that instructors should help students break the ice through warm-up activities and give students opportunities to choose their learning partners and group members in pair and group work activities. That student said, 'Professors [should] provide space where students meet one another before being put in breakout rooms' for group work. Additionally, student (# 2) suggested that instructors use 'group activities, breakout rooms, and quizlet challenges' to increase students' collaborative learning.

Difficulty of developing a sense of community

Our participating students underscored the difficulty of building a sense of community in the online context; this echoes what Biwer and others (2021) claimed about the reduced feeling of community and connectedness in such a context. For example, Student # 1 said, 'Sense of community fades away [in online context]' and attributed this to 'absence of real communication.' This highlights the need for real-life, task-based, project-based, and active learning rather than sticking to didactic and rote learning. Participants also blamed the lack of sense of community on the difficulty of forming impressions about peers whom they had not collaborated or bonded with and the difficulty of appreciating different perspectives and views because they had rarely had 'deep discussions' using the Target Language (MSA) and that they could not form impressions about their peers when they switch their video cameras off. The critical role of putting video cameras on and how it positively affects forming peer impressions have been highlighted by Maimaiti and others (2023) and Castelli et al. (2021).

Participant # 12 suggested instructors train students '*to be able to voice their opinions and critique ideas in a respectful way.*' Other participants encouraged instructors to set clear peer negotiation rules, guidelines, and rubrics and ensure students adhered to these. Student # 1 suggested creating break-out rooms for students' collaborative learning and communication. In addition to the instructors' role in helping students know and collaborate, more students – e.g., Students # 2 and 4 – suggested that students themselves form their learning communities, using media such as WhatsApp, to communicate and bond outside of class. Student # 5 commended the idea, saying, '*The sense of community outside of class can be a great idea.*' Student # 11 suggested that instructors '*allow students to speak and share their ideas and feedback*' as this may help them '*bond and cooperate*' with their peers and will help them '*feel more comfortable.*'

As Figures 7.1–7.4 illustrates, the second group of our participants reported that difficulty in developing a sense of community was the most challenging for them if we tally both challenging and most challenging (N=33), next was insufficient communication (N=32), and the least challenging was lack of peer collaboration (N=26). This underscores the significance of building a sense of community, belonging, and communication for enhancing students' social wellbeing in an online context.

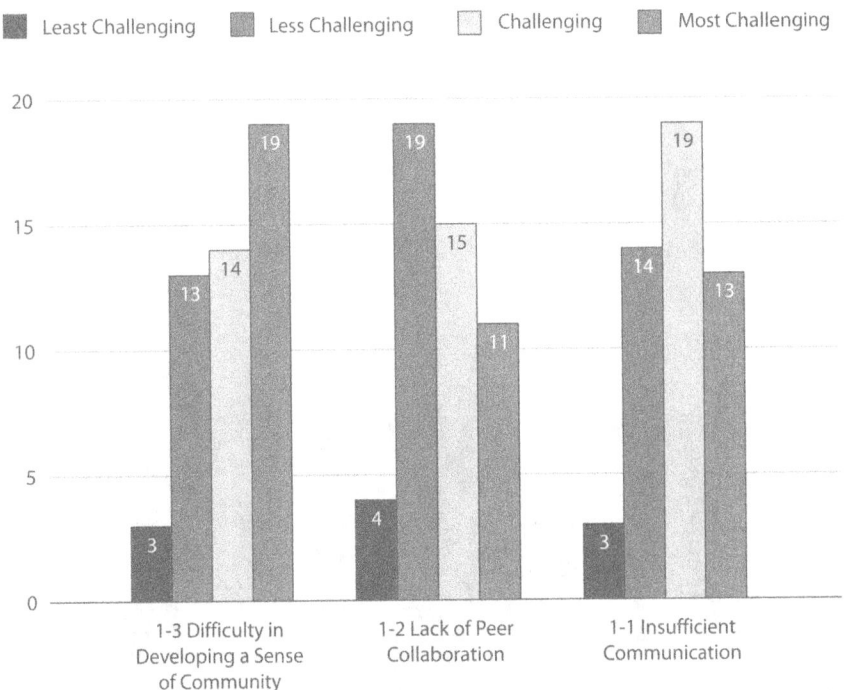

Figure 7.1 Ranking of Social Wellbeing Challenges.

Physical wellbeing

Participants underscored the lack of physical wellbeing associated with their online Arabic course and the adverse impact of these on their cognitive and social wellbeing. For general screen fatigue, Student # 1 said, '*Increased screen time causes fatigue and dizziness.*' These have been also underscored by Agarwal and others (2022). Participants explained that general fatigue lowered their motivation and '*discouraged [their] exploration [of using TL] outside of class time*' (Student # 4). Participants also described how extended screen time causes '*headache, back pain, loss of sense of time*' in addition to eye strain (Student # 8). This aligns with what Sharma and Sharma (2021) found regarding the adverse impact of screen time on eyesight and what Shahriar and Koly (2021) reported regarding headaches caused by excessive screen time. In addition to its adverse impact on concentration and motivation, our participants reported that physical fatigue, back pain, and eye strain lowered their participation in online classes and their 'peer-to-peer interaction' and communication. To overcome these challenges, our participants suggested that instructors ask students to use paper and pens/pencils to do paper-based activities and work individually or collaboratively to perform out-of-class, project-based activities. They also recommended that students do role plays as part of pair and group work, which requires students to stand up and move during the online class. They also advised instructors to design short, engaging activities and insert stretch-ups

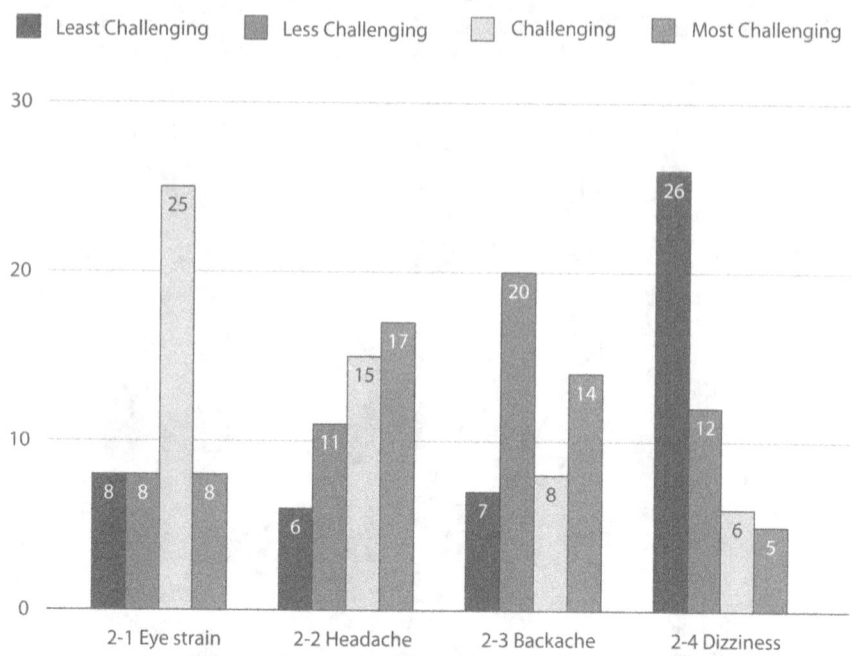

Figure 7.2 Ranking of Physical Wellbeing Challenges

among these activities and that instructors do these stretch-ups with the students to maintain their physical wellness.

As Chart 2 shows, the second group of our participants found that the severest challenge for them (N=33) was eye strain; next was headache (N=32) and backache (N=22), while they ranked dizziness as less/least challenging. This can be attributed to the risk posed by screen time on eyesight and its relation to headaches. Backache and dizziness can last as students could stand up or move their legs while in online classes. However, we should have discussed this ranking with our participating students.

Mental/emotional/psychological wellbeing

Anxiety

Our participants claimed that online and virtual learning contexts in general, and their Arabic courses in particular, triggered anxiety and intimidation. For instance, Student # 7 claimed that even group discussions in break-out rooms could be '*anxiety-inducing*' if students do not know their peers in the group. This was reiterated by Student # 11, who emphasized that students need to know each other and break the ice before the instructor puts them in pairs or groups. Other students such as # 12 attributed such anxiety to having to receive the instructor's feedback in the presence of other students. Damayanti and Listyani (2020) argued that fear of being judged makes students anxious to speak in class. While giving presentations face-to-face in class is intimidating, some of our participants explained that presenting in online classes is double intimidating as they may not see the faces of their audience. To increase self-confidence in Arabic online classes, our participants proposed that instructors do warm-up, ice-breaking, engaging pair and group speaking activities, as well as task and project-based assignments that help students participate and collaborate in online classes. This supports what Yaniafari and Rihardini (2021) suggested, namely, that engaging students in speaking activities in a safe and relaxed learning environment decreases their anxiety. Our participants also suggested that instructors give students more credit for '*researching [language-related topics] beyond the class content*' (Student # 7). Student # 8 recommended practicing Arabic even with oneself to build confidence, saying, '*I go back to the basics and hold up a conversation with myself.*' Probably, they meant talking to themselves in the mirror.

Low motivation

As explained above, being in an online course could be associated with lowered motivation due to physical factors, such as fatigue and eye strain, or social factors, such as the inability to communicate, collaborate, or bond with peers in class. The adverse effect of lack of communication and collaboration in online courses on lowering students' motivation was reported by Biwer and others (2021). Participant # 4 attributed lack of motivation to lowered '*concentration*,' which, in turn, was blamed on physical hardships and lack of interaction and communication with peers and instructors. Participants also attributed their low motivation to their instructors' inability to link what they teach in class to their real lives or students' inability to apply what they learned in real-life situations. As Student # 7 said, '*[I'm] not feeling motivated to go beyond class content.*' Another student attributed their lack of motivation to use the language outside of class to their inability to do so because they did not have time (Student # 8).

Other participants also attributed their lack of motivation in their online Arabic courses to their instructors' inability to use real-life, engaging activities, sticking to their textbook, instructors' tendency to use turn-taking for students to answer or participate, and having to get instructors' permission whenever they need to talk or participate. While our participants reported how turn-taking and instructors' control of who to participate lowered their motivation, Mayer (2012) and Molinari and others (2013) underscored the adverse effect of turn-taking and instructors' control of students' participation on students' engagement. Student # 3, for example, complained that '*online activities were mostly related to the [text]book, and not everyday context*' and proposed '*it would be helpful if activities from newspaper, articles, or movies ... are included as well.*' This is consistent with what Student # 5 suggested, namely, that instructors use materials and activities related to '*different*

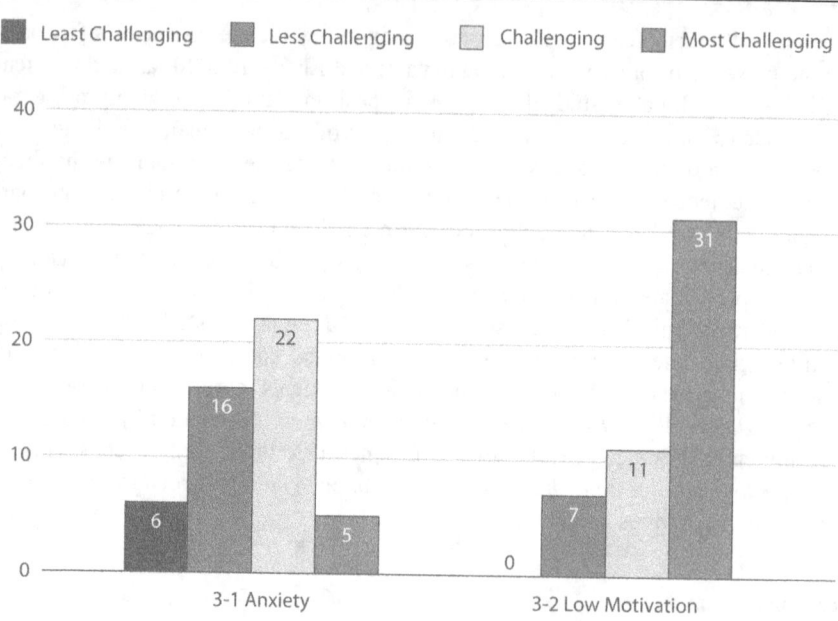

Figure 7.3 Mental/Psychological Wellbeing Challenges

interesting topics: cultural, economic and current events.' Students also considered some activities in their online courses to be too challenging and were rushed by the instructor due to time constraints. Student # 5 said, '*Practice drills ... were not easy.*'

As Chart 3 illustrates, most of our participating students (N=42) in the second group considered low motivation more challenging than anxiety as experienced in online courses. This underscores the key significance of motivation for online learning.

Cognitive/intellectual wellbeing

Our participants reported weak concentration in online classes, indicating they could not reflect on their learning and apply what they learned, especially in speaking MSA outside their classes. They did not receive sufficient, constructive feedback from their Arabic instructors.

Insufficient instructor's constructive feedback

Participants complained about a lack of timely, detailed, personalized, and constructive feedback and a lack of a comfortable, safe environment for receiving feedback. They also complained about the instructor's inability to give personalized feedback in a formative, ongoing way that could have helped them enhance their learning. Ariani and Tawali (2021) reported a lack of feedback in online courses due to time constraints. Student # 4 said, '*Timely feedback wasn't always there.*' and added, '*Providing feedback would have been helpful and encouraging if it is personalized.*' In line with this, Student # 2 suggested that their work should be assessed '*on time*' and that instructors should modify their instructional plans to accommodate students' learning needs and use office hours to provide extra support and detailed, personalized feedback for students who need it. Student # 7 said that they received only '*grades*' without '*clear rubrics as to how/why someone received the marks they got.*' For example, Student # 8 – wished the instructor had provided a '*detailed explanation of [their] understanding of the language and how [they] can improve it.*' In addition to feedback, students pointed out they needed instructors' explanations and '*encouragement*' to improve their learning. Emphasizing the need for appropriate context for giving and receiving feedback, Student # 12 said, '*Having a safe, comfortable environment where mistakes [errors] are accepted and not judged or ridiculed is the key to creating a safe, thriving space for learning.*'

Lack of students' reflection on their learning

Our participants underscored the lack of reflection on their learning in the online Arabic courses due to intensive course content, rush, lack of instructors' recap and revision of past learning, and lack of self-assessment techniques that could have enhanced their meta-cognitive skills. Rahman and others (2022) and Ariani and Tawali (2021) highlighted how insufficient feedback caused a lack of student reflection. For instance, Student # 4 said, '*There often was not enough time or attention from the instructor to repeated/detailed explanations, and I wish the instructor paid more attention to repeating and explaining new concepts, especially when seeing students struggling.*' Emphasizing the need for reflection, Student # 5 said, '*Reflection would have been beneficial; many of the mistakes [errors] that we made were repeated ones.*' This sheds light on the need for training students on how to reflect on their learning using techniques such as exit tickets, through which students identify what they learned and what they need to improve. While exit tickets are used at the end of a learning session/class, instructors could have used the KWL model at the beginning and the end of their online instructional sessions. In the beginning, they get their students to identify what they know about a particular concept of the Target Language and what they want to learn. At the end of the learning session, students ask themselves and share what they learned during the session/class. The KWL model engages students in identifying what they need to learn and helps them reflect on what they learned at the end of each class (AlAdwani et al., 2022).

Difficulty of applying the target language

As mentioned in the section on low motivation above, our participants reported that it was difficult for them to apply the target language, especially speaking in

MSA, outside their online classes; they attributed this challenge to factors such as the diglossic nature of Arabic, which has a high variation called 'Fus-ha' in Arabic, and other low variations (dialects), especially in the spoken form. Additionally, it was difficult for them to practice spoken MSA – while being locked down in their countries under COVID-19. Moreover, native and Arabic heritage speaking classmates tended to communicate either in their relevant colloquial Arabic or in a fluent second language, e.g., English. The course focuses on MSA more than spoken dialects added to the difficulty of using MSA outside classes. The challenge of applying MSA speaking due to the diglossic nature of Arabic was addressed in the literature. Harbi (2022) highlighted such a hardship for non-native learners of Arabic and recommended that they need to be trained on how to use MSA to communicate in real life. Similarly, Albirini (2014) addressed how hard it is even for AHL to use MSA outside of classrooms.

Highlighting the adverse impact of being in online courses, Student # 1 said, '*My confidence in speaking Arabic with natives decreased as a result of the online mode of instruction.*' Reiterating this, Student # 9 said, '*I was in my home country and had no one to speak Arabic to.*' Student # 2 attributed the challenge of speaking in MSA versus dialects to the lack of '*entertainment content*' in MSA online compared to that in dialects and the fact that their Arab colleagues prefer to speak and practice Arabic in their respective dialects rather than MSA – which is more challenging. Student # 3 reiterated the difficulty in applying 'Fus-ha,' saying, '*I did not find it [Fus-ha] very much applicable to everyday usage in speaking.*' However, they underscored that studying MSA did help them read and understand written texts. In the same vein, while Student # 4 said, '*Studying MSA ... brings a lot of challenge with application to real life,*' Study # 5 thought of it as a *mental hurdle*' that is very hard to overcome. In order to overcome this challenge, our participants proposed that their instructors train them more on speaking MSA in class using role plays and formal interviews and dialogues. For example, Student # 9 recommended '*encouraging more speaking interactions during classes.*' Student # 12 urged instructors to build students '*confidence in speaking and writing*' on everyday topics. They also proposed conducting open debates on everyday issues, using media content in MSA from sources such as the Al Jazeera Arabic network.

Lowered concentration

While scholars attributed lowered concentration in an online context to various factors, including poor course design (Gao and Li, 2022) and lack of attractive animations and Hollister and others (2022) to unreliable internet connection, some of our participants attributed it to extended screen time during online classes. For example, Student # 11 said, '*You doze off and are unable to focus in class.*' Other participants claimed that even instructors may lose focus due to increased screen time and associated fatigue. The fatigue experienced in online classes, in addition to the didactic approach, drove some students to say, '*I often tend to forget what I learnt from the course.*' (Student # 3). As illustrated above, our participants

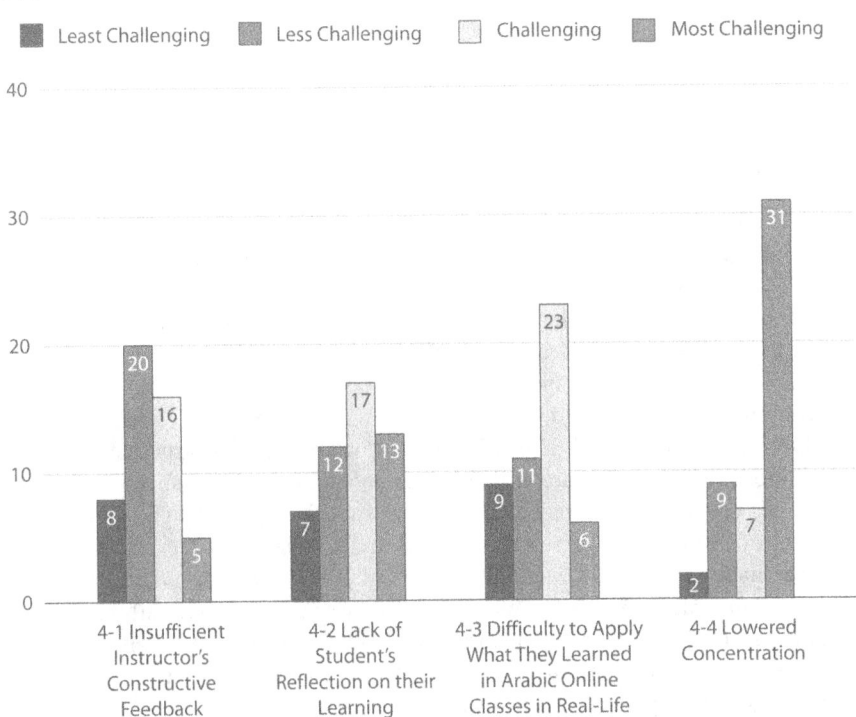

Figure 7.4 Cognitive Wellbeing Challenges

suggested that instructors apply engaging and diversified activities in their online courses and use various methods so that students take the lead in their learning during online classes.

As illustrated in Chart 4, participants in the second group ranked the above four types of cognitive wellbeing challenges, from the most challenging to the least challenging, in the following order: (1) lowered concentration (N=38), (2) lack of students' reflection (N=30), (3) difficulty to apply what they learned in Arabic online classes in real-life (N=29), and (4) insufficient instructor's constructive feedback (N=21).

Limitations and further research

Although this chapter is based on empirical qualitative and quantitative data, adopts the exploratory-sequential mixed method approach, and fills in a gap in the literature about this particular topic, the authors would have liked to increase the number of participants in both phases of the research, especially the second one where quantitative data is collected. In addition, we would have liked to discuss the ranking of the challenges with a sample of the second group in a focus group.

The researchers intend to do so in the future and would like to invite other researchers to engage with the findings presented in this chapter and replicate and extend the methodology followed here.

Conclusion and recommendations

This chapter aimed to provide an understanding of student perceptions of wellbeing within an online and blended Arabic course context. The findings revealed that students reported challenges across the social, physical, mental, and cognitive aspects of wellbeing. More specifically, the following themes emerged: insufficient communication, inadequate collaborative learning and peer collaboration, inability to socialize in or outside of class, eye strain, headaches, back pain, low motivation, anxiety, lowered concentration, lack of student reflection, difficulty to apply what they in real-life, and insufficient instructor's constructive feedback. In addition, students provided a number of potential solutions to the challenges identified. Given that the student self-reported wellbeing challenges reiterate the findings of researchers such as Damayanti and Listyani (2020), Mayer (2012), Molinari and others (2013), Maimaiti and others (2023), Castelli and others (2021), Sederevičiūtė-Pačiauskienė and others (2022), Garwal and others (2022), Sharma and Sharma (2021), Shahriar and Koly (2021), and Yaniafari and Rihardini (2021), it is essential for foreign language educators to consider reported student self-identified wellbeing challenges and solutions such as:

- Requiring student participation and use of video cameras
- Creating opportunities for students to form a sense of community via peer collaboration opportunities
- Incorporating opportunities for physical movement/stretching during class to combat physical fatigue
- Engaging students in warm-up speaking activities to decrease anxiety
- Providing students with feedback and time for self-reflection on their learning in the online context when designing and implementing online foreign language instruction courses.

Additionally, given the cultural implications of practices within the Arabian Gulf region (i.e., the Muslim practice of female modesty and covering), it is not uncommon for female students to refrain from turning on the video camera in remote learning situations and/or meetings. Instructors who are teaching online and/or blended Arabic language courses to heritage language learners should consider the convergence of culture, online instruction, and wellbeing. Based on student reports of difficulty in building a sense of community in the online context, instructors should highlight the requirement for the online/blended learning context to mirror the formal face-to-face learning context, thereby requiring students to turn their cameras on. While this applies to numerous academic subjects, it is crucial for foreign language classes such as Arabic, which require students to engage with each other and/or the instructor during conversational exchanges/repetition. Requiring students to turn on their video cameras will not only impact the student's sense of community but may also affect student engagement.

Due to the limited sample size coupled with the modified instruction methodology that occurred as a result of the COVID-19 pandemic, this study should be replicated with a larger sample size that is more familiar with online instruction methods. This should include exploring wellbeing related to more content-specific curriculum areas to investigate if student self-perception of wellbeing is impacted by more interactive and/or academically challenging content curricula (i.e., stem vs humanities). These findings could be used to inform curriculum-specific student wellbeing considerations and solutions for course design. Additionally, these findings highlight the need to promote active, engaging, and collaborative learning activities as well as use real-life examples and simulations in online and blended learning Arabic teaching contexts.

The findings also underscore the need for training Arabic instructors on creating safe and comfortable learning and teaching online environments, where students are encouraged to make errors, use target language, and try self and peer correction and teaching. Moreover, the findings encourage Arabic programs in similar contexts to be prepared with engaging online content and activities and to train Arabic instructors and students in working online (synchronous and asynchronous) and in blended teaching and learning contexts. It is also important that Arabic instructors are trained to give constructive, personalized feedback in these contexts. Finally, we recommend that Arabic instructors in similar contexts train their students how to reflect on their learning and ensure their students' physical, social, psychological, and cognitive wellbeing.

References

Actfl.org. 2021. *Home. ACTFL* [online]. Available at: https://www.actfl.org/ [Accessed 24 January 2024].

Adams, T. B., Bezner, J. R., Drabbs, M. E., Zambarano, R. J., & Steinhardt, M. A. (2000). Conceptualization and measurement of the spiritual and psychological dimensions of wellness in a college population. *Journal of American College Health*, 48(4), 165–173. https://doi.org/10.1080/07448480009595692

Agarwal, K., Manza, P., Tejeda, H. A., Courville, A. B., Volkow, N. D., & Joseph, P. V. (2023). Risk assessment of maladaptive behaviors in adolescents: nutrition, screen time, prenatal exposure, childhood adversities-adolescent brain cognitive development study. *Journal of Adolescent Health*. https://doi.org/10.1016/j.jadohealth.2023.08.033

Agarwal, R., Tripathi, A., Khan, I. A., & Agarwal, M. (2022). Effect of increased screen time on eyes during COVID-19 pandemic. *Journal of Family Medicine and Primary Care*, 11(7), 3642. https://doi.org/10.1080/07448480009595692

AlAdwani, A., AlFadley, A., AlGasab, M., & Alnwaiem, A. F. (2022). The effect of using KWL (know-want-learned) strategy on reading comprehension of 5th grade EFL students in Kuwait. *English Language Teaching*, 15(1), 79–91. https://doi.org/10.5539/elt.v15n1p79

Albirini, A. (2014). The role of the colloquial varieties in the acquisition of the standard variety: The case of Arabic heritage speakers. *Foreign Language Annals, 47*(3), 447–463. https://doi.org/10.1111/flan.12087

Al-Kahtany, A. H. (1997). The 'problem' of diglossia in the Arab world: An attitudinal study of modern standard Arabic and the Arabic dialects. *al-'Arabiyya, 30*, 1–30.

Arbaugh, J. B., Cleveland-Innes, M., Diaz, S. R., Garrison, D. R., Ice, P., Richardson, J. C., & Swan, K. P. (2008). Developing a community of inquiry instrument: Testing a measure of the community of inquiry framework using a multi-institutional sample. *The Internet and Higher Education, 11*(3–4), 133–136. https://doi.org/10.1016/j.iheduc.2008.06.003

Ariani, S., & Tawali, T. (2021). Problems of online learning during Covid-19 pandemic in speaking for professional context class. *Jo-ELT (Journal of English Language Teaching) Fakultas Pendidikan Bahasa & Seni Prodi Pendidikan Bahasa Inggris IKIP, 8*(1), 32–37. https://doi.org/10.33394/jo-elt.v8i1.3783

Bahruddin, U., & Febriani, S. R. (2020). Student's perceptions of Arabic online learning during COVID-19 emergency. *Journal for the Education of Gifted Young Scientists, 8*(4), 1483–1492. https://doi.org/10.17478/jegys.763705

Biwer, F., Wiradhany, W., Oude Egbrink, M., Hospers, H., Wasenitz, S., Jansen, W., & De Bruin, A. (2021). Changes and adaptations: How university students self-regulate their online learning during the COVID-19 pandemic. *Frontiers in Psychology, 12*, 642593. https://doi.org/10.3389/fpsyg.2021.642593

Braun, V., & Clarke, V. (2012). *Thematic analysis*. American Psychological Association. https://doi.org/10.1037/13620-004

Breslow, L. (1972). A quantitative approach to the World Health Organization definition of health: Physical, mental and social well-being. *International Journal of Epidemiology, 1*(4), 347–355. https://doi.org/10.1093/ije/1.4.347

Castelli, F. R., & Sarvary, M. A. (2021). Why students do not turn on their video cameras during online classes and an equitable and inclusive plan to encourage them to do so. *Ecology and Evolution, 11*(8), 3565–3576. https://doi.org/10.1002/ece3.7123

Choo, J., Bakir, N., Scagnoli, N. I., Ju, B., & Tong, X. (2020). Using the community of inquiry framework to understand students' learning experience in online undergraduate business courses. *TechTrends, 64*, 172–181. https://doi.org/10.1007/s11528-019-00444-9

Damayanti, M. E., & Listyani, L. (2020). An analysis of students' speaking anxiety in academic speaking class. *Eltr Journal, 4*(2), 152–170. https://doi.org/10.37147/eltr.v4i2.70

Elshami, W., Taha, M. H., Abuzaid, M., Saravanan, C., Al Kawas, S., & Abdalla, M. E. (2021). Satisfaction with online learning in the new normal: Perspective of students and faculty at medical and health sciences colleges. *Medical Education Online, 26*(1), 1920090. https://doi.org/10.1080/10872981.2021.1920090

Febriani, S. R. (2021). Investigating the problems of learning Arabic for Islamic universities in the era of COVID-19 pandemic. *International Journal of Language Education, 5*(4), 324–336. https://scholar.uinib.ac.id/id/eprint/276; https://doi.org/10.26858/ijole.v5i4.19732

Ferguson, C. A. (1959). Diglossia. *Word, 15*(2), 325–340. https://doi.org/10.1080/00437956.1959.11659702

Fetters, M. D., Curry, L. A., & Creswell, J. W. (2013). Achieving integration in mixed methods designs—Principles and practices. *Health Services Research, 48*(6pt2), 2134–2156. https://doi.org/10.1111/1475-6773.12117

Gao, Q., & Li, S. (2022). Impact of online courses on university student visual attention during the COVID-19 pandemic. *Frontiers in Psychiatry, 13*, 848844. https://doi.org/10.3389/fpsyt.2022.848844

Garrison, D. R., Anderson, T., & Archer, W. (2010). The first decade of the community of inquiry framework: A retrospective. *The Internet and Higher Education, 13*(1–2), 5–9. https://doi.org/10.1016/j.iheduc.2009.10.003

Garrison, D. R., & Archer, W. (2000). A transactional perspective on teaching and learning: A framework for adult and higher education. *Advances in learning and instruction series*. Elsevier Science, Inc.

Harbi, A. M. (2022). Arabic diglossia and its impact on the social communication and learning process of non-native Arabic learners: Students' perspective. *Arab World English Journal*, *1*, 46. https://dx.doi.org/10.24093/awej/th.283

Hardy, D., Holdsworth, J., Suwanwiwat, A. H., Bandara, W., Altena, S., Watson, J., & Myers, T. (2023). *Enhancing social presence while balancing teacher and student wellbeing*. Report. Australian Council of Deans of Information and Communications Technology (ACDICT), Wadalba, NSW, Australia. Retrieved from: https://researchonline.jcu.edu.au/80197/

Hollister, B., Nair, P., Hill-Lindsay, S., & Chukoskie, L. (2022). Engagement in online learning: Student attitudes and behavior during COVID-19. *Frontiers in education* (Vol. 7, p. 851019). Frontiers Media SA. https://doi.org/10.3389/feduc.2022.851019

Keyes, C. L. M. (1998). Social well-being. *Social Psychology Quarterly*, *60*, 121–140. https://doi.org/10.2307/2787065

Kofoed, M., Gebhart, L., Gilmore, D., & Moschitto, R. (2021). *Zooming to class?: Experimental evidence on college students' online learning during Covid-19*. IZA discussion paper (14356). https://papers.ssrn.com/sol3/papers.cfm?abstract_id=3846700

Lin, T. J., Jadallah, M., Anderson, R. C., Baker, A. R., Nguyen-Jahiel, K., Kim, I. H., Kuo, L. J., Miller, B. W., Dong, T. & Wu, X. (2015). Less is more: Teachers' influence during peer collaboration. *Journal of Educational Psychology*, *107*(2), 609. https://doi.org/10.1037/a0037758

Maimaiti, G., Jia, C., & Hew, K. F. (2023). Student disengagement in web-based videoconferencing supported online learning: An activity theory perspective. *Interactive Learning Environments*, *31*(8), 4883–4902. https://doi.org/10.1080/10494820.2021.1984949

Maksoud, N. F. A. (2018). When virtual becomes better than real: Investigating the impact of a networking simulation on learning and motivation. *International Journal of Education and Practice*, *6*(4), 253–270.

Mayer, S. J. (2012). Classroom discourse and democracy: Making meanings together. *Educational psychology: Critical pedagogical perspectives* (Vol. 13). Peter Lang.

Molinari, L., Mameli, C., & Gnisci, A. (2013). A sequential analysis of classroom discourse in Italian primary schools: The many faces of the IRF pattern. *British Journal of Educational Psychology*, *83*(3), 414–430. https://doi.org/10.1111/j.2044-8279.2012.02071.x

Pahargyan, T. (2021). Anxiety in speaking English during distance learning. *UC Journal: ELT, Linguistics and Literature Journal*, *2*(1), 1–13. https://doi.org/10.24071/uc.v2i1.3240

Paris, B. (2022). Instructors' perspectives of challenges and barriers to providing effective feedback. *Teaching and Learning Inquiry*, *10*. https://doi.org/10.20343/teachlearninqu.10.3

Petillion, R. J., & McNeil, W. S. (2020). Student experiences of emergency remote teaching: Impacts of instructor practice on student learning, engagement, and well-being. *Journal of Chemical Education*, *97*(9), 2486–2493. https://doi.org/10.1021/acs.jchemed.0c00733

Rahman, M. A., Novitasari, D., Handrianto, C., & Rasool, S. (2022). Challenges in online learning assessment during the Covid-19 pandemic. *Kolokium Jurnal Pendidikan Luar Sekolah*, *10*(1), 15–25. https://doi.org/10.24036/kolokium.v10i1.517

Reio, T. G., Jr, & Crim, S. J. (2013). Social presence and student satisfaction as predictors of online enrollment intent. *American Journal of Distance Education*, *27*, 122–133. https://doi.org/10.1080/08923647.2013.775801

Ryding, K. C. (1991). Proficiency despite diglossia: A new approach for Arabic. *Modern Language Journal*, 212–218. https://doi.org/10.2307/328829

Sedaghat, M., Abedin, A., Hejazi, E., & Hassanabadi, H. (2011). Motivation, cognitive engagement, and academic achievement. *Procedia-Social and Behavioral Sciences*, *15*, 2406–2410. https://doi.org/10.1016/j.sbspro.2011.04.117

Sederevičiūtė-Pačiauskienė, Ž, Valantinaitė, I., & Asakavičiūtė, V. (2022). Should I turn on my video camera?'The students' perceptions of the use of video cameras in synchronous distant learning. *Electronics, 11*(5), 813. https://doi.org/10.3390/electronics11050813

Shahriar, S., & Koly, F. J. (2021). A cross-sectional study on Bangladeshi students regarding physiological challenges of online education. *Pharmacy Education, 21*, 267–275. https://doi.org/10.46542/pe.2021.211.267275

Sharma, M., & Sharma, P. (2021). Effect of online classes on physical and mental well-being of students during COVID-19. *Indian Journal of Physical Therapy and Research, 3*(2), 98–101. https://doi.org/10.4103/ijptr.ijptr_57_21

Swan, K., Shea, P., Richardson, J., Ice, P., Garrison, D. R., Cleveland-Innes, M., & Arbaugh, J. B. (2008). *Validating a measurement tool of presence in online communities of inquiry. e-mentor, 2*(24). https://www.e-mentor.edu.pl/_xml/wydania/24/543.pdf

Syahputri, V. N., Rahma, E. A., Setiyana, R., Diana, S., & Parlindungan, F. (2020). Online learning drawbacks during the Covid-19 pandemic: A psychological perspective. *EnJourMe (English Journal of Merdeka): Culture, Language, and Teaching of English, 5*(2), 108–116. https://doi.org/10.26905/enjourme.v5i2.5005

World Health Organization. (2001). *The world health report 2001: Mental health: New understanding, new hope.* World Health Organization.

World Health Organization. 2024. *Promoting well-being* [online]. Available at: https://www.who.int/activities/promoting-well-being [Accessed 11 February 2024].

Yaniafari, R. P., & Rihardini, A. A. (2021). Face-to-face or online speaking practice: A comparison of students' foreign language classroom anxiety level. *JEELS (Journal of English Education and Linguistics Studies), 8*(1), 49–67. https://doi.org/10.30762/jeels.v8i1.3058

Chapter 8

Beyond borders

Understanding wellbeing in higher education through culturally appropriate measures

Herdiyan Maulana and Gumgum Gumelar

Introduction

The rising incidence and severity of mental health issues among students pose a significant concern for universities worldwide. During the pandemic academic year 2020–2021, the WHO World Mental Health International College Student initiative launched an extensive poll in eight countries to estimate the prevalence of mental health issues among college students (Chen & Lucock, 2022). The survey results indicated that over one-third of first-year college students met to be diagnosed with at least one mental health problem. Overall, 45.5% of the responses indicated the presence of DSM-IV mental disorders categories, including major depression, anxiety, panic disorder, alcohol dependency, and substance use disorder. Similar to the world trend above, the prevalence of mental health issues among young people is also considered a significant public health threat in Asian higher education sector (Hernández-Torrano et al., 2020). Recent data reveals that approximately one-fifth of Asian students experienced mental health issues over the course of the 12-month period amid the COVID-19 pandemic (Lipson et al., 2022). This issue is further exacerbated by the challenging conditions in low and middle-income countries (LMICs) in a number of Asian countries, where mental health resources are limited and counseling services are not routinely provided in the universities.

Optimal mental health is an essential component of one's overall state of wellbeing. Good mental health is associated with a greater sense of wellbeing, feelings of competence, and the ability to effectively manage life stressors (Hernández-Torrano et al., 2020). The relationship between mental health and wellbeing is bidirectional. Poor mental health can lead to reduced overall quality of life, which potentially leads to individual mental health issues and vice versa. A considerable body of evidence serves a support of the link between an individual's sense of wellbeing and positive outcomes in aspects of life, including personal health, financial stability, and educational success. Research has demonstrated a strong correlation between wellbeing and improved physical health (Davidson et al., 2010), increased job satisfaction (Yuan, 2015), and enhanced academic achievement among students (Rüppel et al., 2015).

DOI: 10.4324/9781003491613-8

The presence of wellbeing and positive psychological functions substantially contribute to the level of success among university students (Suldo et al., 2006). According to the Organisation for Economic Co-operation and Development (OECD) report (Durand, 2015), students' psychological satisfaction is just as important as their intellectual capacities in the classroom for predicting academic success. Psychological wellbeing plays an important role for university students as it regulates a wide array of skills and traits that are essential for effective learning. These include academic preparedness, emotional resilience, social adaptation, and independent living skills. These skills assist students in effectively maneuvering through the intricate and frequently demanding academic environment, leading to enhancing possibility of their overall success.

Considering the importance of wellbeing in shaping an individual's quality of life, numerous international institutions and nations have incorporated wellbeing as a key component in their national education policies (e.g., Finland, New Zealand, Canada, and Australia) (Cummins et al., 2003; Kelly, 2012). These countries have chosen to prioritize their higher educational approach focusing on promoting physical and psychological wellbeing, social-emotional learning, and inclusivity that involves community partners and educators. This effort is seen as not just a moral obligation but a practical necessity for nurturing well-rounded, successful students.

The concept of wellbeing has been extensively studied in the field of psychology and relevant areas over the past 30 years (Diener et al., 1999, 2018). Nevertheless, the majority of wellbeing research has been carried out in Western countries, such as Australia, Europe, and North America. This area of study identifies essential aspects and models of wellbeing that are currently used by scholars worldwide. Literature suggests that there were numerous ways to measure wellbeing and saw that it could be assessed in both unidimensional and multidimensional ways (Cummins et al., 2003). The unidimensional scale aims to measure wellbeing as a single construct that evaluates particular individual aspect separately (e.g., satisfaction with life, positive/negative emotions). The multidimensional perspective suggests wellbeing as a condition where people feel and think about their lives based on their psychological, social, and cultural contexts. This assessment approach took account both individual universal needs, such as physical health and financial condition, as well as relative socio-cultural demands, which refer to things that are mostly valued by individuals respective to their social and cultural context.

While the effort to fully comprehend wellbeing has made significant progress, a persistent challenge consists in figuring out how this concept is assessed in a cross-cultural setting, given that the existing model and instrument practices are mainly Western-oriented. An accurate assessment of individual wellbeing levels is an important step toward establishing a foundation for developing programs and policies that would help students, academic community, and the existing resources to achieve the highest possible level of wellbeing. This chapter seeks to elucidate the importance of measuring wellbeing in cross-cultural context and the continuing advances in this attempt within the academic sphere. In addition, this chapter will also offer arguments on the significance of measuring wellbeing in a way that is attuned to diverse cultural nuances of students in higher education context.

Wellbeing in the higher education context

Throughout history, humans have engaged in a deep reflection to inquire what is happiness. The origins of wellbeing theory may be traced back to the early philosophers in multiple cultures and traditions (e.g., Aristotle, Al-Ghazali). These early thinkers engaged in discussions of happiness within the context of ethical and moral theories, which laid the foundation for the evolution of the modern wellbeing theory (Polansky, 2014). Early Greek thinkers identified two primary paradigms of wellbeing: the eudaimonia and the hedonistic approaches (Waterman, 1993). The eudaimonia derived from the Greek word means "happiness or welfare" and denotes a completely individual functional existence to achieve what is best in life (Ryff, 1989). The hedonic perspective of wellbeing is rooted from the normative hedonism theory, which focuses on the individual desires for satisfaction and the avoidance of pain (Kahneman et al., 1999). This hedonic perspective of happiness is frequently translated as the subjective wellbeing (SWB) term, which is the sum of the scores of an individual sense of life satisfaction level and emotional equilibrium (Diener et al., 1985).

Additionally, the concept of happiness has evolved and is now commonly referred to as wellbeing within the field of psychology and related disciplines. The American Psychological Association (APA) defines wellbeing as the condition of an individual who holds an optimistic viewpoint on life, experiences happiness, feels minimal levels of stress, becomes satisfied with their life, and enjoys physical and mental health. While most of the Western-based published works defined wellbeing as both personal satisfaction and successful accomplishments (e.g., Huppert, 2009), this concept involves individual experience of positive emotions like fulfillment and joy, as well as realizing one's potential, having autonomy, finding purpose, and fostering positive interpersonal relationships.

Existing studies have demonstrated that students who demonstrate higher levels of wellbeing have a reduced likelihood of encountering various psychological and interpersonal issues, such as depression, general anxiety disorder, and challenges in making connection with others (e.g., Durand, 2015; Evans et al., 2018). Adolescents who engage in physical fitness and healthy behaviors, such as eating nutritious foods and getting enough exercise, have also been found possessing higher level of wellbeing. Conversely, a high prevalence of substance use, including smoking, alcohol, and marijuana, is associated with negative wellbeing (Allen & Holder, 2014). In the classroom setting, teachers report fewer incidents of student misbehavior, greater levels of self-control, and regulation compliance among students with higher level of psychological wellbeing.

Following the facts above, university life presents a unique set of challenges and experiences that require individual psychological preparedness. This psychological capacity will help students deal with stress and problems that come up while they are studying. Students entering university often encounter a significant social transition that demands adaptability, resilience, and a range of psychological and social skills (Slavich & Auerbach, 2018). College students are considered to be in the emerging adulthood stage of mental development, which spans the years between childhood and early adulthood. Characteristics of social development at this age include growing independence from parents and other adults, a preoccupation with the future, changes in roles in society, and volatility in interpersonal relationships. They often face instability during this transition, which can lead to decreased social support and heightened distress levels.

A longitudinal study among university students revealed a U-shaped developmental trajectory that influenced student's life satisfaction during their time at the university (Shek et al., 2017). Specifically, there was a decline in the second year followed by a consistent improvement in the third and fourth years. Research conducted by Hernández-Torrano et al. (2020) demonstrates that a lower sense of wellbeing among university students can have both immediate and long-term effects on their psychological health functions. Students with lower level of wellbeing have been found to have negative impacts on college attendance, academic performance, social engagement, and course completion in the short run (e.g., Antaramian, 2015; King & Datu, 2017). The long-term consequences include relationship problems (Kerr et al., 2017), recurring mental health issues, termination of studies, decreased rates of employment, and lower income (Ferguson et al., 2007).

A recent study involving first-year students from institutions in Europe, Asia, Western Pacific, and the Americas discovered notable connections between low level of wellbeing and individual social capital. Students who possessed poorer social capital at both the interpersonal level (such as having low confidence in others, less close friendships, and least involvement in community activities) and the macro level (such as the low social-economic background of their family/community) exhibited a greater likelihood of experiencing lower level of wellbeing. Predominant research findings have also found a strong correlation between students' social-economic status and wellbeing. It has been observed that students who are dealing with financial challenges tend to have a lower level of wellbeing. However, a recent study suggests that the correlation mentioned above may become stronger as the pandemic continues to impact society worldwide (Yan & Gai, 2022).

The challenges in learning situations escalated during the COVID-19 pandemic due to the prevalent uncertainty related to the post-pandemic period and anticipated economic downturn. Researchers believe that considering the effects of COVID-19 pandemic and anticipated social changes in society which are responsible for mental health vulnerability among adolescents, it is crucial for policymakers and higher education professionals to place their attention on the concept of wellbeing (Dessauvagie et al., 2022). Universities being closed and students transitioning to online education, a departure from the traditional learning experience, may have heightened students' apprehensions about successfully completing the academic year. This situation is increasing the risk of learning losses, which could have a detrimental impact on the mental health of vulnerable students (Chu & Li, 2022).

Numerous studies conducted during the pandemic have indicated that university students could have been specially susceptible to mental health disorders as a result of the challenging academic life. These psychological conditions arise from the pressure of striving for success in times of uncertainty, social isolation due to direct social interaction no longer taking place, and financial issues that might encountered during studying. Problems with mental health can have far-reaching consequences, and if neither the students nor the institution take action to address them, they can escalate into larger problems with financial and physical consequences (Donohue & Bornman, 2021).

Based in our discussion above, we conclude that there are a number of factors that would help students to achieve wellbeing during their study period at the university. These factors can be classified as internal and external sources. Internal factors include individual personality traits (DeNeve & Cooper, 1998), intrinsic motivation (Ryan & Deci, 2001), self-esteem (X. Li & Zheng, 2014), and subjective life evaluations (Diener & Chan, 2011). By contrast, external factors encompass an individual's cultural and social backgrounds. These include a range of influences from economic circumstances and social norms to religious beliefs, demographic characteristics, and environmental conditions (Delle Fave et al., 2023; Jovanović, 2016; Stubbe et al., 2005). Meanwhile Lomas (2015) classifies wellbeing-related factors as either universal or culturally relative. Universal factors comprise all human needs and conditions that are supposed to be fulfilled irrespective of individual cultural or social backgrounds (e.g., traditions, customs, and beliefs). Relative factors refer to the psychological needs or traits that reflect the cultural and social variations of an individual, such as the significance attributed to certain things within individual traditions or norms perspective.

Nevertheless, several studies demonstrate the inconsistency in using these indicators to predict student wellbeing in the higher education setting. For example, research has shown that while wealth is a reliable indicator of wellbeing in developed countries, students in middle- to low-income countries with greater socio-economic status do not always experience higher levels of wellbeing (Ferrer-i-Carbonell, 2005). A cross-cultural investigation conducted by Oshio et al. (2011) indicates that in relation to happiness, individuals from Asian cultures (e.g., Japan and Korea) prefer to consider the standard of living of their reference group (e.g., family and relatives) rather than their own financial status as a significant factor contributing to their happiness.

Wellbeing in Asian social-cultural context

In response to the previous concern on wellbeing in higher education context, extensive research focus on this topic has been initiated worldwide; however, most of these studies were primarily conducted in the WEIRD (Western, Educated, Industrialized, Rich, and Democratic) nations (Hernández-Torrano et al., 2020). The majority of wellbeing research conducted in these nations defines wellbeing in the context of individualism and secularism. The ideological underpinnings of this framework were responsible for a significant impact on the development of theories and assessment methods for wellbeing globally.

On the other hand, comprehensive wellbeing research in non-Western countries, which primarily consist of low- and middle-income societies (LMIS), is limited. As a result, discussion about factors contributing to wellbeing research and discussions often do not adequately consider non-Western social and personal values perspectives. Lu (2005) explains that research on wellbeing in Western societies focuses on individual attributes, such as autonomy, freedom, and personal achievement as the primary factors in predicting wellbeing. However, the discussion of traditional Eastern cultural values' impact on wellbeing has received little attention. These values, including a sense of belonging, spirituality, and social bonding, have been identified as essential markers of individual mental health but have received little attention in Western studies as variables driving wellbeing.

Recent literature has emphasized that different social-cultural settings, such as a nation's socio-economic conditions and cultural orientations, may result in distinct understandings of wellbeing and varied patterns of connection among key factors related to it. Knoop and Delle Fave (2013) suggest that prevalent meaning of wellbeing is likely to be varied and non-Western developing nations, characterized by distinct cultural and value systems, may present challenges for the generalizability of existing wellbeing understandings.

Social and cultural perspectives encompass a set of social norms, values, and systems that develop in certain geographical regions, commonly associated with both Western and Eastern cultural classifications (Markus & Kitayama, 1991). In Western societies, there is a strong emphasis on individualism, where personal interest, autonomy, and preferences take precedence over social interests (Jetten et al., 2002). Individuals are encouraged to be competitive and motivated by personal interests in pursuit of the highest living standard. When assessing the individual's quality of life, these values assign significant importance. The notion of self within this society is intricately linked to the general belief that individuals possess the right to make decisions following their own personal preferences. Secularism is a prominent value that is closely linked to this society as it holds a significant influence on individual daily life practices, including how people perceive what a satisfactory life is.

Li and Bond (2010) illustrate how different factors can have varying effects on wellbeing in different cultural contexts. Their research posits that the presence of robust religious values serves as a predictor of individual satisfaction; however, this relationship may be more intricate than initially perceived. Further investigations have revealed that the Human Development Index (HDI) suggests that the alignment between individual and societal values plays a crucial role in how religious values impact life satisfaction in a particular society (Yin et al., 2023). For instance, European countries with high HDI levels tend to have significantly higher life satisfaction compared to countries with low HDI (Yin et al., 2023). Many of the countries with low HDI are located in Asia and Africa. This demonstrates how HDI serves as a social catalyst, reshaping people's perspectives and fundamental values about what constitutes a good quality of life. Most European countries with high HDI levels tend to embrace secularism in their social life, while many countries with low HDI have a cultural foundation rooted in strong religious values. This leads to societal shifts, as stated by Allen et al. (2007), with the West and developed countries endorsing secularist principles, such as individual autonomy, equality, and freedom, as benchmarks for a meaningful life in typical Western societies.

Conversely, Eastern societies are primarily shaped by the collectivistic culture (Hofstede, 1991), which prioritizes group affiliation and loyalty above individual interests (Hofstede & Hofstede, 2005). Priority is given to group aspirations and harmony over personal matters in these societies, including those in Asia. Group affiliation holds significant importance since it serves as the foundation for constructing an individual's social identity. The Eastern society highly recommended for individuals to participate in various societal groups, including family, local community, jobs, and education institutions.

Asian culture typically displays a hierarchy in the allocation of power and positions which are often influenced by gender orientation (Jetten et al., 2002). Males are often seen as caretakers of the family and act as breadwinners, while females typically bear the responsibility of nurturing the family and managing domestic tasks. In the Eastern society, family and kinship connections are highly regarded as a significant social reference point. As a result, parents and other relatives have a considerable influence on an individual's personal life. As an illustration, MacDonald and other researchers (2012) demonstrate that Asian couples place significant importance on obtaining family acceptance as a crucial aspect for the sustainability of their relationship, rather than only relying on personal choices. Following that, age was also identified as a significant determinant of interpersonal interactions in the Eastern society. Trommsdorff and Schwarz (2007) discovered that individuals from Asian backgrounds often prioritize avoiding conflict through acts of respect and deference toward elders, striving to uphold societal harmony. Additionally, it is noted that communities within Asian communities are distinguished by their strong cultural traditions and significant spiritual aspirations, which are deeply embedded and play an important role in guiding both communal and personal conduct. In short, Asian civilization is deeply rooted in tradition and incorporates religious principles into nearly every facet of daily life.

Studies on wellbeing in the Eastern developing country are still considered as insufficient, relative to the large number of studies conducted in Western contexts. However, several wellbeing studies done in Asian countries have yielded interesting results. For example, Davey et al. (2009) reported important findings about how socio-economic status is not associated with the perception of quality of life in traditional Chinese villages. A similar finding was also concluded in a study by Nielsen et al. (2010) on Beijing urban worker's wellbeing. Other research conducted among the Indian population by Agrawal et al. (2011) reveals that there are significant differences in perceptions of happiness throughout the socio-demographic factors in India, where variations among gender, income, marital status, and education resulted in a variation on wellbeing dimensions. Another study by Parnami et al. (2013) showed that apart from their gender, religion played an important role in promoting happiness among Indian people. Subsequently, religious differences elicited a different sense of social identity in Indian society, where social identification with the group also played a substantial role in achieving happiness (Kumar et al., 2013).

Due to the growing concerns mentioned above, Diener (2009) initially emphasized the importance of accuracy in defining wellbeing in cross-cultural research. This involves careful attention to how wellbeing is understood and translated into culturally relevant tool for analysis. This phase is important to ensure that the measures we used are suitable and appropriate for the target society.

Findings: wellbeing measures in Asian cross-cultural context

The existing literature confirms that wellbeing is a multidimensional concept that encompasses multiple indicators of measurement (Bérenger & Verdier-Chouchane, 2007; Diener, 2009). Various scales exist for assessing these multiple dimensions of wellbeing, spanning a wide range of formats and categories. Linton et al. (2016) presented evidence of the existence of at least 99 instruments to assess wellbeing. Combined, these instruments include 190 distinct dimensions of wellbeing. The researchers synthesized six key dimensions covered by these current wellbeing measures, including mental health, social relations, physical health, spiritually, and psychological functioning (Linton et al., 2016). Researchers have systematically attempted to translate some of these scales into local languages; however, in-depth responses to the question of whether these surveys are culturally suitable for different populations in varied social-cultural context remain elusive (Sousa & Rojjanasrirat, 2011).

The multidimensional approach suggests certain wellbeing indicators are culturally subjective and pertain to specific societies, whereas others are universally objective and applicable across nations. Delle Fave and other researchers (2016) conducted a cross-cultural study involving 12 nations, which revealed diverse extended conceptions of wellbeing among participants. For instance, when using on Hofstede's cultural categorization (individualist/collectivist), individuals from highly individualistic nations (like New Zealand) are more likely to use high-arousal emotions (like joy, enthusiasm, and vitality) as measures of happiness than those from less individualistic nations (like India). A noteworthy development on the research agenda is the suggestion to examine wellbeing and culture in conjunction in order to attain a more thorough comprehension of the notion.

Furthermore, there has been a recent growth in the number of studies aiming at developing culturally sensitive wellbeing measures. The Chinese Happiness Inventory, developed by Lu and Shih (1997), is one of the first attempts at developing a cross-cultural wellbeing measure. The scale was one of the earliest to include a local interpretation of wellbeing in its measuring approach. This scale was developed through examining the factors that contribute to happiness in Chinese society using a thorough qualitative approach. The scale consists of 47 items that were created to gage the Chinese understanding of wellbeing by incorporating personal and social dimensions, such as the harmony relationships with family and friends, social connection, respect, fulfillment of material needs, work achievement, obtaining pleasure from helping others, and contentment with life. The psychometric properties of the scale have been validated and it has been consistently used to assess the level of happiness among Chinese participants (Barsasella et al., 2021; Lu & Hu, 2005; Zhang et al., 2009).

There is a growing momentum in the development of scales that adhere to different cultural themes. Some examples include the Inner Well-being (IWB) questionnaire developed by White et al. (2014), the Korean Community Well-being Index by Kim and Lee (2014), and the Singapore Mental Well-being Scale by Fen et al. (2013). The IWB was created to assist individuals in rural areas with lower socio-economic backgrounds. The scale was developed by the researchers using samples of people from rural areas in India. The scale was designed to give an alternative means of measuring wellbeing for individuals living in low social-economic conditions residing in developing countries. The IWB questionnaire assesses how individuals perceive their overall wellbeing, taking into account various aspects of their lives, including the political and cultural context. Another scale was developed by Manuela and Sibley (2015) using the Pacific Identity and Wellbeing Scale (PIWBS-R), which consists of six sub-scales that assess the perception of wellbeing among Pacific Islanders in multiple social domains. These domains include family, society as a whole, national identity, group membership, religious beliefs, and cultural unity. The scale was particularly designed for the collectivist cultural context of Pacific Islanders.

In their study, Maulana et al. (2019) developed the Indonesian Well-being Scale (IWS) which comprises 20 questions that assess four main components of wellbeing: basic necessities, relationships with others, self-acceptance, and spirituality. These components provide a distinct viewpoint on the Indonesian population's sense of happiness. The scale simultaneously considers universally recognized elements of wellbeing, such as personal interests, and places significant importance on culturally nuanced aspects of wellbeing specific to Indonesians, such as social connections and spirituality.

Given that wellbeing is a complex concept that is influenced by social and cultural factors, it is critical to acknowledge different cultural perspectives when choosing the correct approach to assess wellbeing. This attempt is particularly important within the university setting, as there are a growing number of inter-cultural interactions among students in academic institutions worldwide. Traditionally, wellbeing measures have been predominantly developed within the framework of the Western paradigm, emphasizing individualistic ideals. There is a growing recognition of the value of implementing culturally appropriate wellbeing indicators and measures with the aim to accommodate the increasing inter-cultural interaction in the university environment.

Discussion

Despite the global surge in research attention on the topic of wellbeing, there remains an urgent need to find an effective approach for deploying this concept into practical interventions, especially in cross-cultural educational settings. Researchers suggest that initiating an effective program relies upon obtaining an accurate definition and assessment of wellbeing (Lindert et al., 2015). Recent study findings highlight an increasing trend toward employing wellbeing measurement tools tailored to specific cultural and contextual realities, as evidenced by works from Collomb et al. (2012), Greco and Polli (2021), and Manuela and Sibley (2013). This movement reflects a deeper understanding that wellbeing is a complex, multifaceted concept that cannot be adequately captured by generic instruments. The development of these specialized tools is essential for improving the precision and relevance of wellbeing assessments across diverse demographic groups. Despite this trend, the field continues to rely on universal measures of wellbeing, such as the Satisfaction With Life Scale (Diener et al., 1985), SPANE (Diener et al., 2010), WEMWBS (Tennant et al., 2007), and the Personal Wellbeing Index (International Wellbeing Group, 2013). These tools aim for broad applicability but face challenges in balancing universality with the need to reflect context-specific aspects of wellbeing. This reliance underscores a critical tension in wellbeing research between the pursuit of a common metric and the recognition of diverse human experiences, including their diverse social-cultural backgrounds.

A systematic review conducted by Dessauvagie et al. (2022) on mental health studies among university students in Asian nations revealed that just 3 out of the 34 available studies employed culturally compatible instruments. The authors note the advantages of using a culturally specific, multidimensional instrument for measuring wellbeing. By employing a multidimensional approach to evaluating wellbeing, we could obtain a more comprehensive understanding of the particular factors that contribute to an attempt to establish an effective wellbeing program in higher education settings. As a result, we could be assured that the aspects of wellbeing assessed are pertinent to the target population.

Recent studies indicate that college students may be more prone to experiencing generalized anxiety disorder or depression or even thoughts of suicide and related behaviors in comparison to individuals of the same age who are not pursuing higher education. The situation is being referred to be a mental health crisis in higher education by Evans et al. (2018). The challenges are even greater as students' mental health has been greatly impacted by multiple concerns they encountered because of prior pandemic online learning.

Wellbeing is a psychological concept that is closely linked to an individual's subjective experiences, which are significantly shaped by social and cultural factors. This extends to individuals enrolled in universities. Higher education presents a wide range of challenges, including navigating inter-cultural relationships with fellow students, lecturers, and university staff. Therefore, it is crucial to take into account cross-cultural perspectives in the assessment of wellbeing.

There are significant shifts in most university students' mental health concerns over time with three main observations. First, students' life satisfaction has significantly worsened due to the impact of the shift to online learning during the pandemic. Second, following the above condition, there is a surge in demand for mental health support in the university contexts. Last, while our knowledge of mental health management in university settings has progressed, further investigation is needed to establish an accurate definition of happiness and a culturally appropriate assessment tool.

Over the past few decades, the number of young people from foreign nations who enroll in the West higher education institution has grown rapidly throughout the world. Although this higher education mobility has persisted for a while in the context of higher education, it frequently goes unnoticed that international students' enrollment in foreign institutions carries significant ramifications for the overall mental health of students hailing from diverse cultural backgrounds. According to the latest 2023 OECD data, there are significant increases in the migration of international students to the US, Canada, Australia, South Korea, and Japan in 2022. The number of permits issued to international students has increased by 42% relative to 2021, and by 30% across OECD European countries. Most international students come from China, India, and Vietnam, with close to 60% in 2021. This international students' mobilization gives rise to a social process called acculturation, which is described as a way of finding a balance between one's own culture and the culture of the country that one has migrated to.

The acculturation process is another significant factor that also contributes to the high prevalence of current mental health vulnerability among university students. Acculturation requires an individual psychological adaptation skill toward new environment and is an attempt to manage the anticipated psychological induced effect of cross-cultural interaction and transition. Acculturation is the result of individuals migrating across nations or regions, a phenomenon that is accelerating as a result of globalization, which has facilitated the exchange of knowledge and learning opportunities among individuals from different nations and cultures, leading to a wide range of remarkable possibilities and variances in higher education learning experiences. As a consequence of this, there is a process of cultural interchange or acculturation taking place. Nevertheless, the process of acculturation is frequently depicted as a source of stress for students studying abroad. One important attempt made by the university is initiating wellbeing programs that may help in assisting international students to navigate this transition.

Enhancing wellbeing at the university level encompasses more than simply helping individuals to maintain their academic achievement; it is essential for the university to adapt and foster optimal learning experiences. Emphasizing the importance of wellbeing in higher education policy is not only advantageous for students' mental health but also contributes to the improvement of the wellbeing of faculty, staff, and the academic community as a whole. The existing literature indicates that students who are better at managing stress, feeling satisfied with their self and academic performance, and establish healthy social relationship tend to perform better in social and academic lives (Niemiec et al., 2010).

Wellbeing should not be regarded as a supplementary element that could be deliberated upon or discounted in the event of additional time. The concept of wellbeing is indispensable and inherent to the essence of higher education learning. From this point of view, wellbeing is an essential attribute that every individual possesses, yet possibly to varying extents. Higher education institutions are expected to provide facilities and learning experiences that promote wellbeing. In spite of all of the challenges and chances that arise in students' learning experiences, university life signifies a unique phase that provides a valid and reliable wellbeing measurement tool.

Dessauvagie et al. (2022) argue that utilizing established wellbeing measures developed in Western contexts in a distinct cultural setting has many constraints. As previously noted, different cultural backgrounds may have different ways of experiencing, communicating, and interpreting mental health situations. In addition, individuals from low-income developing nations may face challenges with literacy and language comprehension when trying to understand and interpret the contextual meaning of the scale. Each of these challenges could point out bias and validity issues related to the instruments. Therefore, an important step for the universities to provide comprehensive mental health services for students would be to prioritize the development of a wellbeing assessment instrument that is attuned to individual social and cultural backgrounds. This culturally appropriate instrument would also have a significant role in the early detection of students' quality of life and mental health states.

This chapter presented an overview of the important implications of mental health policies and strategies designed to promote wellbeing in the university setting. We provide information demonstrating higher education institutions that consistently have adopted policies and practices involving wellbeing support programs are likely to observe not just enhanced student involvement and academic performance in a class but also an increasingly healthy academic community. To ensure the effective delivery of wellbeing programs in university settings, it is recommended that universities adopt a multitier strategy that involves establishing an accurate description of wellbeing and developing a culturally suitable wellbeing instrument.

Conclusion

Mental health issues are prevalent among university students worldwide. As a result, there has been an increasing pressure on universities to provide support services for students who are facing mental health issues. It is critical to take the required precautions to reduce the negative effect that may follow from the rise in international student mobility globally. While most university students report required mental health services available at their university, international students frequently find that the program and facilities are insufficient.

The university's inability to provide sufficient mental health support and providing an accurate as well as reliable wellbeing instrument for the international students has been identified as factors that contribute to the emergence of chronic behavioral disorders and exacerbates academic setbacks for vulnerable students. Universities are more than institutions that confer a degree; they also provide possibilities for social interaction and personal growth. Finally, we believe that the present chapter would lay an empirical basis for higher education researchers, practitioners, and policymakers to further explore the development and implementation of wellbeing measurements in higher education settings that are more adaptable to varied social and cultural contexts.

References

Agrawal, J., Murthy, P., Philip, M., Mehrotra, S., Thennarasu, K., John, J. P., Girish, N., Thippeswamy, V., & Isaac, M. (2011). Socio-demographic correlates of subjective well-being in urban India. *Social Indicators Research*, *101*(3), 419–434. https://doi.org/10.1007/s11205-010-9669-5

Allen, J., & Holder, M. D. (2014). Marijuana use and well-being in university students. *Journal of Happiness Studies*, *15*(2), 301–321. https://doi.org/10.1007/s10902-013-9423-1

Allen, M. W., Ng, S. H., Ikeda, K., Jawan, J. A., Sufi, A. H., Wilson, M., & Yang, K. S. (2007). Two decades of change in cultural values and economic development in eight East Asian and Pacific Island Nations. *Journal of Cross-Cultural Psychology*, *38*(3), 247–269. https://doi.org/10.1177/0022022107300273

Antaramian, S. (2015). Assessing psychological symptoms and well-being. *Journal of Psychoeducational Assessment*, *33*(5), 419–429. https://doi.org/10.1177/0734282914557727

Barsasella, D., Liu, M. F., Malwade, S., Galvin, C. J., Dhar, E., Chang, C.-C., Li, Y.-C. J., & Syed-Abdul, S. (2021). Effects of virtual reality sessions on the quality of life, happiness, and functional fitness among the older people: A randomized controlled trial from Taiwan. *Computer Methods and Programs in Biomedicine*, *200*, 105892. https://doi.org/10.1016/j.cmpb.2020.105892

Bérenger, V., & Verdier-Chouchane, A. (2007). Multidimensional measures of wellbeing: Standard of living and quality of life across countries. *World Development*, *35*(7), 1259–1276. https://doi.org/10.1016/j.worlddev.2006.10.011

Chen, T., & Lucock, M. (2022). The mental health of university students during the COVID-19 pandemic: An online survey in the UK. *PLOS ONE*, *17*(1), e0262562. https://doi.org/10.1371/journal.pone.0262562

Chu, Y.-H., & Li, Y.-C. (2022). The impact of online learning on physical and mental health in university students during the COVID-19 pandemic. *International Journal of Environmental Research and Public Health*, *19*(5), 2966. https://doi.org/10.3390/ijerph19052966

Collomb, J.-G. E., Alavalapati, J. R., & Fik, T. (2012). Building a multidimensional wellbeing index for rural populations in northeastern Namibia. *Journal of Human Development and Capabilities*, *13*(2), 227–246. https://doi.org/10.1080/19452829.2011.645532

Cummins, R. A., Eckersley, R., Pallant, J., van Vugt, J., & Misajon, R. (2003). Developing a national index of subjective wellbeing: The Australian unity wellbeing index. *Social Indicators Research*, *64*(2), 159–190. https://doi.org/10.1023/A:1024704320683

Davidson, K. W., Mostofsky, E., & Whang, W. (2010). Don't worry, be happy: Positive affect and reduced 10-year incident coronary heart disease: The Canadian Nova Scotia Health Survey. *European Heart Journal*, *31*(9), 1065–1070. https://doi.org/10.1093/eurheartj/ehp603

Davey, G., Chen, Z., & Lau, A. (2009). 'Peace in a thatched hut --that is happiness': Subjective wellbeing among peasants in rural China. *Journal of Happiness Studies, 10*, 239–252. https://doi.org/10.1007/s10902-007-9078-x

Delle Fave, A., Brdar, I., Wissing, M. P., Araujo, U., Castro Solano, A., Freire, T., Hernández-Pozo, M. D. R., Jose, P., Martos, T., Nafstad, H. E., Nakamura, J., Singh, K., & Soosai-Nathan, L. (2016). Lay definitions of happiness across nations: The primacy of inner harmony and relational connectedness. *Frontiers in Psychology, 7*. https://doi.org/10.3389/fpsyg.2016.00030

Delle Fave, A., Wissing, M. P., & Brdar, I. (2023). Beyond polarization towards dynamic balance: Harmony as the core of mental health. *Frontiers in Psychology, 14*. https://doi.org/10.3389/fpsyg.2023.1177657

DeNeve, K. M., & Cooper, H. (1998). The happy personality: A meta-analysis of 137 personality traits and subjective well-being. *Psychological Bulletin, 124*(2), 197–229. https://doi.org/10.1037/0033-2909.124.2.197

Dessauvagie, A. S., Dang, H.-M., Nguyen, T., & Groen, A. T. (2022). Mental health of university students in Southeastern Asia: A systematic review. *Asia Pacific Journal of Public Health, 34*(2–3), 172–181. https://doi.org/10.1177/10105395211055545

Diener, E. (2009). *Subjective well-being* (pp. 11–58). https://doi.org/10.1007/978-90-481-2350-6_2

Diener, E., & Chan, M. Y. (2011). Happy people live longer: Subjective well-being contributes to health and longevity. *Applied Psychology: Health and Well-Being, 3*(1), 1–43. https://doi.org/10.1111/j.1758-0854.2010.01045.x

Diener, E., Emmons, R. A., Larsen, R. J., & Griffin, S. (1985). The satisfaction with life scale. *Journal of Personality Assessment, 49*(1), 71–75. https://doi.org/10.1207/s15327752jpa4901_13

Diener, E., Lucas, R. E., & Oishi, S. (2018). Advances and open questions in the science of subjective well-being. *Collabra: Psychology, 4*(1). https://doi.org/10.1525/collabra.115

Diener, E., Suh, E. M., Lucas, R. E., & Smith, H. L. (1999). Subjective well-being: Three decades of progress. *Psychological Bulletin, 125*(2), 276–302. https://doi.org/10.1037/0033-2909.125.2.276

Diener, E., Wirtz, D., Tov, W., Kim-Prieto, C., Choi, D., Oishi, S., & Biswas-Diener, R. (2010). New well-being measures: Short scales to assess flourishing and positive and negative feelings. *Social Indicators Research, 97*(2), 143–156. https://doi.org/10.1007/s11205-009-9493-y

Donohue, D. K., & Bornman, J. (2021). Academic well-being in higher education: A cross-country analysis of the relationship between perceptions of instruction and academic well-being. *Frontiers in Psychology, 12*. https://doi.org/10.3389/fpsyg.2021.766307

Durand, M. (2015). The OECD better life initiative: *How's life?* and the measurement of well-being. *Review of Income and Wealth, 61*(1), 4–17. https://doi.org/10.1111/roiw.12156

Evans, T. M., Bira, L., Gastelum, J. B., Weiss, L. T., & Vanderford, N. L. (2018). Evidence for a mental health crisis in graduate education. *Nature Biotechnology, 36*(3), 282–284. https://doi.org/10.1038/nbt.4089

Fen, C. M., Isa, I., Chu, C. W., Ling, C., & Ling, S. Y. (2013). Development and validation of a mental wellbeing scale in Singapore. *Psychology, 04*(07), 592–606. https://doi.org/10.4236/psych.2013.47085

Ferguson, H., Bovaird, S., & Mueller, M. (2007). The impact of poverty on educational outcomes for children. *Paediatrics & Child Health, 12*(8), 701–706. https://doi.org/10.1093/pch/12.8.701

Ferrer-i-Carbonell, A. (2005). Income and well-being: An empirical analysis of the comparison income effect. *Journal of Public Economics, 89*(5–6), 997–1019. https://doi.org/10.1016/j.jpubeco.2004.06.003

Greco, F., & Polli, A. (2021). Security perception and people well-being. *Social Indicators Research, 153*(2), 741–758. https://doi.org/10.1007/s11205-020-02341-8

Hernández-Torrano, D., Ibrayeva, L., Sparks, J., Lim, N., Clementi, A., Almukhambetova, A., Nurtayev, Y., & Muratkyzy, A. (2020). Mental health and well-being of university students: A bibliometric mapping of the literature. *Frontiers in Psychology, 11*. https://doi.org/10.3389/fpsyg.2020.01226

Hofstede, G. (1991). Empirical models of cultural differences. In *Contemporary issues in cross-cultural psychology* (pp. 4–20). Swets & Zeitlinger Publishers.

Hofstede, G., & Hofstede, G. J. (2005). *Culture and organizations—Software of the mind: Intercultural cooperation and its importance for survival* (2nd ed.). McGraw Hill.

Huppert, F. A. (2009). Psychological well-being: Evidence regarding its causes and consequences†. *Applied Psychology: Health and Well-Being, 1*(2), 137–164. https://doi.org/10.1111/j.1758-0854.2009.01008.x

International Wellbeing Group (2013). *Personal Wellbeing Index: 5th Edition*. Australian Centre on Quality of Life, Deakin University http://www.acqol.com.au/instruments#measures

Jetten, J., Postmes, T., & McAuliffe, B. J. (2002). "We're all individuals": Group norms of individualism and collectivism, levels of identification and identity threat. *European Journal of Social Psychology, 32*(2), 189–207. https://doi.org/10.1002/ejsp.65

Jovanović, V. (2016). Trust and subjective well-being: The case of Serbia. *Personality and Individual Differences, 98*, 284–288. https://doi.org/10.1016/j.paid.2016.04.061

Kahneman, D., Diener, E., & Schwarz, N. (1999). *Well-being: The foundations of hedonic psychology* (D. Kahneman, E. Diener, & N. Schwarz, Eds.). Russell Sage Foundation. https://psycnet.apa.org/record/1999-02842-000

Kelly, A., Papadopoulos, A., Oyebode, J., Bäckmark Goodwill, H., & Halloran, E. (2012). The development of the Wellbeing Evaluation Scale. *British Journal of Mental Health Nursing, 1*(3), 162–170. https://doi.org/10.12968/bjmh.2012.1.3.162

Kerr, D. C. R., Gini, G., & Capaldi, D. M. (2017). Young men's suicidal behavior, depression, crime, and substance use risks linked to childhood teasing. *Child Abuse & Neglect, 67*, 32–43. https://doi.org/10.1016/j.chiabu.2017.02.026

Kim, Y., & Lee, S. J. (2014). The development and application of a community wellbeing index in Korean metropolitan cities. *Social Indicators Research, 119*(2), 533–558. https://doi.org/10.1007/s11205-013-0527-0

King, R. B., & Datu, J. A. (2017). Happy classes make happy students: Classmates' well-being predicts individual student well-being. *Journal of School Psychology, 65*, 116–128. https://doi.org/10.1016/j.jsp.2017.07.004

Knoop, H. H., & Delle Fave, A. (Eds.). (2013). *Well-being and cultures* (Vol. 3). Springer. https://doi.org/10.1007/978-94-007-4611-4

Kumar, D., Afroz, S., & Rao, M. K. (2013). Social identity and subjective well-being among Hindu and Muslim community. *Indian Journal of Health and Wellbeing, 4*(4), 872–874. https://www.proquest.com/scholarly-journals/social-identity-subjective-well-being-among-hindu/docview/1511429064/se-2?accountid=35143

Li, L. M. W., & Bond, M. H. (2010). Does individual secularism promote life satisfaction? The moderating role of societal development. *Social Indicators Research, 99*(3), 443–453. https://doi.org/10.1007/s11205-010-9591-x

Li, X., & Zheng, X. (2014). Adult attachment orientations and subjective well-being: Emotional intelligence and self-esteem as moderators. *Social Behavior and Personality: An International Journal, 42*(8), 1257–1265. https://doi.org/10.2224/sbp.2014.42.8.1257

Lindert, J., Bain, P. A., Kubzansky, L. D., & Stein, C. (2015). Well-being measurement and the WHO health policy health 2010: Systematic review of measurement scales. *The European Journal of Public Health, 25*(4), 731–740. https://doi.org/10.1093/eurpub/cku193

Linton, M.-J., Dieppe, P., & Medina-Lara, A. (2016). Review of 99 self-report measures for assessing well-being in adults: Exploring dimensions of well-being and developments over time. *British Medical Journal Open, 6*(7), e010641. https://doi.org/10.1136/bmjopen-2015-010641

Lipson, S. K., Zhou, S., Abelson, S., Heinze, J., Jirsa, M., Morigney, J., Patterson, A., Singh, M., & Eisenberg, D. (2022). Trends in college student mental health and help-seeking by race/ethnicity: Findings from the national healthy minds study, 2013–2021. *Journal of Affective Disorders, 306*, 138–147. https://doi.org/10.1016/j.jad.2022.03.038

Lomas, T. (2015). Positive cross-cultural psychology: Exploring similarity and difference in constructions and experiences of wellbeing. *International Journal of Wellbeing, 5*(4), 60–77. https://doi.org/10.5502/ijw.v5i4.437

Luo, L. (2005). In pursuit of happiness: The cultural psychological study of SWB. *Chinese Journal of Psychology, 47*(2), 99–112. http://dx.doi.org/10.6129/CJP.2005.4702.01

Lu, L., & Hu, C.-H. (2005). Personality, leisure experiences and happiness. *Journal of Happiness Studies, 6*(3), 325–342. https://doi.org/10.1007/s10902-005-8628-3

Lu, L., & Shih, J. B. (1997). Personality and happiness: Is mental health a mediator? *Personality and Individual Differences, 22*(2), 249–256. https://doi.org/10.1016/S0191-8869(96)00187-0

MacDonald, G., Marshall, T. C., Gere, J., Shimotomai, A., & Lies, J. (2012). Valuing romantic relationships. *Cross-Cultural Research, 46*(4), 366–393. https://doi.org/10.1177/1069397112450854

Markus, H. R., & Kitayama, S. (1991). Cultural variation in the self-concept. In *The self: Interdisciplinary approaches* (pp. 18–48). Springer.

Manuela, S., & Sibley, C. G. (2013). The Pacific Identity and Wellbeing Scale (PIWBS): A culturally-appropriate self-report measure for Pacific peoples in New Zealand. *Social Indicators Research, 112*(1), 83–103. https://doi.org/10.1007/s11205-012-0041-9

Manuela, S., & Sibley, C. G. (2015). The Pacific Identity and Wellbeing Scale-Revised (PIWBS-R). *Cultural Diversity and Ethnic Minority Psychology, 21*(1), 146–155. https://doi.org/10.1037/a0037536

Maulana, H., Khawaja, N., & Obst, P. (2019). Development and validation of the Indonesian Well-being Scale. *Asian Journal of Social Psychology, 22*(3), 268–280. https://doi.org/10.1111/ajsp.12366

Nielsen, I., Paritski, O., & Smyth, R. (2010). Subjective well-being of Beijing taxi drivers. *Journal of Happiness Studies, 11*(6), 721–733. https://doi.org/10.1007/s10902-009-9170-5

Niemiec, C. P., Ryan, R. M., & Deci, E. L. (2010). Self-determination theory and the relation of autonomy to self-regulatory processes and personality development. In *Handbook of personality and self-regulation* (pp. 169–191). Blackwell Publishing Inc.

Oshio, T., Nozaki, K., & Kobayashi, M. (2011). Relative income and happiness in Asia: Evidence from nationwide surveys in China, Japan, and Korea. *Social Indicators Research, 104*(3), 351–367. https://doi.org/10.1007/s11205-010-9754-9

Parnami, M., Mittal, U., & Hingar, A. (2013). Impact of religiosity on subjective well-being in various groups: A comparative study. *Indian Journal of Health and Wellbeing, 4*, 903–908. https://api.semanticscholar.org/CorpusID:148693524

Polansky, R. (Ed.). (2014). *The Cambridge companion to Aristotle's Nicomachean Ethics*. Cambridge University Press. https://doi.org/10.1017/CCO9781139022484

Rüppel, F., Liersch, S., & Walter, U. (2015). The influence of psychological well-being on academic success. *Journal of Public Health, 23*(1), 15–24. https://doi.org/10.1007/s10389-015-0654-y

Ryan, R. M., & Deci, E. L. (2001). On happiness and human potentials: A review of research on hedonic and eudaimonic well-being. *Annual Review of Psychology, 52*(1), 141–166. https://doi.org/10.1146/annurev.psych.52.1.141

Ryff, C. D. (1989). Happiness is everything, or is it? Explorations on the meaning of psychological well-being. *Journal of Personality and Social Psychology, 57*(6), 1069–1081. https://doi.org/10.1037/0022-3514.57.6.1069

Shek, D. T. L., Yu, L., Wu, F. K. Y., Zhu, X., & Chan, K. H. Y. (2017). A 4-year longitudinal study of well-being of Chinese university students in Hong Kong. *Applied Research in Quality of Life, 12*(4), 867–884. https://doi.org/10.1007/s11482-016-9493-4

Slavich, G. M., & Auerbach, R. P. (2018). Stress and its sequelae: Depression, suicide, inflammation, and physical illness. In *APA handbook of psychopathology: Psychopathology: Understanding, assessing, and treating adult mental disorders* (Vol. 1, pp. 375–402). American Psychological Association. https://doi.org/10.1037/0000064-016

Sousa, V. D., & Rojjanasrirat, W. (2011). Translation, adaptation and validation of instruments or scales for use in cross-cultural health care research: A clear and user-friendly guideline. *Journal of Evaluation in Clinical Practice, 17*(2), 268–274. https://doi.org/10.1111/j.1365-2753.2010.01434.x

Stubbe, J. H., Posthuma, D., Boomsma, D. I., & De Geus, E. J. (2005). Heritability of life satisfaction in adults: A twin-family study. *Psychological Medicine, 35*(11), 1581–1588. https://doi.org/10.1017/S0033291705005374

Suldo, S. M., Riley, K. N., & Shaffer, E. J. (2006). Academic correlates of children and Adolescents' life satisfaction. *School Psychology International, 27*(5), 567–582. https://doi.org/10.1177/0143034306073411

Tennant, R., Hiller, L., Fishwick, R., Platt, S., Joseph, S., Weich, S., Parkinson, J., Secker, J., & Stewart-Brown, S. (2007). The Warwick-Edinburgh Mental Well-being Scale (WEMWBS): Development and UK validation. *Health and Quality of Life Outcomes, 5*(1), 63. https://doi.org/10.1186/1477-7525-5-63

Trommsdorff, G., & Schwarz, B. (2007). The 'Intergenerational Stake Hypothesis' in Indonesia and Germany. *Current Sociology, 55*(4), 599–620. https://doi.org/10.1177/0011392107077641

Waterman, A. S. (1993). Two conceptions of happiness: Contrasts of personal expressiveness (eudaimonia) and hedonic enjoyment. *Journal of Personality and Social Psychology, 64*(4), 678–691. https://doi.org/10.1037/0022-3514.64.4.678

White, S. C., Gaines, S. O., & Jha, S. (2014). Inner wellbeing: Concept and validation of a new approach to subjective perceptions of wellbeing—India. *Social Indicators Research, 119*(2), 723–746. https://doi.org/10.1007/s11205-013-0504-7

Yan, Y., & Gai, X. (2022). High achievers from low family socioeconomic status families: Protective factors for academically resilient students. *International Journal of Environmental Research and Public Health, 19*(23), 15882. https://doi.org/10.3390/ijerph192315882

Yin, R., Lepinteur, A., Clark, A. E., & D'Ambrosio, C. (2023). Life satisfaction and the human development index across the world. *Journal of Cross-Cultural Psychology, 54*(2), 269–282. https://doi.org/10.1177/00220221211044784

Yuan, L. (2015). The happier one is, the more creative one becomes: An investigation on inspirational positive emotions from both subjective well-being and satisfaction at work. *Psychology, 06*(03), 201–209. https://doi.org/10.4236/psych.2015.63019

Zhang, J., Yang, Y., & Wang, H. (2009). Measuring subjective well-being: A comparison of China and the USA. *Asian Journal of Social Psychology, 12*(3), 221–225. https://doi.org/10.1111/j.1467-839X.2009.01287.x

Chapter 9

Challenges to wellbeing of faculty and leaders in higher education in the Gulf Cooperation Council

Rita W. El-Haddad and Stavros P. Hadjisolomou

Introduction

Subjective wellbeing, which involves experiencing positive emotions, life satisfaction, and a sense of purpose (Busseri & Sadava, 2013; Diener, 1984; Tov & Diener, 2013), is a crucial component of an individual's overall quality of life. In workplaces, occupational wellbeing encompasses the emotional and psychological satisfaction derived from one's work, relating to how job roles, expectations, and the work environment contribute to or take away from one's sense of purpose and satisfaction within their work context (Cotton & Hart, 2003; Mudrak et al., 2018). For faculty and leaders in higher education, occupational wellbeing is a critical component of their overall wellbeing that merits further investigation, particularly in the context of the Gulf Cooperation Council (GCC) region, where cultural norms, religious beliefs, and traditions may shape expectations and challenges in unique ways impacting their emotional, psychological, and social wellbeing.

Although there is a substantial body of literature on wellbeing among higher education faculty (Hammoudi Halat et al., 2023; Larson et al., 2019; Mudrak et al., 2018; Roos & Borkoski, 2021; Sabagh et al., 2022; Salimzadeh et al., 2020; Samad et al., 2022), research focusing specifically on faculty and leader occupational wellbeing within non-Western settings, such as the Arabian Gulf, is comparatively scarce. This gap in the literature highlights the need for studies that consider diverse cultural and educational systems, as cultural norms and institutional structures can vary significantly when comparing the GCC region to Western contexts. For example, in the GCC region, traditional gender role expectations might impact female leaders or create additional pressures for female faculty to balance academic and family responsibilities. Similarly, the religious and cultural context strongly emphasizes responsibilities surrounding family and community, which may create unique work-life balance challenges for faculty and leaders attempting to navigate these cultural expectations while striving to meet demanding work tasks such as fulfilling international accreditation standards in higher education.

Investigating the challenges faculty and leaders face in the GCC requires a nuanced approach that considers the region's unique socio-cultural context, including the sizeable expatriate population. The GCC's distinct learning environment, local regulations, and many expatriate academics create a context where a range of potential issues could impact the wellbeing of faculty and leaders. Expatriate faculty members, who make up a significant portion of the academic workforce in the GCC, may face challenges different from those of local faculty, which can significantly impact their occupational wellbeing. Examining these factors within the GCC context contributes to a more comprehensive understanding of faculty and leader wellbeing in the region and offers insights that may be applicable to other non-Western contexts. Understanding and addressing these challenges could help the GCC's ambition to become a regional leader in higher education.

In this chapter, we will first review existing research to identify challenges to faculty and leader wellbeing that are common across cultural contexts. We will then focus on the GCC region, exploring how cultural factors and the expatriate experience can influence the wellbeing of faculty and leaders in higher education institutions. By identifying gaps in the current literature, we aim to propose potential strategies and interventions that could improve wellbeing and foster a more supportive workplace environment, taking into account the specific needs of academics in the GCC, with a particular focus on the expatriate experience. The findings and recommendations presented in this chapter have implications for theory, practice, and future research in the field of wellbeing in higher education, particularly in the context of the GCC region and other non-Western settings. This chapter begins by discussing the GCC context, its higher education systems, and its academic population.

Gulf Cooperation Council context

The GCC comprises Bahrain, Kuwait, Oman, Qatar, Saudi Arabia, and the United Arab Emirates (UAE) in the Arabian Gulf. These countries share cultures and customs similar to yet distinct from other Arab countries in the Middle East and North Africa (MENA) region (Metwally, 2010). The GCC is characterized by its significant expatriate population; in some countries, the expatriates outnumber the nationals. This unique demographic composition presents distinct societal dynamics that may influence the wellbeing of faculty and leaders in higher education.

Higher education in the GCC: demographics, regulatory frameworks, and the role of accreditation

Similar to other regions, the GCC's higher education landscape includes public and private institutions, many adopting American, British, or Canadian curricula. Some private institutions have affiliations with Western universities, such as the American University of Kuwait's (AUK's) partnership with Dartmouth College. In other cases, an institution is an international branch campus of a well-known Western university, such as New York University (NYU) Abu Dhabi and Northwestern University in Qatar.

GCC universities are subject to local higher education laws and regulations based on the country (Healey, 2015; Kelly, 2011; Wilkins, 2010; Wilkins & Neri, 2019), and some may simultaneously seek international, usually Western, accreditation (Hijazi et al., 2020; Kelly, 2011; Noori & Anderson, 2013). One example is the American University of Sharjah (AUS) in the UAE, accredited by the Middle States Commission on Higher Education. International accreditation serves as a quality indicator (Hijazi et al., 2020; Noori & Anderson, 2013), allowing an institution additional academic prestige, which can attract a higher caliber of students and faculty (Noori & Anderson, 2013). As such, GCC institutions seeking international accreditation must fulfill rigorous demands set by international accreditors while maintaining local standards and regulations. This delicate balancing act can cause stress to faculty and leaders who have to deal with pressure from two separate entities, resolve potential identity conflicts that may arise, and deal with the required professional development opportunities to push the processes forward (Healey, 2015; Hijazi et al., 2020; Noori & Anderson, 2013).

The nationality of students, faculty, and leaders varies widely across GCC institutions, reflecting the region's diversity. At the same time, public universities cater mainly to local students, such as UAE University (UAEU), where 84% of students are UAE nationals (UAEU, n.d.). In contrast, private universities often cater to a mix of nationalities. For example, local students make up the majority of the student body at AUK (AUK, n.d.), but the minority at NYU Abu Dhabi and the AUS (AUS, n.d.; NYUAD, n.d.). Generally, private institutions are co-educational, while some public institutions may have gender-segregated campuses or classes. Recently, the UAE has started to slowly adopt co-education within its educational system, beginning with K–12 schools in 2018, so experiencing gender segregation for the entirety of one's schooling will decline (Gender segregation, 2024).

The nationalities of faculty and leadership are also diverse, with private institutions usually being more multinational. In Saudi Arabia, for the years 2020–2022, more than half of the professors at public universities were of Saudi nationality (Ministry of Education, n.d.). In contrast, less than 20% of faculty are locals at UAEU (UAEU, n.d.). Some private universities may not only have faculty that are majority expatriate (AUK, n.d.; AUS, n.d.) but they may also promote how international their faculty are (AUK, n.d.; AUS, n.d.; NYUAD, n.d.) even stating on their websites exactly how many are from North America specifically (AUK, n.d.; AUS, n.d.). This can highlight the institution's diversity to potential students and employees so that students may have an international experience while still staying in the GCC. Depending on the institution, the multicultural and multinational makeup of faculties and leadership teams could pose challenges or benefits to wellbeing. In some institutions, it may manifest as cultural tensions; in others, it could be a path to community building and cross-cultural communication.

Expatriate academics

Many academic expatriates come to the GCC region due to being offered tax-free salaries, which may be higher than what they could earn in their home countries

(Asif et al., 2020; Austin et al., 2014; Chapman et al., 2014; Kelly, 2011; Przytula, 2023; Schoepp & Forstenlechner, 2012; Tahir, 2023; Wilkins & Neri, 2019). Additionally, academics receive extensive benefits from higher education institutions, such as housing provision or allowance, school tuition allowance for dependents, annual flights home, and health insurance (Austin et al., 2014; Chapman et al., 2014; Kelly, 2011; Tahir, 2023). The geographic location of the GCC is also beneficial due to the ease of international travel for conferences and collaboration (Austin et al., 2014; Tahir, 2023). For non-GCC Arab expatriates, the GCC has the added advantage of being close to their home countries in the MENA region (Austin et al., 2014; Chapman et al., 2014). Finally, some GCC institutions may further entice academics with research funding, travel support for international conferences, or other types of professional development (Austin et al., 2014; Chapman et al., 2014; Kelly, 2011).

Methodology

This narrative review consists of a traditional approach to examining the existing literature, focusing on qualitatively interpreting existing knowledge on challenges to faculty and leader wellbeing in the GCC region. Following the methodologies recommended by Sylvester et al. (2013) and Green et al. (2006), this review aims to summarize and synthesize the information written on the topic without generalizing from the reviewed literature.

We aimed to present an in-depth examination of the existing body of literature and to emphasize the importance of recent studies. Through identifying gaps in the literature, narrative reviews serve as a method that generates research ideas and questions and allows the development of hypotheses. Following Levy and Ellis (2006), this chapter's review process involved three steps: literature search and screening, data extraction and analysis, and writing the review. During the literature search and screening, we focused on the relevance to faculty and leader wellbeing in the GCC, methodological rigor, and contributions to the field of higher education.

Academic Search Ultimate, Google Scholar, and the AUK library catalog ("Search all" function) were used to search for all material related to the topic until 2023. Searches included various combinations of the following keywords: "leaders," "well-being," "higher education," "university," "faculty," "professors," "coping strategies," and "expatriate." When searching for GCC-specific information, either "GCC" or a specific country was added, for example, "expatriate AND leaders AND higher education AND UAE." Relevant papers were also found by searching the reference lists of sources.

Narrative review findings

The occupational wellbeing of faculty and leaders in higher education in the GCC region is a complex issue that requires a contextually sensitive and culturally responsive approach. Some challenges, such as work-life balance, may be similar to those faced by academics globally. However, the unique cultural, political, and social characteristics of the GCC necessitate a discussion of wellbeing occurring outside of Western values and norms. There are plenty of studies on faculty job satisfaction in the GCC (Ababneh, 2020; Ababneh & Hackett, 2019; Ahmad et al., 2021; Aldosari, 2020; Al Kuwaiti et al., 2020; Bin Bakr & Almagati, 2023; Sawalha et al., 2019) and other qualitative studies which directly focus on the faculty or leaders' experience of wellbeing or of being an academic in the GCC (e.g., Alanazi & Alkouatli, 2023; Austin et al., 2014). However, there do not appear to be studies on faculty or leaders in the GCC whose primary focus is occupational wellbeing, as measured through standardized scales. By synthesizing the existing literature on faculty and leader experiences in the GCC, this review aims to highlight the distinctive challenges faced by academics in the region and propose strategies for enhancing wellbeing that take into account the specific needs and contexts of the GCC.

Universal responsibilities

The roles and responsibilities of faculty and leaders in higher education are necessary for higher education institutions to run and thrive. In this section, we explore the nature of these responsibilities and what is needed to have an environment conducive to learning and engagement.

Faculty responsibilities

Faculty members typically have a "tripartite" workload: teaching, research, and service (Hammoudi Halat et al., 2023; Link et al., 2008; Price & Cotten, 2006; Przytula, 2023; Salimzadeh et al., 2020; Schoepp & Forstenlechner, 2012; Trembath, 2016). Teaching entails designing coursework, lecturing, and assessing students. Research often involves applying for grants, conducting studies, and disseminating results through publications and presentations. Service includes duties like participating in university committees, mentoring students, and reviewing work for academic journals.

While academic work as a faculty member offers a degree of autonomy and flexibility, it also introduces challenges. Though courses have pre-set schedules, professors largely self-direct office hours, research, and service tasks and must ensure they self-impose their deadlines where needed (Ackerman & Gross, 2007; Link et al., 2008).

Leader responsibilities

Academic leadership can come in many forms, from Department Chairs to Provosts and University Presidents. Some leadership roles, such as Department Chairs, often include teaching and research obligations alongside administrative duties.

Others, particularly high-level roles such as Deans, prioritize administrative responsibilities exclusively. Regardless of level, leaders shoulder various operational duties, including budget management, staff oversight, and ensuring the university's objectives are met (Al-Swailem & Elliott, 2013; Gonaim, 2019; Morris & Laipple, 2015). Leaders may also support and mentor faculty and staff, ensuring they are on track regarding their teaching, research, and service obligations (Alnassar & Dow, 2013; Bowen, 2021; Fedoruk, 2021; Gonaim, 2019). Leaders may also be called in to help mediate student issues or complaints when problems escalate.

Leaders might be involved in maintaining quality assurance, seeing that standards are met, and arranging appropriate professional development opportunities to support faculty and staff in meeting their goals (Al-Swailem & Elliott, 2013; Bowen, 2021). In addition, leaders may oversee institutional efforts to adhere to government regulations and comply with specific standards such as accreditation entities. Hence, they work to confirm the alignment of the institution's mission and vision with what is done on the ground. Finally, leaders may be involved in strategic planning of the institution's vision and promoting what they perceive as the institutional "brand" to help attract students and faculty (Al-Swailem & Elliott, 2013; Wilkins, 2010).

Universal challenges

Common challenges for faculty and leaders

Though faculty and leaders occupy different academic roles, they may experience common challenges. Here, we will describe common challenges to wellbeing that both groups face that are similar to what faculty and leaders experience globally. Thus, we will emphasize some of the "universal" challenges of academics, regardless of the cultural context.

WORK-LIFE BALANCE AND TIME MANAGEMENT

Faculty and leaders must balance their workload and may struggle to achieve a work-life balance (Alanazi & Alkouatli, 2023; Alotaibi, 2020; Alsubhi et al., 2018; Bin Bakr, 2022; Bojiah & Gulei, 2020; Bowen, 2021; Kinman, 2014; Mohamed & Mohamed, 2016; Morris & Laipple, 2015; Mudrak et al., 2018; Sabagh et al., 2022). As such, they may work long hours and potentially miss out on family time (Alanazi & Alkouatli, 2023; Kinman, 2014; Morris & Laipple, 2015). Leaders must not only balance between their obligations but also determine the workload of faculty. Leaders must ensure classes are filled and assign a specific teaching load to faculty while monitoring their scholarly output (Smith & Abouammoh, 2013). Thus, leaders must provide enough research support to faculty while determining realistic expectations for scholarly production based on their context (Smith & Abouammoh, 2013).

BURNOUT

Considering how much time is devoted to being an academic, it is thus not surprising that burnout is a common concern (Alzahmi et al., 2022; Hammoudi Halat et al., 2023; Kinman, 2014; Lackritz, 2004; Morris & Laipple, 2015; Roos & Borkoski, 2021; Sabagh et al., 2022; Salimzadeh et al., 2020). Burnout is a reaction to consistent workplace stressors that involves "overwhelming exhaustion, feelings of cynicism and detachment from the job, and a sense of ineffectiveness and lack of accomplishment" (Maslach et al., 2001, p. 399). Burnout can negatively influence many aspects of employees' lives, including decreased productivity, increased health issues, interpersonal problems with coworkers, and turnover (Maslach et al., 2001). Academics who experience burnout may experience low job satisfaction or feel like they are no longer effective in their work (Hammoudi Halat et al., 2023; Kinman, 2014; Lackritz, 2004; Maslach et al., 2001).

Faculty-specific challenges

Academic faculty in the GCC and internationally share some challenges that can negatively impact wellbeing, distinct from what leaders face. Specifically, faculty often directly deal with students who become antagonistic. They may have complaints about how the professor is teaching, or they may feel entitled to higher grades and try to negotiate with or convince faculty to submit grade changes (Hammoudi Halat et al., 2023; Hudgins et al., 2023; Kelly, 2011; Wilkins, 2010; Wilkins & Neri, 2019). Experiencing a consistent flow of students arguing about grades, needing to repeatedly explain why changes are not warranted, and having students, and sometimes their families, threaten or complain to the administration is draining.

In addition to dealing with student concerns directly, faculty may also be in regular contact with academic colleagues, Student Affairs and Library staff members, disability service offices, Department Chairs, Deans, and Provosts about student issues. The sheer number of people with whom faculty interact to deal with student concerns can contribute to faculty stress levels.

Leader-specific challenges

Leaders in the GCC and internationally also share challenges that can negatively impact wellbeing, distinct from what faculty face. As leaders frequently start as faculty members, especially those who become Department Chairs and Deans, they may not have had formal leadership training. Feeling unprepared or not having sufficient management skills when taking on a leadership role would negatively impact the wellbeing of leaders. Hence, leaders report they want proper training in this area (Abalkhail, 2017; Akbar et al., 2023; Alotaibi, 2020; Alsubhi et al., 2018; Al-Swailem & Elliott, 2013; Fenech et al., 2023; Floyd et al., 2023; Gonaim, 2019; Jarrett, 2021; Morris & Laipple, 2015; Smith & Abouammoh, 2013).

GCC-specific challenges

While there are several areas in which challenges to faculty and leader wellbeing align with some of the same issues seen abroad, there also appear to be certain ones that are unique to the GCC. Here, we will review some specific considerations for faculty and leaders based on their location in the GCC.

Challenges common to faculty and leaders in the GCC

As stated earlier, the GCC region has many expatriates in each country. Thus, it is understandable that many challenges specific to the GCC revolve around expatriate academics. When reviewing the literature, it was found that particular challenges linked to being in the GCC were common to expatriate both faculty and leaders. Such challenges are short employment contracts, lack of tenure, higher turnover, sponsoring dependents/visa issues, homesickness and pessimism, and perceived inequality between expats and locals. In a later section, we will explore challenges specific to faculty, distinct from leaders and vice versa.

SHORT EMPLOYMENT CONTRACTS

Expatriates are in the GCC on short employment contracts based on work visas, which are renewed after a fixed period, usually from one to three years (Ababneh, 2020; Austin et al., 2014; Chapman et al., 2014; Farrugia, 2012; Kelly, 2011; Noori & Anderson, 2013; Romanowski & Nasser, 2015; Schoepp & Forstenlechner, 2012; Tahir, 2023), but this depends on the institution and country. An expatriate's residency in a GCC country is linked to their work as GCC nations do not readily grant permanent residency to expatriates; they must be employed to stay. If they resign or are terminated, they must find other work or face a prompt return to their country (Austin et al., 2014; Chapman et al., 2014; Kelly, 2011). That said, the UAE now issues Golden Visas to allow expats to stay longer (up to ten years) (Golden Visa, 2024), which may change how some expatriates approach working in the UAE if opportunities exist for more stable employment.

LACK OF TENURE

Since employment contracts are time-limited, by extension, this means that there generally is a lack of tenure at universities in the GCC region (Ababneh, 2020; Austin et al., 2014; Kelly, 2011; Noori & Anderson, 2013; Romanowski & Nasser, 2015; Schoepp & Forstenlechner, 2012; Tahir, 2023). An exception to this would be some Western branch campuses, such as NYU Abu Dhabi, which do have tenure because they are working based on the policies of the original campus rather than the host country (Schoepp & Forstenlechner, 2012). As a result of a lack of tenure and limited-time contracts, professors and leaders may feel their positions are insecure and that they are expendable (Asif et al., 2020; Austin et al., 2014;

Chapman et al., 2014; Trembath, 2016). Additionally, if academics perceive that they could be fired indiscriminately (Asif et al., 2020; Noori & Anderson, 2013; Trembath, 2016) or that the promotion process is unfair or not based on merit (Przytula, 2023), they will not be motivated to produce their best work.

HIGHER TURNOVER

Short contracts may also influence whether professors and leaders choose to leave their positions, leading to higher turnover, as they may not feel attached to their institutions (Austin et al., 2014; Chapman et al., 2014; Farrugia, 2012; Noori & Anderson, 2013; Schoepp & Forstenlechner, 2012; Tahir, 2023; Trembath, 2016). This makes it challenging for academics who want to stay long-term as it is difficult to establish collaborative relationships with other professors as it is uncertain if projects will be followed through (Farrugia, 2012; Romanowski & Nasser, 2015). This has downstream effects of limiting the type of research professors may conduct, negatively impacting their productivity.

SPONSORING DEPENDENTS/VISA ISSUES

Since expatriate faculty are in the GCC on work visas, dependent sponsorship issues may also be a source of confusion or stress (Przytula, 2023; Tahir, 2023). Generally speaking, a male professor hired at a GCC university can sponsor his wife and children as dependents if he meets specific requirements set by the institution and country. However, the reverse is untrue; not all GCC countries allow women to sponsor their husbands as dependents. In Kuwait, for example, a man cannot obtain residency through his wife (Al-Seyassah, 2024a). Thus, when a married female academic receives a job offer from Kuwait, she not only considers whether she will accept the offer but whether she will move there alone. Subsequently, the couple must decide how long they will stay apart should he not find employment. On the other hand, in the UAE, a female professor could sponsor her husband if she met specific salary and other requirements (Husain, 2022).

Granting of visas and sponsorship rules may also change suddenly. Kuwait restricted the issuance of family visas in August 2022 (Study on consequences of family visa halt gets nod, 2023) and only recently reinstated them, allowing a larger number of expatriates the ability to apply for them (Al-Seyassah, 2024b). Finally, the above considerations are only granted to legally married couples, prompting the additional decision to marry should one partner be offered a job to allow for visa sponsorship and ensure a legal stay in the same accommodation.

HOMESICKNESS AND PESSIMISM

Once they arrive in the GCC, expatriates may miss the comforts of home and may not easily adapt to the local culture (Przytula, 2023). Some expatriates relish the opportunity to explore their new environment, visit tourist attractions and cultural landmarks, learn Arabic, try local cuisine, and meet and befriend locals (Asif et al., 2020; Austin et al., 2014; Chapman et al., 2014; Fenech et al., 2020; Przytula, 2023; Tahir, 2023; Trembath, 2016; Wilkins & Neri, 2019). Indeed, research findings show that the more culturally competent expatriate faculty are (which increases with time), the easier their adjustment to the country (Fenech et al., 2020).

Other expatriates have a more difficult time (Przytula, 2023; Trembath, 2016; Wilkins & Neri, 2019), especially if this is their first time abroad. They may feel isolated (Przytula, 2023; Romanowski & Nasser, 2015; Trembath, 2016; Wilkins & Neri, 2019), not interact with locals, and only associate with and befriend others like them (Przytula, 2023; Tahir, 2023). They may compare life back home to the GCC region, regret coming at all, and view their situation pessimistically (Przytula, 2023). This negativity can be contagious and lead to complaining about what is "different" or "worse" in the GCC. Further, they may feel "stuck" in their current positions (Asif et al., 2020). Perhaps they came to the GCC for the attractive packages but feel unable to leave because they are financially supporting family back home or paying off personal or educational debts (Asif et al., 2020). This pessimism and complaining can weaken productivity, reinforce their negative feelings, and demotivate others.

PERCEIVED INEQUALITY BETWEEN EXPATRIATES AND LOCALS

A unique consideration of the GCC region is that based on the laws of different countries, expatriate professors may feel they are treated differently compared to or worse than local GCC nationals (Asif et al., 2020; Romanowski & Nasser, 2015; Tahir, 2023; Trembath, 2016). The difference may be financial, with locals receiving higher salaries or benefits from the government to which expatriates do not have access (Austin et al., 2014; Chapman et al., 2014; Kelly, 2011; Romanowski & Nasser, 2015). For example, some expatriates indicate that they do not have the same opportunities to receive government research funding compared to locals, as locals appear to be prioritized over expatriates (Kelly, 2011; Tahir, 2023). Thus, expatriates would need to involve a local researcher to receive funding, but this usually means forfeiting being the first author (Tahir, 2023). While locals reap the benefits of job security (Chapman et al., 2014; Kelly, 2011), expatriates may feel a sense of being a "guest in their country" and avoid bringing up issues with faculty or staff who are locals (Romanowski, & Nasser, 2015, p. 664). This leads to underlying resentment and a sense of injustice for expatriate faculty, which would undoubtedly contribute to negative wellbeing.

Based on all this, it is unsurprising that local faculty in a Saudi Arabian study reported significantly higher job satisfaction than expatriates (Al Kuwaiti et al., 2020). That said, some leaders at institutions in the UAE stated that they felt that "UAE nationals are not interested in pursuing an academic career," which is why they only hire expatriates (Wilkins & Neri, 2019, p. 460). Such sweeping assumptions and statements certainly would not contribute to healthy relations between locals and expatriates. In a study about expatriates in Saudi Arabia, one participant expressed that local academics feel resentful that expatriates are taking job opportunities away (Asif et al., 2020). Thus, neither group is immune to the potentially negative impacts of local laws and institutional decisions on their wellbeing.

Faculty-specific challenges in the GCC

Faculty in the GCC also face distinct challenges from leaders, specifically restricted academic freedom, decreased research productivity, challenges with students' academic and language abilities, and a lack of a faculty senate.

RESTRICTED ACADEMIC FREEDOM

In the GCC, faculty may report feeling that their academic freedom is restricted (Ababneh, 2020; Costandi et al., 2019). As a result, they may purposely avoid researching or teaching controversial subjects. By "playing it safe" in their professional and personal lives, faculty feel they are safeguarding their positions and livelihoods since their residency in the country remains based on employment (Austin et al., 2014; Chapman et al., 2014; Kelly, 2011; Noori & Anderson, 2013; Romanowski & Nasser, 2015; Trembath, 2016). Faculty thus lose out on rich, nuanced pedagogical and scholarly discussions and may feel bitter about this state of reality.

DECREASED RESEARCH PRODUCTIVITY

Some institutions base promotions on research output but may still require heavy teaching loads and high service commitments. When such institutions do not offer sufficient funding, sabbaticals, or teaching releases for research, faculty may fall behind in their research responsibilities (Ababneh, 2020; Ababneh & Hackett, 2019; Aboelenein et al., 2022; Austin et al., 2014; Chapman et al., 2014; Kelly, 2011; Przytula, 2023; Romanowski & Nasser, 2015; Tahir, 2023). As a result, professors may feel they are not academically on par with their international peers, especially if they think they are primarily completing tasks that are not research-related (Przytula, 2023).

While some universities in the GCC may not require professors to conduct and publish research compared to other institutions (Austin et al., 2014), these professors may no longer be competitive candidates for universities in their home or other countries (Kelly, 2011; Przytula, 2023). Consequently, they must choose between leaving the institution to improve their skills and research portfolios and staying due to the lack of opportunities. This is a difficult choice that faculty likely would not have to face had they stayed in their home countries.

ACADEMIC/LANGUAGE ABILITY OF STUDENTS

Undergraduate students in the GCC have differing levels of ability based on different secondary schooling, ranging from segregated, Arabic-language public schools to co-educational American international schools. Thus, some may not be prepared for the Western-style education many universities offer (Lee, 2021). This is usually because there would be less of a focus on memorization compared to what students are accustomed to in their secondary schooling, especially in public schools (Asif et al., 2020; Eppard et al., 2021; Hamdan Alghamdi, 2014; Lee, 2021). As a result, there may be a learning curve for students to adjust to a new way of learning, and faculty will need to adapt their teaching to accommodate student needs (Asif et al., 2020; Eppard et al., 2021; Hamdan Alghamdi, 2014; Healey, 2015; Wilkins & Neri, 2019) and to be culturally appropriate. Another issue that may be a more considerable obstacle for faculty is the English language ability of students. Students tend to be non-native speakers and may struggle to perform in a classroom where English is the primary language of instruction (Aboelenein et al., 2022; Eppard et al., 2021; Przytula, 2023). Thus, these extra considerations and adjustments add to the level of work and stress for GCC faculty who must teach in a language and system to which many students are not accustomed.

LACK OF FACULTY SENATE

Faculty often feel unable to contribute to institutional decision processes (Ababneh, 2020; Austin et al., 2014; Chapman et al., 2014; Costandi et al., 2019; Schoepp & Forstenlechner, 2012). GCC higher education institutions may not typically have a faculty senate, and faculty, in general, do not have a clear say in institutional decision-making processes (Austin et al., 2014; Chapman et al., 2014; Kelly, 2011; Schoepp & Forstenlechner, 2012). This may make them feel less connected to their institution and have less of a sense of loyalty or wanting to stay long-term (Austin et al., 2014; Chapman et al., 2014; Schoepp & Forstenlechner, 2012). Interestingly, leaders themselves may think it does not make sense for faculty to have a say in shaping institutional policies. The reasoning is that if there is such high turnover among faculty anyway, then they would not have long-term goals in mind (Chapman et al., 2014). This is an interesting conundrum that arises due to the ramifications of short employment contracts affecting multiple areas "down the line."

Leader-specific challenges in the GCC

Similar to faculty in the GCC, leaders face particular challenges that are distinct from faculty and international peers. These include competing pressures of local and international standards, resistance to changes in leadership styles, and gender-based issues.

COMPETING PRESSURES OF LOCAL AND INTERNATIONAL STANDARDS

As in other countries, GCC leaders need to manage conflicting pressures from various regulatory bodies to ensure that the institution is running according to the provided standards (Healey, 2015; Smith & Abouammoh, 2013; Wilkins, 2010).

However, leaders in the GCC have the additional challenge of wanting to apply, usually Western, standards and expectations (such as in accreditation) while also ensuring that the institution is running in accordance with local regulations but also with cultural norms and expectations (Al-Swailem & Elliott, 2013; Healey, 2015; Kelly, 2011; Noori & Anderson, 2013; Smith & Abouammoh, 2013). Such a balance may be challenging to achieve, especially if some of these pressures may be at odds with each other (Noori & Anderson, 2013; Smith & Abouammoh, 2013).

RESISTANCE TO CHANGES IN LEADERSHIP STYLES

In other cases, leaders in the GCC need to be aware of how the implementation of new systems or even leadership styles may work (or not) in the local context. For example, in the GCC and Arab cultures generally, leadership tends to be more top-down and follows a specific hierarchy (Austin et al., 2014). If institutions want to implement something such as servant leadership, there may be pushback from others at the institution for whom this is an entirely new way of understanding leadership (Fenech et al., 2023; Gonaim, 2019). They may not view servant leadership as helpful or effective, and it would require a cultural shift within the institution, adding additional work and stress for leaders (Gonaim, 2019).

GENDER-BASED ISSUES

Granted that there is variety in how gender segregation is implemented (if at all) in higher education institutions in the GCC, there are unique considerations for female leaders. Much research in Saudi Arabia emphasizes that women in higher education institutions experienced gender-based bias, discrimination, the limited scope of their leadership power, and a lack of institutional policies that would support women in being promoted to leadership positions (Abalkhail, 2017; Alotaibi, 2020; Alsubaie & Jones, 2017; Alsubhi et al., 2018; Bin Bakr, 2022). One study found that in female-only and co-educational institutions in Saudi Arabia, women felt they could thrive in leadership positions (Akbar et al., 2023). However, in partially segregated institutions in Saudi Arabia (where a majority-male campus also has a women's campus within it), women faced challenges related to leadership (Abalkhail, 2017; Akbar et al., 2023). While women may have been in charge of the women's campus in partially segregated campuses, men still made campus-wide decisions and did not consult with female leaders (Abalkhail, 2017; Akbar et al., 2023). It is important to note that the experience of female leaders in other GCC countries may differ. For example, expatriate and local female leaders in Qatar reported generally positive leadership experiences at their institutions (Floyd et al., 2023).

Discussion

The findings of this narrative review underscore the importance of adopting a culturally responsive and contextually sensitive approach to understanding and promoting wellbeing among faculty and leaders in higher education in the GCC region. While some challenges, such as work-life balance and burnout, are universal, the unique cultural, political, and social characteristics of the GCC create distinctive challenges that require a discussion of wellbeing that occurs outside of Western norms and values. Challenges such as short employment contracts, lack of tenure, and issues surrounding expatriate status highlight the complexity of the common experiences faculty and leaders face in this region. These factors, in addition to cultural considerations and the regulatory environment of the GCC, can significantly impact the wellbeing of faculty and leaders, which not only shapes their professional experiences but also influences their personal lives.

We also found several faculty-specific challenges faced in the GCC, such as restricted academic freedom, decreased research productivity, difficulties related to students' academic and language abilities, and a lack of voice in institutional decision-making. Leader-specific challenges include the management of conflicting pressures from local and international standards, resistance to changes in leadership styles, and gender-based issues in leadership roles, which primarily affect women. These findings indicate a need for further investigation of the unique experiences of faculty and leaders in the GCC and the development of targeted support strategies.

Research gaps

The gaps identified in the literature, such as the need for large-scale studies on occupational wellbeing, the underrepresentation of certain GCC countries, and the need for more focus on local academics, highlight the importance of further research that takes into account the specific contexts and experiences of academics in the region. Addressing such gaps will contribute to a more comprehensive understanding of faculty and leader wellbeing in the GCC and inform the development of culturally responsive and contextually sensitive strategies for promoting wellbeing in higher education in the region.

Geographical gaps

Based on the literature review, there is a body of research available from various GCC countries focusing on faculty and leader experiences and aspects of their wellbeing (e.g., job satisfaction, stress, and work-life balance). However, such research typically comes from Saudi Arabia and the UAE, with less from Qatar and Oman, and the least from Bahrain and Kuwait. Thus, there is a need for increased representation from the understudied GCC countries.

Need large-scale studies on occupational wellbeing

Additionally, the literature review has uncovered a lack of research on faculty and leaders' current state of occupational wellbeing across the GCC region. There is a need for systematic, large-scale, quantitative studies using standardized measures encompassing occupational wellbeing (e.g., stress, work engagement, burnout, emotional regulation, and job satisfaction) rather than primarily focusing on job satisfaction. These measures can be administered to faculty and leaders across different institutions and countries of the GCC. Such large-scale studies would allow us to determine and compare wellbeing across institutions and countries. They could also measure the impact of institutionally administered interventions or other policies on wellbeing.

Increased research focusing on academic leaders

Similar to what is seen in international research, there is comparatively less research on academic leaders' wellbeing compared to GCC faculty. Thus, there is a need to study leaders specifically, as this area is understudied.

Focus on local faculty and leaders

While there is plenty of research on expatriate academics in the GCC, there is a need for more research that focuses explicitly on local faculty and leaders. This is especially important in countries where the majority of the population are expatriates (Kuwait, Qatar, and the UAE). Understanding and comparing the wellbeing of local faculty and leaders in institutions where locals are the minority will provide helpful insights on how to support them in their unique environment.

Recommendations

The proposed institutional and governmental interventions, such as increased support for research, the creation of faculty senates, leadership training programs, and changes to employment contracts and visa policies, have the potential to significantly enhance the wellbeing of faculty and leaders in higher education in the GCC. By addressing the unique challenges faced by academics in the region and creating a more supportive and inclusive work environment, such interventions can contribute to a discussion of wellbeing in higher education based on the specific needs and contexts of the GCC.

Institutional interventions

Offering faculty enough support for conducting and publishing research will help to address general faculty concerns about decreased research productivity and burnout, as well as homesickness for expatriates.

Institutions can provide professors with thorough research-focused mentoring or other research-based training initiatives (Ababneh, 2020; Ababneh & Hackett, 2019; Chapman et al., 2014; Farrugia, 2012; Hijazi et al., 2020; Knight, 2014; Przytula, 2023; Smith & Abouammoh, 2013; Trembath, 2016; Wilkins & Neri, 2019). This will help support faculty in keeping up with their international peers, and having higher research output will raise the institution's profile as a whole. Increased support for research can also allow expatriate professors to work on issues of local relevance with immediate results rather than only focusing on research that advances their careers but does not produce change in the larger community. This might help expatriate faculty feel more integrated within the local community rather than being spectators until they return to their home countries. Thus, this may help decrease turnover and help faculty who wish to establish collaborative research relationships in the country.

Regarding wellbeing specifically, there is a need for institutionally backed initiatives on stress management and promoting work-life balance, which would positively impact wellbeing (Bojiah & Gulei, 2020; Hammoudi Halat et al., 2023; Kinman, 2014; Mohamed & Mohamed, 2016; Roos & Borkoski, 2021; Sabagh et al., 2022). This could help create a more inclusive and supportive environment for academics. Finally, institutions may implement programs to support expatriate academics to adjust to life in a new country to help decrease feelings of isolation, homesickness, and pessimism (Isakovic & Forseth Whitman, 2013; Trembath, 2016; Wilkins & Neri, 2019).

CREATE FACULTY SENATES

Allowing faculty to be part of the institutional decision-making process will benefit faculty, making them more satisfied at the workplace and potentially making them feel more connected to the institution (Ababneh, 2020; Schoepp & Forstenlechner, 2012). While the transience of faculty is an understandable concern that leaders may have, not being able to have a voice will only increase feelings of detachment from the institution. If institutions hope to encourage faculty to stay long-term, then all faculty should have a say, even if some may leave sooner rather than later.

IMPLEMENT LEADERSHIP TRAINING PROGRAMS

Since many leaders do not feel they have sufficient preparation before becoming administrators, they think they would benefit from training programs (Abalkhail, 2017; Abdulla et al., 2023; Al-Swailem & Elliott, 2013; Bin Bakr, 2022; Fenech et al., 2023; Floyd et al., 2023; Gonaim, 2019; Jarrett, 2021; Morris & Laipple, 2015; Samad et al., 2022; Smith & Abouammoh, 2013). Research in Saudi Arabia also mentions the necessity of specific training programs targeted at women who want to seek leadership roles as well as a need for a shift in prevalent norms and expectations about women (Abalkhail, 2017; Alotaibi, 2020; Alsubaie & Jones, 2017; Alsubhi et al., 2018; Bin Bakr, 2022). This would allow for an institutional environment that is generally more supportive but specifically would help women (Abalkhail, 2017; Alotaibi, 2020; Bin Bakr, 2022). Researchers studying female leaders in Saudi Arabia suggested changing partially segregated campuses to fully co-educational or fully segregated (women-only), as those environments had the fewest gender-based issues (Akbar et al., 2023). This is something other GCC countries that are also implementing a partially segregated model should consider.

IMPLEMENTING DIFFERENT LEADERSHIP STYLES

Leadership styles such as transformational, servant, and participative-supportive leadership have been found to positively impact higher education institutions, including wellbeing and job satisfaction, in both the GCC and international contexts (Ahmad et al., 2021; Fenech et al., 2023; Gonaim, 2019; Hammoudi Halat et al., 2023; Samad et al., 2022). Though there may be resistance at first to such a new leadership style, it may be worth implementing in institutions as it helps increase the job satisfaction of faculty and improve employee retention (Fenech et al., 2023; Samad et al., 2022). In a review by Hammoudi Halat et al. (2023), they suggest that if higher education emphasized having a supportive workplace that focuses on mental health, faculty would be less likely they are to experience stress, burnout, and other adverse effects, and thus, positive impacts to wellbeing.

Governmental policies

LONGER CONTRACTS/VISAS

If widespread implementation of tenure is not feasible, then having longer employment contracts (Schoepp & Forstenlechner, 2012), which would necessitate longer visas, can help increase feelings of job security and belongingness to an institution. Academics with more job security and belongingness would be more likely to stay, thus improving employee retention. Additionally, this could help to address faculty concerns about restricted academic freedom. If faculty are in a supportive environment with a say in institutional decision-making, having job security on top of that may make them feel freer to delve more deeply into controversial topics in their teaching or research.

The UAE is already making strides in providing opportunities for expats to have more stability in their residencies. Their Golden Visa is a long-term residence visa that lasts up to ten years and is renewable (Golden Visa, 2024). While this is limited for those in highly specialized fields that are of specific priority to the UAE, the existence of such an opportunity is a positive step forward.

Conclusion

The findings and recommendations presented in this chapter contribute to the ongoing effort to develop a culturally responsive and contextually sensitive understanding of wellbeing in higher education in the GCC region. By highlighting the unique challenges faced by faculty and leaders in the region and proposing strategies for addressing them, this review lays the groundwork for future research and interventions that prioritize academics' specific needs and experiences in the GCC.

References

Ababneh, K. I. (2020). Effects of met expectations, trust, job satisfaction, and commitment on faculty turnover intentions in the United Arab Emirates (UAE). *International Journal of Human Resource Management, 31*(2), 303–334. https://doi.org/10.1080/09585192.2016.1255904

Ababneh, K. I., & Hackett, R. D. (2019). The direct and indirect impacts of job characteristics on faculty organizational citizenship behavior in the United Arab Emirates (UAE). *Higher Education, 77*(1), 19–36. https://doi.org/10.1007/s10734-018-0252-3

Abalkhail, J. M. (2017). Women and leadership: Challenges and opportunities in Saudi higher education. *Career Development International, 22*(2), 165–183. https://doi.org/10.1108/CDI-03-2016-0029

Abdulla, A., Fenech, R., Kinsella, K., Hiasat, L., Chakravarti, S., White, T., & Rajan, P. B. (2023). Leadership development in academia in the UAE: Creating a community of learning. *Journal of Higher Education Policy and Management, 45*(1), 96–112. https://doi.org/10.1080/1360080X.2022.2116667

Aboelenein, M., Salnikova, D., Karabchuk, T., & Shomotova, A. (2022). Universities research performance in the United Arab Emirates and Oman: Challenges of higher education systems. *Journal of Higher Education Policy and Leadership Studies, 3*(4), 28–48. https://doi.org/10.52547/johepal.3.4.28

Ahmad, A. R., Alhammad, A. H. Y., & Jameel, A. S. (2021). National culture, leadership styles and job satisfaction: An empirical study in the United Arab Emirates. *Journal of Asian Finance, Economics and Business, 8*(6), 1111–1120. https://doi.org/10.13106/jafeb.2021.vol8.no6.1111

Akbar, H., Al-Dajani, H., Ayub, N., & Adeinat, I. (2023). Women's leadership gamut in Saudi Arabia's higher education sector. *Gender, Work and Organization*, 1–27. https://doi.org/10.1111/gwao.13003

Al Kuwaiti, A., Bicak, H. A., & Wahass, S. (2020). Factors predicting job satisfaction among faculty members of a Saudi higher education institution. *Journal of Applied Research in Higher Education, 12*(2), 296–310. https://doi.org/10.1108/JARHE-07-2018-0128

Alanazi, R., & Alkouatli, C. (2023). Sources of wellbeing amongst Saudi Arabian women academic leaders: An explorative study. *Societies, 13*(4). https://doi.org/10.3390/soc13040088

Aldosari, S. A. M. (2020). The methods of selecting academic leaders (faculty members) at new Saudi universities and its relationship to some variables. *International Journal of Higher Education, 9*(4), 69–83. https://doi.org/10.5430/ijhe.v9n4p69

Alnassar, S. A., & Dow, K. L. (2013). Delivering high-quality teaching and learning for university students in Saudi Arabia. In *Higher education in Saudi Arabia: Achievements, challenges and opportunities* (Vol. 40, pp. 49–60). https://doi.org/10.1007/978-94-007-6321-0_5

Alotaibi, F. T. (2020). Saudi women and leadership: Empowering women as leaders in higher education Institutions. *Open Journal of Leadership, 09*(03), 156–177. https://doi.org/10.4236/ojl.2020.93010

Al-Seyassah, M. N. (2024a, January 28). Here is what you need to know: Females' can also Sponsor Family Visa. *Arab Times*. https://www.arabtimesonline.com/news/here-is-what-you-need-to-know-females-can-also-sponsor-dependent-visa/

Al-Seyassah, M. N. (2024b, February 5). Kuwait reintroduces visit visas for expat families, tourists etc.... *Arab Times*. https://www.arabtimesonline.com/news/kuwait-reintroduces-visit-visas-for-expat-families-tourists-etc/

Alsubaie, A., & Jones, K. (2017). An overview of the current state of women's leadership in higher education in Saudi Arabia and a proposal for future research directions. *Administrative Sciences, 7*(4). https://doi.org/10.3390/admsci7040036

Alsubhi, A. A., Hoque, K. E., & Abdul Razak, A. Z. (2018). Workplace barriers and leadership conflicts experienced by the women in higher education in Saudi Arabia. *International Journal of Learning and Development*, *8*(2), 1. https://doi.org/10.5296/ijld.v8i2.13007

Al-Swailem, O., & Elliott, G. (2013). The learning experiences of Saudi Arabian higher education leadership: Characteristics for global success. *Higher Education Dynamics*, *40*, 37–47. https://doi.org/10.1007/978-94-007-6321-0_4

Alzahmi, E. A., Belbase, S., & Al Hosani, M. (2022). Teacher burnout and collegiality at the workplace in higher education institutions in the Arab Gulf region. *Education Sciences*, *12*(10). https://doi.org/10.3390/educsci12100718

Ackerman, D. S., & Gross, B. L. (2007). I can start that JME manuscript next week, can't I? The task characteristics behind why faculty procrastinate. *Journal of Marketing Education*, *29*(2), 97–110. https://doi.org/10.1177/0273475307302012

Asif, U., Bano, N., & Najjar, H. A. (2020). Experiences of expatriate university teachers in a health science university in Saudi Arabia – A qualitative study. *Pakistan Journal of Medical Sciences*, *36*(4), 799–803. https://doi.org/10.12669/pjms.36.4.1896

AUK. (n.d.). *Institutional research.* American University of Kuwait. https://www.auk.edu.kw/about-auk/administration/institutional-research

AUS. (n.d.). *Fast facts – Fall 2023.* American University of Sharjah. https://www.aus.edu/about/aus-at-a-glance/facts-and-figures/fast-facts-fall-2023

Austin, A. E., Chapman, D. W., Farah, S., Wilson, E., & Ridge, N. (2014). Expatriate academic staff in the United Arab Emirates: The nature of their work experiences in higher education institutions. *Higher Education*, *68*(4), 541–557. https://doi.org/10.1007/s10734-014-9727-z

Bin Bakr, M. B. (2022). Women and leadership: Challenges to women empowerment in academic leadership roles in Saudi Arabia. *Journal of Positive Psychology and Wellbeing*, *6*(2), 1645–1658.

Bin Bakr, M. B., & Almagati, H. T. (2023). Job empowerment and its relationship to job satisfaction among faculty members in higher education – Saudi Arabia. *Journal of Positive Psychology & Wellbeing*, *7*(1), 126–148.

Bojiah, J., & Gulei, N. (2020). Managing work-life predicaments: A study on the selected female employees at Gulf University in Bahrain. *International Journal on Emerging Technologies*, *11*(3), 1134–1139. www.researchtrend.net

Bowen, J. (2021). Being a leader. In K. Jarrett & S. Newton (Eds.), *The practice of leadership in higher education: Real-world perspectives on becoming, being and leaving* (pp. 206–210). Routledge. https://doi.org/10.1177/019263657305737605

Busseri, M. A., & Sadava, S. W. (2013). A review of the tripartite structure of subjective well-being: Implications for conceptualization, operationalization, analysis, and synthesis. *Personality and Social Psychology Review*, *15*(3), 290–314. https://doi.org/10.1177/1088868310391271

Chapman, D., Austin, A., Farah, S., Wilson, E., & Ridge, N. (2014). Academic staff in the UAE: Unsettled journey. *Higher Education Policy*, *27*(1), 131–151. https://doi.org/10.1057/hep.2013.19

Costandi, S., Hamdan, A., Alareeni, B., & Hassan, A. (2019). Educational governance and challenges to universities in the Arabian Gulf region. *Educational Philosophy and Theory*, *51*(1), 70–86. https://doi.org/10.1080/00131857.2018.1434621

Cotton, P., & Hart, P. M. (2003). Occupational wellbeing and performance: A review of organisational health research. *Australian Psychologist*, *30*(2), 118–127. https://doi.org/10.1080/00050060310001707117

Diener, E. (1984). Subjective well-being. *Psychological Bulletin*, *95*(3), 542–575.

Eppard, J., Bailey, F., Mckeown, K., & Singh, H. (2021). Expatriate faculty and student perspectives on teaching and learning in a United Arab Emirates university. *Issues in Educational Research*, *31*(2), 458–475.

Farrugia, C. A. (2012). Universities and innovation networks in the UAE. *Sheikh Saud Bin Saqr Al Qasimi, 4*, 12.
Fedoruk, L. (2021). Being a leader. In K. Jarrett & S. Newton (Eds.), *The practice of leadership in higher education: Real-world perspectives on becoming, being and leaving* (pp. 215–219). Routledge. https://doi.org/10.1097/DCR.0000000000003002
Fenech, R., Abdulla, A., Zairi, A., Kinsella, K., & Misra, A. (2023). Culture of excellence in academia in the UAE: A model of transformational leadership and leadership development. *Journal of Research on Leadership Education.* https://doi.org/10.1177/19427751231188388
Fenech, R., Baguant, P., & Abdelwahed, I. (2020). Cultural learning in the adjustment process of academic expatriates. *Cogent Education, 7*(1). https://doi.org/10.1080/2331186X.2020.1830924
Floyd, A., Qadhi, S. M., Al-Thani, H., Chaaban, Y., & Du, X. (2023). An integrated systems model for understanding experiences of academic leadership development in Qatar. *Journal of Higher Education Policy and Management, 45*(6), 690–705. https://doi.org/10.1080/1360080X.2023.2225148
Gender segregation. (2024). The United Arab Emirates' Government Portal. https://u.ae/en/information-and-services/education/school-education-k-12/gender-segregation
Golden visa. (2024). The United Arab Emirates' Government Portal. https://u.ae/en/information-and-services/visa-and-emirates-id/residence-visas/golden-visa
Gonaim, F. A. (2019). Leadership in higher education in Saudi Arabia: Benefits, constraints and challenges of adopting servant leadership model by department chairs. *International Journal of Education and Practice, 7*(2), 101–111. https://doi.org/10.18488/journal.61.2019.72.101.111
Green, B. N., Johnson, C. D., & Adams, A. (2006). Writing narrative literature reviews for peer-reviewed journals: Secrets of the trade. *Clinical Update, 5*(3), 101–117.
Hamdan Alghamdi, A. K. (2014). The road to culturally relevant pedagogy: Expatriate teachers' pedagogical practices in the cultural context of Saudi Arabian higher education. *McGill Journal of Education, 49*(1), 201–226. https://doi.org/10.7202/1025778ar
Hammoudi Halat, D., Soltani, A., Dalli, R., Alsarraj, L., & Malki, A. (2023). Understanding and fostering mental health and well-being among university faculty: A narrative review. *Journal of Clinical Medicine, 12*(13). https://doi.org/10.3390/jcm12134425
Healey, N. (2015). Managing international branch campuses: What do we know? *Higher Education Quarterly, 69*(4), 386–409. https://doi.org/10.1111/hequ.12082
Hijazi, R., Hassan, Y., & Husain, Z. (2020). Deans' perceptions of challenges facing business education in the Arabian Gulf. *Journal of Education for Business, 95*(1), 10–22. https://doi.org/10.1080/08832323.2019.1595502
Hudgins, T., Layne, D., Kusch, C. E., & Lounsbury, K. (2023). Disruptive academic behaviors: The dance between emotional intelligence and academic incivility. *Journal of Academic Ethics, 21*(3), 449–469. https://doi.org/10.1007/s10805-022-09454-4
Husain, Z. (2022, June 29). Can a wife sponsor her husband in Dubai? Here is all you need to know. *Gulf News.* https://gulfnews.com/living-in-uae/visa-immigration/can-a-wife-sponsor-her-husband-in-dubai-here-is-all-you-need-to-know-1.1656513841813
Isakovic, A. A., & Forseth Whitman, M. (2013). Self-initiated expatriate adjustment in the United Arab Emirates: A study of academics. *Journal of Global Mobility, 1*(2), 161–186. https://doi.org/10.1108/JGM-09-2012-0011
Jarrett, K. (2021). Developing leaders from within. In K. Jarrett & S. Newton (Eds.), *The practice of leadership in higher education: Real-world perspectives on becoming, being and leaving* (pp. 20–42). Routledge. https://doi.org/10.4324/9780367823849-22
Kelly, M. (2011). Balancing cultures at the American University of Kuwait. *Journal of Arabian Studies, 1*(2), 201–229. https://doi.org/10.1080/21534764.2011.630893
Kinman, G. (2014). Doing more with less? Work and wellbeing in academics. *Somatechnics, 4*(2), 219–235. https://doi.org/10.3366/soma.2014.0129

Knight, J. (2014). Professional development for faculty and staff in Ras Al Khaimah's Higher Education Institutions. *Al Qasimi Foundation.* https://doi.org/10.18502/aqf.0096

Lackritz, J. R. (2004). Exploring burnout among university faculty: Incidence, performance, and demographic issues. *Teaching and Teacher Education, 20*(7), 713–729. https://doi.org/10.1016/j.tate.2004.07.002

Larson, L. M., Seipel, M. T., Shelley, M. C., Gahn, S. W., Ko, S. Y., Schenkenfelder, M., Rover, D. T., Schmittmann, B., & Heitmann, M. M. (2019). The academic environment and faculty well-being: The role of psychological needs. *Journal of Career Assessment, 27*(1), 167–182. https://doi.org/10.1177/1069072717748667

Lee, S. S. (2021). A precarious balancing act. *Contemporary Arab Affairs, 14*(1), 113–133. https://doi.org/10.1525/caa.2021.14.1.113

Levy, Y., & Ellis, T. J. (2006). A systems approach to conduct an effective literature review in support of information systems research. *Informing Science Journal, 9,* 181–212.

Link, B. A. N., Swann, C. A., & Bozeman, B. (2008). A time allocation study of university faculty, *Economics of Education Review, 27*(4), 363–374.

Maslach, C., Schaufeli, W. B., & Leiter, M. P. (2001). Job burnout. *Annual Review of Psychology, 52,* 397–422. https://doi.org/10.1146/annurev.psych.52.1.397

Metwally, M. M. (2010). Gulf cooperation council. In K. A. Reinert L. S. Davis & R. S. Rajan (Eds.), *The Princeton encyclopedia of the world economy.* Princeton University Press.

Ministry of Education, n.d. Saudi Ministry of Education Website.https://moe.gov.sa/en

Mohamed, A. G., & Mohamed, L. K. (2016). Occupational stress and coping strategies among academicians at Hafr al-Batin University, Saudi Arabia. *International Organization of Scientific Research (IOSR) Journal of Nursing and Health Science, 5*(5), 23–30. https://doi.org/10.9790/1959-0505072330

Morris, T. L., & Laipple, J. S. (2015). How prepared are academic administrators? Leadership and job satisfaction within US research universities. *Journal of Higher Education Policy and Management, 37*(2), 241–251. https://doi.org/10.1080/1360080X.2015.1019125

Mudrak, J., Zabrodska, K., Kveton, P., Jelinek, M., Blatny, M., Solcova, I., & Machovcova, K. (2018). Occupational well-being among university faculty: A job demands-resources model. *Research in Higher Education, 59*(3), 325–348. https://doi.org/10.1007/s11162-017-9467-x

Noori, N., & Anderson, P.-K. (2013). Globalization, governance, and the diffusion of the American model of education: Accreditation agencies and American-style universities in the Middle East. *International Journal of Politics, Culture, and Society, 26*(2), 159–172. https://doi.org/10.1007/s10767-013-9131-1

NYUAD. (n.d.). Fast facts. *NYU Abu Dhabi.* https://nyuad.nyu.edu/en/about/nyuad-at-a-glance/fast-facts.html

Price, J., & Cotten, S. R. (2006). Teaching, research, and service: Expectations of assistant professors. *The American Sociologist, 37,* 5–21. https://doi.org/10.1007/s12108-006-1011-y

Przytula, S. (2023). Expatriate academics: What have we known for four decades? A systematic literature review. *Journal of Global Mobility.* https://doi.org/10.1108/JGM-03-2023-0024

Romanowski, M. H., & Nasser, R. (2015). Identity issues: Expatriate professors teaching and researching in Qatar. *Higher Education, 69*(4), 653–671. https://doi.org/10.1007/s10734-014-9795-0

Roos, B. H., & Borkoski, C. C. (2021). Attending to the teacher in the teaching: Prioritizing faculty well-being. *Perspectives of the ASHA Special Interest Groups, 6*(4), 831–840. https://doi.org/10.1044/2021_persp-21-00006

Sabagh, Z., Hall, N. C., Saroyan, A., & Trépanier, S. G. (2022). Occupational factors and faculty well-being: Investigating the mediating role of need frustration. *Journal of Higher Education, 93*(4), 559–584. https://doi.org/10.1080/00221546.2021.2004810

Salimzadeh, R., Hall, N. C., & Saroyan, A. (2020). Stress, emotion regulation, and wellbeing among Canadian faculty members in research-intensive universities. *Social Sciences*, *9*(12), 1–37. https://doi.org/10.3390/socsci9120227

Samad, A., Muchiri, M., & Shahid, S. (2022). Investigating leadership and employee wellbeing in higher education. *Personnel Review*, *51*(1), 57–76. https://doi.org/10.1108/PR-05-2020-0340

Sawalha, N., Kathawala, Y., & Magableh, I. (2019). Educator organizational citizenship behavior and job satisfaction moderation in the GCC expatriate-dominated market. *International Journal of Organizational Analysis*, *27*(1), 19–35. https://doi.org/10.1108/IJOA-09-2017-1247

Schoepp, K., & Forstenlechner, I. (2012). Self-initiated expatriate faculty in the UAE: Balancing the profession and financial rewards. *International Journal of Business and Globalisation*, *8*(4), 454–470. https://doi.org/10.1504/IJBG.2012.047081

Smith, L., & Abouammoh, A. (2013). Challenges and opportunities for higher education in Saudi Arabia: An exploratory focus group. *Higher Education Dynamics*, *40*, 167–179. https://doi.org/10.1007/978-94-007-6321-0_16

Study on consequences of family visa halt gets nod. (2023, November 28). *Arab Times*. https://www.arabtimesonline.com/news/study-on-consequences-of-family-visa-halt-gets-nod/

Sylvester, A., Tate, M., & Johnstone, D. (2013). Beyond synthesis: Re-presenting heterogeneous research literature. *Behaviour and Information Technology*, *32*(12), 1199–1215. https://doi.org/10.1080/0144929X.2011.624633

Tahir, R. (2023). Expatriate academics: An exploratory study of western academics in the United Arab Emirates. *International Journal of Management Practice*, *16*(1), 1. https://doi.org/10.1504/ijmp.2023.10055146

Tov, W., & Diener, E. (2013). Subjective well-being. In *The encyclopedia of cross-cultural psychology first edition*. https://ink.library.smu.edu.sg/soss_research/1395

Trembath, J. L. (2016). The professional lives of expatriate academics: Construct clarity and implications for expatriate management in higher education. *Journal of Global Mobility*, *4*(2), 112–130. https://doi.org/10.1108/JGM-04-2015-0012

UAEU. (n.d.). *Annual report 2021-2022*. United Arab Emirates University (UAEU). https://www.uaeu.ac.ae/en/vc/uod/publications/annual-report-21-22.pdf

Wilkins, S. (2010). Higher education in the United Arab Emirates: An analysis of the outcomes of significant increases in supply and competition. *Journal of Higher Education Policy and Management*, *32*(4), 389–400. https://doi.org/10.1080/1360080X.2010.491112

Wilkins, S., & Neri, S. (2019). Managing faculty in transnational higher education: Expatriate academics at international branch campuses. *Journal of Studies in International Education*, *23*(4), 451–472. https://doi.org/10.1177/1028315318814200

Chapter 10

Conclusion

Abdellatif Sellami and Igor Michaleczek

This volume emphasizes the significance of contextualized wellbeing in higher education, with a specific focus on the Global South. Rather than adhering to simplistic interpretations of wellbeing, it invites us to engage in a deeper investigation of the multi-faceted nature of this concept—one that not only acknowledges but also embraces the complex web of factors shaping our mental, emotional, and physical wellbeing within the context of higher education. The central argument of the book posits that while existing scholarship on wellbeing predominantly emanates from social, cultural, political, and economic settings in the Global North, there exists a conspicuous void in our understanding of wellbeing when viewed through the lens of other world regions, with their distinct characteristics. In response, this volume offers an alternative conceptualization of wellbeing that resonates with the realities of higher education in the Global South, drawing upon the rich narratives, perceptions, and experiences articulated by university students, faculty, and staff in the region.

The chapters compiled in this work highlight the need for a holistic, culturally sensitive approach that takes into account the complex nature of wellbeing and the myriad factors that influence it. This collection argues in favor of a transformative paradigm shift, one that fosters environments nurturing holistic flourishing and resilience among individuals engaged in higher education within developing societies. Combined, the chapters discuss the growing interest in wellbeing in higher education contexts, triggered by external challenges spanning social issues to economic crises, environmental disasters, and conflicts. The authors argue that even amid these external pressures, students still need to grapple with inherent challenges in higher education. The collection emphasizes the importance of promoting wellbeing in higher education and identifies several salient pedagogical benefits. The authors caution against conflating mental health with overall wellbeing and advocate instead for a comprehensive wellbeing-for-all stance.

Beyond the confines of mere academic pursuits, this book recognizes that the concept of wellbeing transcends the boundaries of the classroom. By weaving together insights from multiple disciplines, alongside empirical research and contextualized real-world experiences, it paints a vivid picture of the complex multi-faceted nature of wellbeing when viewed within specific settings. In this edited volume, the contributors have covered a broad spectrum of issues related to wellbeing in higher education across diverse cultural and geographical contexts from the Global South.

The first chapter introduces its focus on redefining wellbeing in higher education, emphasizing the need for a contextually sensitive and culturally responsive approach. While research on student wellbeing in higher education has surged, particularly in response to external challenges like economic crises and the COVID-19 pandemic, there is a dearth of studies from the Global South. The chapter proposes an alternative conceptualization of wellbeing, challenging Western-centric definitions and advocating for a more inclusive approach that considers the diverse socio-cultural, political, and economic contexts of the Global South. The chapter further discusses the complexities of defining wellbeing, drawing on hedonic and eudaimonic perspectives, and highlights the need to move beyond individualistic views to consider relational and contextual dimensions. Additionally, it addresses the importance of infusing wellbeing into higher education policies and practices, particularly in supporting students through proactive measures rather than reactive interventions. The chapter advocates for a holistic understanding of wellbeing that encompasses social, emotional, physical, intellectual, and spiritual dimensions, emphasizing their interconnectedness. It also stresses the importance of context and culture in shaping wellbeing, advocating for a structured framework that acknowledges the multi-dimensional nature of wellbeing and rejects reductionist perspectives.

In Chapter 2, Eybers presented a model that deconstructs coloniality and fulfills emancipatory obligations toward culturally diverse communities in the African continent. In exploring the integration of Afrofuturist and Afrocentric principles into academic literacies to enhance the holistic wellbeing of novice scholars, particularly in higher education, he emphasized the need for a departure from traditional academic literacy models, advocating for a more contextually aware and inclusive paradigm. To address the epistemic violence of colonization and centuries of marginalization of traditional and autochthone knowledge, Eybers considers the interplay of two key conceptual frameworks, Afrofuturism and Afrocentrism, in order to relocate traditional knowledge at the center of intellectual and academic projection. In the different case studies presented in this chapter, it is clearly noticeable that young academics recognize academic wellbeing as intimately interrelated to a traditional and culturally situated framework. To respond to these aspirations and perceived necessity, the chapter proposed the implementation of multimodal, multilingual learning experiences and collaborative learning environments in order to foster a pre-colonial and a-colonial analysis and framing of learning experiences. This approach aligns with Afrocentric principles that center on students' wellbeing and indigeneity. The chapter concluded by stressing the need to shift toward a more contextualized and inclusive approach to academic literacy which addresses the shortcomings inherent in relying solely on textual constructs of literacy.

Chapter 3, titled "Exploring well-being in the Arab higher education context: A scoping review", explores the academic research on wellbeing in the Arab region. Academic wellbeing research in the Arab world is embedded and situated within the region-specific socio-cultural context, marked among others by conflict and inherent religious identity. The research also uncovers the reliance of higher education research on wellbeing on external tools and framework rooted in Western European and American background. Despite the dependence on imported research tools, the need and aspiration for wellbeing intervention in higher education is also acknowledged. This chapter highlights the interesting case of developing the wellbeing concept in a socio-cultural context other than the Global North, as wellbeing is perceived as flexible and open to local setting contextualization. It exposes the will and aspiration to develop wellbeing in the Arab world alongside the dependence on imported tools and epistemic description from an academic context dominated by former colonizers. It also highlights the opportunity that wellbeing represents to promote alternative ontological understanding and epistemic implementations. Academics in this region need to seize this opportunity to contextualize their social, historical, and intellectual capital so they free themselves from a dependence on tools and concepts imported from a hegemonic academic context.

In Crookes' chapter, the narrative shifts to the Pacific Oceania region, focusing on the mental health and academic stressors experienced by students in the context of the University of the South Pacific (USP). The findings revealed, despite significant distress and mental health risks, a high subjective wellbeing across the region. The chapter highlighted the unique socio-environmental challenges these students encounter, including lower enrollment rates, higher withdrawal rates, and a greater prevalence of mental health issues compared to their white European peers. It emphasizes the key role of university support services in helping students during their academic transitions, developing coping skills, resilience, and facilitating access to formal mental health services. In her research, Crooks emphasized the importance of considering the specific context of Pacific students, particularly the role of family and community in their perception of wellbeing. She contextualized the concept of wellbeing by integrating two conceptual frameworks. The first, the Fonofale model, encompasses family, community, spiritual, and cultural history. Additionally, Crooks incorporated Tinto's wellbeing model, which links culture and identity with spiritual and physical health, thereby offering a holistic and contextualized approach to wellbeing. This chapter is a good example of culturally sensitive and responsive support systems that concluded by advocating for further research on student wellbeing in the Pacific Oceania region. But more importantly, this research highlights the importance of decentralizing and contextualizing wellbeing support for Pacific students in higher education. It also highlights the importance that university can play in supporting Pacific students' wellbeing and academic transition while respecting their cultural and historical identity.

In Chapter 5, Donaldson and Koci discussed the application of positive psychology and the PERMA+4 framework in higher education across cultures. The chapter emphasized that academic success is strongly related to student wellbeing. The framework includes nine major building blocks (i.e., positive emotions, engagement, relationships, meaning and purpose, accomplishment, physical health, positive mindset, environment, and economic security) and provides a guide for assessing and developing student wellbeing. The researchers stressed the importance of contextually sensitive and culturally responsive approaches in implementing positive psychology practices and interventions. The chapter concluded by encouraging universities to use evidence-based approaches to promote student wellbeing in order to enhance the quality of the educational experience and preventing pathological conditions such as anxiety and depression.

Al-Wattary, Al-Thani, and Ahmadi's chapter delved into the impact of mindfulness-based instruction and behavioral changes on the wellbeing of college students. Their study focused on students who were instructed to modify their smartphone usage habits, resulting in increased productivity and improved wellbeing. The authors emphasized the importance of addressing students' struggles beyond academia and involving them in policy and decision-making processes. They advocated for providing resources such as counseling, career advice, and mental health interventions. The chapter concluded by discussing the effects of burnout on public school teachers in Qatar, linking emotional exhaustion to decreased mental wellbeing and depersonalization, and calling for the development of non-academic skills to support mental health and wellbeing. Furthermore, this research identified the positive outcomes of a culturally contextualized wellbeing intervention on students at three different levels. These included increased emotional wellbeing, with reduced hopelessness and increased optimism; enhanced recognition of the spiritual dimension, leading to greater inner peace and satisfaction; and improved cognitive efficacy, by fostering a sense of purpose and engagement in learning. Additionally, it reinforced social wellbeing by developing a sense of community and connection among students. These results were achieved through a socio-cultural situated intervention that acknowledged the importance of local values and the spiritual identity of students. The intervention demonstrated the significance of integrating students' identity aspirations in adapting external wellbeing models.

Chapter 7 examined the challenges students encountered when engaging in an online Arabic course during the COVID-19 lockdown. In their study, Mahgoub, Fazza, and Elie adopted a mixed-method exploratory-sequential approach and used an open-ended questionnaire to collect qualitative data. Their findings revealed that students reported challenges across social, physical, mental, and cognitive aspects of wellbeing. These challenges include insufficient communication, inadequate collaborative learning, inability to socialize, physical discomforts like eye strain and back pain, low motivation, anxiety, lowered concentration, difficulty in applying what they learned in real-life, and insufficient instructor's constructive feedback. The authors presented potential solutions to these challenges as suggested by students themselves. The chapter concluded by proposing policy recommendations to promote students' engagement in online Arabic courses in the future. The chapter also highlighted that students as embedded within their own cognitive, social, and cultural context are able to identify and propose contextualized and adapted solutions to existing challenges for their academic and individual wellbeing. These practical recommendations may appear simple but respond to students' perceived challenges within their own understood reality.

Chapter 8 discussed the importance of mental health and wellbeing in the context of higher education. More specifically, it focused on the mental health issues prevalent among university students worldwide. In this chapter, Maulana and Gumelar contended that there is an increasing need for universities to provide adequate support services, suggesting universities should adopt a multi-tier strategy that includes defining wellbeing accurately and developing culturally appropriate wellbeing instruments. They also noted the need for measuring wellbeing in a way that is sensitive to the diverse cultural nuances of students as they observed that the near totality of research on wellbeing in higher education resorts to culturally adapted measuring tools. The findings of the chapter also acknowledge that enhancing students' wellbeing implies an overall relation to students being, and as a result this needs to recognize and promote their socio-cultural identity. To this end, the chapter then concluded by stating that there is a clear and substantial need for developing a socio-cultural relevant measuring framework of wellbeing in order to enable the development of relevant and adapted support.

Chapter 9 discussed the wellbeing of faculty and leaders in higher education, with a particular focus on the Gulf Cooperation Council (GCC) region. In this chapter, Rita W. El-Haddad and Stavros P. Hadjisolomou identified universal and GCC-specific challenges faced by faculty and leaders, though a narrative analysis of the existing academic literature. They identify challenge specific to the GCC that are linked to its demographic and work force structured based on a high proportion of expatriate population. This structural specificity involves key challenges, including short employment contracts, lack of tenure, and issues surrounding expatriate status that negatively impact wellbeing. They also noted decreased research productivity, difficulties related to the academic and language abilities of students, and a lack of individual voice in institutional decision-making. The authors stressed the need for an improved understanding of these salient challenges and the development of targeted support strategies. They list specific recommendations at institutional and governmental aiming at addressing the structural and contextual issues harming faculty wellbeing. They also identified gaps in the literature and emphasized the need for more research on the wellbeing of academic leaders and large-scale studies on subjective wellbeing.

Combined, the chapters included in the book underline the importance of a holistic, culturally sensitive approach that takes into account the complex nature of wellbeing and the myriad factors influencing it. The book calls for interventions and services within university settings to improve students' and other members' wellbeing, critiquing the prevailing focus on Westernized conceptions of wellbeing and advocating instead for interventions tailored to specific cultural and educational contexts. The book encourages higher education institutions to adopt these approaches to foster an inclusive learning environment that promotes the success and flourishing of all members. This conclusion contributes to the broader narrative of the book, emphasizing the importance of contextualized wellbeing in higher education, particularly in the Global South.

The issues related to conceptualization, perception, and implementation of wellbeing-related interventions in higher education institution within the Global South as explored within this volume acknowledge that there are contextual and structural issues. Indeed, academic reliance on external tools and conceptual framework essentially based on a Global North epistemic and ontological essence. This implies that there is a need for developing indigenous frameworks and methodologies that resonate more authentically with the lived experiences of students, faculty, and staff in these regions. These frameworks should draw on local knowledge systems, cultural practices, and social structures to create a more relevant and effective approach to wellbeing. By doing so, higher education institutions in the Global South can better address the unique challenges they face and support the holistic development of their academic communities. This volume, therefore, stands as a critical call to action for researchers, policymakers, and practitioners to prioritize and invest in the development of contextually sensitive and culturally appropriate wellbeing interventions in higher education.

As we conclude this volume, it is evident that the pursuit of wellbeing in higher education within the Global South is not a one-size-fits-all endeavor. Rather, it requires an understanding of the uniqueness of local contexts, a commitment to equity and social justice, and a willingness to engage in transformative practices that empower individuals and communities. It calls for collaborative efforts among educators, policymakers, researchers, and stakeholders to co-create inclusive and empowering learning environments that prioritize the wellbeing of all. Moving forward, it is our hope that the insights, reflections, and recommendations presented in this book will serve as a catalyst for further dialogue, research, and action related to wellbeing in higher education contexts in the developing world. By embracing the richness of diversity, fostering inclusive practices, and centering the voices and experiences of different stakeholders, we can collectively work toward a future where all members of the higher education community can thrive and flourish. In closing, the editors extend our gratitude to all the contributors and reviewers who have contributed to the realization of this work.

Index

academic performance 5, 37, 41, 49–51, 76, 79, 84, 88, 105, 128, 136; *see also* academic achievement 56, 66, 84, 135; academic success 14, 41, 52, 58, 74, 76, 79, 81, 83
agency 11, 14, 16, 30, 54
anxiety 2, 36–37, 49, 60, 62–63, 65, 74, 83, 88, 90–91, 100, 107–108, 114–116, 120, 125, 127, 134, 167
apartheid 10–13, 15, 17–20, 23–24

burnout 56, 78, 100, 148, 155–156, 158, 167

collectivism 40, 54, 131–133; *see also* collectivistic 131
collectivist 40, 54, 131–133; *see also* collectivism
colonial 6, 10–13, 15–20, 23–25, 165; *see also* colonialism 6, 10, 11, 12, 15, 18, 19
contextually sensitive 6–7, 20, 40, 75–76, 81, 83, 145, 154–155, 158, 165, 167, 169; *see also* contextually relevant 40, 41; culturally responsive 6, 7, 24, 39, 75, 76, 81, 82, 83, 84, 89, 154, 155, 158, 165, 167; culturally sensitive 20, 39, 40, 46, 58, 83, 100, 132, 164, 166, 168

depression 2, 36, 53, 60, 62–63, 83, 96, 100, 125, 127, 134, 167

eudaimonic 2, 29, 127, 165; *see also* eudaimonia 127

faith 52, 65, 83, 93
family 14, 20, 54–55, 57–59, 62–68, 81, 128–129, 131, 133, 142, 147, 150–151, 166

Global North 6, 11, 28–29, 164, 166, 169
Global South 6–7, 164–165, 168–169

hedonic 2, 27, 29, 92, 127, 156; *see also* hedonistic 127

identity 11, 14, 20, 24, 35, 45, 53–55, 57–58, 65, 67–69, 131–133, 144, 166–168
indigenous 6, 10–22, 24, 54, 56, 59, 61, 64, 67–68, 169
individualism 12, 54, 129, 130, 132–133, 165; *see also* individualistic 132, 133, 165
intervention 3, 5–6, 35–36, 38–42, 47, 49–50, 75, 77, 79, 81, 83, 87–94, 98–101, 134, 143, 156, 158, 165–169

mental health 2–3, 6–7, 28, 35–38, 40, 47–48, 53–54, 56, 59–65, 68–69, 74–76, 81, 83–84, 87–89, 91–93, 96–97, 100, 104, 125, 127–130, 132–137, 158, 164, 166–168
mental illness 1, 3
mindfulness 37, 48, 90–91, 167
mindset 54, 67–68, 80–81, 83, 98, 166

non-Western 6–7, 69, 89, 130, 142–143

occupational 142–143, 145–146, 155–156
ontology 10–11, 15, 27, 29, 42, 166, 169; *see also* ontological 27, 42, 166, 169
optimal human functioning 28, 75

positive functioning 74–76, 79–81
positive psychology 3–4, 28, 38, 49–51, 74–79, 83–84, 89, 92, 167

quality of life 28, 50, 63, 75, 125–126, 130–131, 136, 142

relationships 4–5, 48–49, 55, 56, 63–64, 66, 79, 83, 98, 100, 105, 127–128, 133–134, 150, 157, 166

satisfaction 5, 27–29, 36, 46–47, 51, 60, 62–63, 78, 88–90, 95–97, 99, 103, 105, 125–128, 130, 134–135, 142, 146, 148, 151, 155–156, 158, 167
selfcare 5, 93
self-determination theory 4, 27, 54
self-realization 94–95
self-regulation 28, 88–89, 95, 106
sense of belonging 35, 55, 98–99, 105, 110, 112, 120, 121, 130, 167; *see also* sense of community
sense of purpose 5, 95, 97, 99, 142, 167

social-emotional 87, 89, 93–94, 98, 100, 126
socio-cultural 4, 6–7, 29, 34, 36, 38–42, 52–53, 57, 100, 126, 142, 165–168
spirituality 54, 83, 93, 130, 133
stress 1–3, 36–37, 40–41, 45, 50, 56–57, 59–65, 68, 90–91, 107–108, 125, 127, 135, 144, 148, 150, 153–158, 166; *see also* stressors

values 5, 7, 14–15, 17, 20, 35–36, 39–40, 52, 55, 89, 92, 95, 98–99, 101, 130–131, 146, 155, 167

Western 6–7, 29–30, 36–40, 52, 58–60, 67, 77, 87, 89, 126–127, 129–131, 133, 136, 142–144, 146, 149, 153–155, 165–166, 168; *see also* Westernized
work-life balance 142, 145, 147, 155, 157

For Product Safety Concerns and Information please contact our EU
representative GPSR@taylorandfrancis.com
Taylor & Francis Verlag GmbH, Kaufingerstraße 24, 80331 München, Germany

www.ingramcontent.com/pod-product-compliance
Lightning Source LLC
Chambersburg PA
CBHW061716300426
44115CB00014B/2710